NATURE, THE SOUL, AND GOD

NATURE, THE SOUL, AND GOD

An Introduction to the Philosophy of Nature

SECOND EDITION

JEAN W. RIOUX

CASCADE *Books* · Eugene, Oregon

NATURE, THE SOUL, AND GOD
An Introduction to the Philosophy of Nature, Second Edition

Cascade Books
An Imprint of Wipf and Stock Publishers
199 W. 8th Ave., Suite 3
Eugene, OR 97401

www.wipfandstock.com

PAPERBACK ISBN: 978-1-6667-0248-4
HARDCOVER ISBN: 978-1-6667-0249-1
EBOOK ISBN: 978-1-6667-0250-7

Cataloging-in-Publication data:

Names: Rioux, Jean W., author.
Title: Nature, the soul, and God : an introduction to the philosophy of nature, second
    editiopn / by Jean W. Rioux.
Description: Eugene, OR : Cascade Books, 2021 | Includes bibliographical references.
Identifiers: ISBN 978-1-6667-0248-4 (paperback) | ISBN 978-1-6667-0249-1
    (hardcover) | ISBN 978-1-6667-0250-7 (ebook)
Subjects: LCSH: Philosophy and religion—Early works to 1800. | Philosophy and
    religion—History. | Philosophers. | Philosophy of nature.
Classification: LCC BD581 R56 2018 (print) | LCC BD581 (ebook)

Contents

Chapter 5 Natural Philosophy, Freedom, and Right Action

Chapter 6 Natural Philosophy and the Human Soul

Chapter 7 Natural Philosophy and the Existence of God

Chapter 8 Elements of Logic

Bibliography

Preface

We are unique among living things in that we can apply our minds, not only to life's mundane problems but also to questions which have no immediate practical consequence. We ask not only how or what but why, and it is the last question Aristotle has foremost in mind when he says that we have a natural desire to know. This distinctive trait is evident even in the very young, as evidenced by the persistent questioning of a child wanting to know why things are as they are.

We accordingly divide human knowing into practical and speculative, or theoretical. Most people (by far) are more familiar with practical knowing than with speculative, if only because it is of great importance in day-to-day life. As engineers, architects, surveyors, or craftsmen find the need to compute the length of the diagonal of a rectangle, they solve the problem by taking the square root of the sum of the squares on two adjacent sides, or, more familiarly, by applying the formula $a^2 + b^2 = c^2$ to the case at hand. Solving the problem in this way, even arriving at such a formula by trial-and-error, is a practical use of reason. But this is not what Aristotle intends when he says we naturally desire to know,

"Man naturally desires to know."

since practical knowledge is itself directed to something else (to the building of a structure or establishing property lines). Speculative knowledge is not a means: here, one simply asks why it is that the sum of the squares on two adjacent sides of a rectangle is equal to the square on the diagonal. Asking this question assumes that one already knows the formula in question, (which is all that would be needed if one had solving some concrete problem in mind). What we desire here is to know, as such. Speculative inquiries are directed to the possession of knowledge itself, as to something desirable and good.

On the other hand, we know from history that even speculative uses of reason have practical results. The developments of our technological age, for example, are partially rooted in speculative disputes about how human beings come to know things. The point here, however, is that speculative reasoning is good to do, whether one gains in a practical way or not. In answer to a question from a student of his, who asked what was to be gained in a study of geometry, Euclid is supposed to have responded "Give the man a coin, seeing that he feels he must profit in some way from what he learns." The profit was in the learning itself—we can only hope that the student got the point.

Mathematics, literature, the arts, human history, natural science, all these and more present themselves as possible areas of a properly speculative study. Moreover, within these several areas, one might go about such a study in different ways. For example: "why are the angles of a triangle equal to two right angles?" which is to say: "upon what basis is this true?" The solution to such a question would be a mathematical one. One might also look at the same subject and ask, "are there such things as triangles in reality?" or even "how do we know the truth of the very starting-points of mathematics?" These latter questions are more properly philosophical ones, and resolving such questions is the work of philosophy, as we know it today.

To say the same thing somewhat differently, philosophy considers the most fundamental questions which arise in all areas of study. As we said, the mathematician would not ask whether triangles exist or not— the question is really not a mathematical one at all. That question is more like asking "is there such a thing as a science of mathematics?" Rather, the mathematician assumes certain things within the study, and proceeds. The philosopher, in turn, asks questions about what is assumed by the mathematician.

In this book, we are concerned with the natural world. As you might expect, there are many ways in which one might study nature. Physics, biology, and chemistry study nature in a manner we call "scientific". They look at nature from a certain perspective, and they make assumptions about studying the natural world in this way. With these starting points in mind, they proceed to deal with more specific questions about nature. In contrast, a philosophical study of nature is "pre-scientific". It is more concerned with the starting points of these sciences than with the detailed conclusions scientists are interested in. While the chemist would assume a certain table of elements, more or less well-established, and proceed to investigate the properties and various combinations of such elements, a philosopher would ask about the nature of elements and compounds themselves—what are they? is a compound merely a group of elements, or something different? While a classical physicist would assume that a body moving in a straight line would continue to do so unless impeded, a philosopher might ask: what is motion? does it really differ from rest, or is this only a seeming difference?

This book deals with properly philosophical questions about the natural world. Consequently, we have included readings from past philosophers to bring out these fundamental questions, and most of the book is concerned directly with these. Further, in order to show what impact one's position on the natural world will have upon other things, we have included readings concerned with the nature and scope of human knowledge, human freedom and right action, the immortality of the human soul, and the existence of God. As will become clear, there are definite and unavoidable connections among our philosophical views—what we hold about some things has a real effect upon what we hold elsewhere. In particular, what we hold regarding the world of nature has a direct impact upon what we hold regarding human nature, as well as God. As one sees nature to be a certain way, one sees human nature in a like vein. Insofar as one regards nature to be of this sort, so one defines what is beyond nature, or the super-natural.

1

DO WE HAVE IT ALL WRONG?

The greatest challenge to a philosophy of nature such as we have described above comes from those who would deny, either that there is anything natural and fixed in the first place, or, if there is, we are unable to know what it is. Sextus Empiricus presents a case for such a fallibilism—essentially, the conviction that, however hard we may try, we can never be sure we are not entirely mistaken about everything. A modern version of this ancient view arises in the writings of David Hume, an eighteenth-century British philosopher, with whose objections to natural knowledge we grapple even to this day.

SEXTUS EMPIRICUS—OUTLINES OFPYRRHONISM

Chapter 1. Of the Main Difference Between Philosophic Systems

The natural result of any investigation is that the investigators either discover the object of search or deny that it is discoverable and confess it to be inapprehensible or persist in their search. So, too, with regard to the objects investigated by philosophy, this is probably why some have claimed to have discovered the truth, others have asserted that it

> *"Some claim to have discovered the truth, others assert that it cannot be apprehended, while still others go on inquiring."*

5 cannot be apprehended, while others again go on inquiring. Those who
10 believe, they have discovered it are the "Dogmatists," specially so-called—Aristotle, for example, and Epicurus and the Stoics and certain others; Cleitomachus and Carneades and other Academics treat it as inapprehensible—the Skeptics keep on searching. Hence it seems reasonable to hold that the main types of philosophy are three—the
15 Dogmatic, the Academic, and the Skeptic. Of the other systems it will best become others to speak: our task it present is to describe in outline the Skeptic doctrines first premising that of none of our future

1

statements do we positively affirm that the fact is exactly as we state it, but we simply record each fact, like a chronicler, as it appears to us at the moment.

Chapter 2. Of the Arguments of Skepticism

Of the Skeptic philosophy one argument (or branch of exposition) is called "general," the other "special." In the general argument we set forth the distinctive features of Skepticism, stating its purport and principles, its logical methods, criterion, and end or aim; the "Tropes," also, or "Modes," which lead to suspension of judgment, and in what sense we adopt the Skeptic formulae, and the distinction between Skepticism and the philosophies which stand next to it. In the special argument we state our objections regarding the several divisions of so-called philosophy. Let us, then, deal first with the general argument, beginning our description with the names given to the Skeptic School.

Chapter 3. Of the Nomenclature of Skepticism

The Skeptic School, then, is also called "Zetetic" from its activity in investigation and inquiry, and "Ephectic" or Suspensive from the state of mind produced in the inquirer after his search, and "Aporetic" or Dubitative either from its habit of doubting and seeking, as some say, or from its indecision as regards assent and denial, and "Pyrrhonean" from the fact that Pyrrho appears to us to have applied himself to Skepticism more thoroughly and more conspicuously than his predecessors.

Chapter 4. What Skepticism Is

Skepticism is an ability, or mental attitude, which opposes appearances to judgments in any way whatsoever, with the result that, owing to the equipollence of the objects and reasons thus opposed, we are brought firstly to a state of mental suspense and next to a state of "unperturbedness" or quietude. Now we call it an "ability" not in any subtle sense, but simply in respect of its "being able." By "appearances" we now mean the objects of sense-perception, whence we contrast them with the objects of thought or "judgments." The phrase "in any way whatsoever" can be connected either with the word "ability," to make us take the word "ability," as we said, in its simple sense, or with the phrase "opposing appearances to judgments"; for inasmuch as we oppose these in a variety of ways—appearances to appearances, or judgments to judgments, or *alternando* appearances to judgments—in order to ensure the inclusion of all these antitheses we employ the phrase "in any way whatsoever." Or, again, we join "in any way whatsoever" to "appearances and judgments" in order that we may not have to inquire how the appearances appear or how the thought-objects are judged but may take these terms in the simple sense. The phrase "opposed judgments" we do not employ in the sense of negations and affirmations only but simply as equivalent to "conflicting judgments." "Equipollence" we use of equality in respect of probability and improbability, to indicate that no one of the conflicting judgments takes precedence of any other as being more probable. "Suspense" is a state of mental rest owing to which we neither deny nor affirm anything. "Quietude" is an untroubled and tranquil condition of soul. And how quietude enters the soul along with suspension of judgment we shall explain in our chapter "Concerning the End."

Chapter 5. Of the Skeptic

In the definition of the system there is also implicitly included that of the Pyrrhonean philosopher: he is the man who participates in this "ability."

Chapter 6. Of the Principles of Skepticism

The originating cause of Skepticism is, we say, the hope of attaining quietude. Men of talent, who were perturbed by the contradictions in things and in doubt as to which of the alternatives they ought to accept, were led on to inquire what is true in things and what false, hoping by the settlement of this question to attain quietude. The main basic principle of the Skeptic system is that of opposing to every proposition an equal proposition; for we believe that as a consequence of this we end by ceasing to dogmatize.

Chapter 7. Does the Skeptic Dogmatize?

When we say that the Skeptic refrains from dogmatizing we do not use the term "dogma," as some do, in the broader sense of "approval of a thing" for the Skeptic gives assent to the feelings which are the necessary results of sense-impressions, and he would not, for example, say when feeling hot or cold "I believe that I am not hot or cold"); but we say that

"he does not dogmatize" using "dogma" in the sense, which some give
it, of "assent to one of the non-evident objects of scientific inquiry"; for
the Pyrrhonean philosopher assents to nothing that is non-evident.
Moreover, even in the act of enunciating the Skeptic formulae
concerning things non-evident—such as the formula "No more (one
thing than another)," or the formula "I determine nothing," or any of the
others which we shall presently mention he does not dogmatize. For
whereas the dogmatizer posits the things about which he is said to be
dogmatizing as really existent, the Skeptic does not posit these formulae
in any absolute sense; for he conceives that, just as the formula "All things
are false" asserts the falsity of itself as well as of everything else, as does
the formula "Nothing is true," so also the formula "No more" asserts
that itself, like all the rest, is "No more (this than that)," and thus cancels
itself along with the rest. And of the other formulae we say the same. If
then, while the dogmatizer posits the matter of his dogma as substantial
truth, the Skeptic enunciates his formulae so that they are virtually
cancelled by themselves, he should not be said to dogmatize in his
enunciation of them. And, most important of all, in his enunciation of
these formulae he states what appears to himself and announces his own
impression in an undogmatic way, without making any positive assertion
regarding the external realities.

Chapter 8. Has the Skeptic a Doctrinal Rule?

We follow the same lines in replying to the question "Has the Skeptic a
doctrinal rule?" For if one defines a "doctrinal rule" as "adherence to a
number of dogmas which are dependent both on one another and on
appearances," and defines "dogma" as "assent to a non-evident
proposition," then we shall say that he has not a doctrinal rule. But if one
defines "doctrinal rule" as "procedure which, in accordance with
appearance, follows a certain line of reasoning, that reasoning indicating
how it is possible to seem to live rightly (the word 'rightly' being taken, not
as referring to virtue only, but in a wider sense) and tending to enable one
to suspend judgment, then we say that he has a doctrinal rule. For we follow
a line of reasoning which, in accordance with appearances, points us to a
life conformable to the customs of our country and its laws and institutions,
and to our own instinctive feelings.

Chapter 9. Does the Skeptic Deal with Physics?

We make a similar reply also to the question "Should the Skeptic deal with physical problems?" For while, on the one hand, so far as regards making, firm and positive assertions about any of the matters dogmatically treated in physical theory, we do not deal with physics; yet, on the other hand, in respect of our mode of opposing to every proposition an equal proposition and of our theory of quietude we do treat of physics. This, too, is the way in which we approach the logical and ethical branches of so-called "philosophy."

Chapter 10. Do the Skeptics Abolish Appearances?

Those who say that "the Skeptics abolish appearances," or phenomena, seem to me to be unacquainted with the statements of our School. For, as we said above, we do not overthrow the affective sense-impressions which induce our assent involuntarily; and these impressions are "the appearances." And when we question whether the underlying object is such as it appears, we grant the fact that it appears, and our doubt does not concern the appearance itself, but the account given of that appearance—and that is a different thing from questioning the appearance itself. For example, honey appears to us to be sweet (and this we grant, for we perceive sweetness through the senses), but whether it is also sweet in its essence is for us a matter of doubt, since this is not an appearance but a judgment regarding the appearance. And even if we do actually argue against the appearances, we do not propound such arguments with the intention of abolishing appearances, but by way of pointing out the rashness of the Dogmatists; for if reason is such a trickster as to all but snatch away the appearances from under our very eyes, surely we should view it with suspicion in the case of things non-evident so as not to display rashness by following it.

Chapter 11. Of the Criterion of Skepticism

That we adhere to appearances is plain from what we say about the Criterion of the Skeptic School. The word "Criterion" is used in two senses: in the one it means "the standard regulating belief in reality or unreality," (and this we shall discuss in our refutation); in the other it denotes the standard of action by conforming to which in the conduct of life we perform some actions and abstain from others; and it is of the latter that we are now speaking. The criterion, then, of the Skeptic School is, we say, the appearance, giving this name to what is virtually the sense-presentation. For since this lies in feeling and involuntary affection, it is not open to question. Consequently, no one, I suppose, disputes that the underlying object has this or that appearance; the point in dispute is whether the object is in reality such as it appears to be.

Adhering, then, to appearances we live in accordance with the normal rules of life, undogmatically, seeing that we cannot remain wholly inactive. And it would seem that this regulation of life is fourfold, and that one part of it lies in the guidance of Nature, another in the constraint of the passions, Another in the tradition of laws and customs, another in the instruction of the arts. Nature's guidance is that by which we are naturally capable of sensation and thought, constraint of the passions is that whereby hunger drives us to food and thirst to drink; tradition of customs and laws, that whereby we regard piety in the conduct of life as good, but impiety as evil; instruction of the arts, that whereby we are not inactive in such arts as we adopt. But we make all these statements undogmatically.

Chapter 12. What is the End of Skepticism?

Our next subject will be the end of the Skeptic system. Now an "end" is "that for which all actions or reasonings are undertaken, while it exists for the sake of none"; or, otherwise, "the ultimate object of appetency." We assert still that the Skeptic's End is quietude in respect of matters of opinion and moderate feeling in respect of things unavoidable. For the skeptic, having set out to philosophize with the object of passing judgment on the sense impressions and ascertaining which of them are true and which false, so as to attain quietude thereby, found himself involved in contradictions of equal weight, and being unable to decide between them suspended judgment; and as he was thus in suspense there followed, as it happened, the state of quietude in respect of matters of opinion. For the man who opines that anything is by nature good or bad is forever being disquieted: when he is without the things which he deems good he believes himself to be tormented by things naturally bad and he pursues after the things which are, as he thinks, good; which when he has obtained he keeps falling into still more perturbations because of his irrational and immoderate elation, and in his dread of a change of fortune he uses every endeavor to avoid losing the things which he deems good.

On the other hand, the man who determines nothing as to what is naturally good or bad neither shuns nor pursues anything eagerly; and, in consequence, he is unperturbed.

The Skeptic, in fact, had the same experience which is said to have befallen the painter Apelles. Once, they say, when he was painting a horse and wished to represent in the painting the horse's foam, he was so unsuccessful that he gave up the attempt and flung at the picture the sponge on which he used to wipe the paints off his brush, and the mark of the sponge produced the effect of a horse's foam. So, too, the Skeptics were in hopes of gaining quietude by means of a decision regarding the disparity of the objects of sense and of thought and being unable to effect this they suspended judgment; and they found that quietude, as if by chance, followed upon their suspense, even as a shadow follows its substance. We do not, however, suppose that the Skeptic is wholly untroubled; but we say that he is troubled by things unavoidable; for we grant that he is cold at times and thirsty, and suffers various affections of that kind. But even in these cases, whereas ordinary people are afflicted by two circumstances—namely, by the affections themselves and, in no less a degree, by the belief that these conditions are evil by nature,—the Skeptic, by his rejection of the added belief in the natural badness of all these conditions, escapes here too with less discomfort. Hence we say that, while in regard to matters of opinion the Skeptic's End is quietude, in regard to things unavoidable it is "moderate affection." But some notable Skeptics have added the further definition "suspension of judgment in investigations."

Chapter 13. Of the General Modes Leading to Suspension of Judgment

Now that we have been saying that tranquility follows on suspension of judgment, it will be our next task to explain how we arrive at this suspension. Speaking generally, one may say that it is the result of setting things in opposition. We oppose either appearances to appearances or objects of thought to objects of thought or alternando. For instance, we oppose appearances to appearances when we say "The same tower appears round from a distance, but square from close at hand"; and thoughts to thoughts, when in answer to him who argues the existence of providence from the order of the heavenly bodies we oppose the fact that often the good fare ill and the bad fare well and draw from this the inference that providence does not exist. And thoughts we oppose to appearances, as when Anaxagoras countered the notion that snow is white with the argument, "Snow is frozen water, and water is black; therefore snow also is black." With a different idea we oppose things present sometimes to things present, as in the foregoing examples, and sometimes to things past or future, as, for instance, when someone propounds to us a theory which we are unable to refute, we say to him in reply, "Just as, before the birth of the founder of the school to which you belong, the theory it holds was not as yet apparent as a sound theory, although it was really in existence, so likewise it is possible that the opposite theory to that which you now propound is already existent, though not yet apparent to us, so that we ought not as yet to yield assent to this theory which at the moment seems to be valid."

But in order that we may have a more exact understanding of these antitheses I will describe the modes by which suspension of judgment is brought about, but without making any positive assertion regarding either their number or their validity; for it is possible that they may be unsound or there may be more of them than I shall enumerate.

Chapter 14. Concerning the Ten Modes

The usual tradition amongst the older skeptics is that the "modes" by which "suspension" is supposed to be brought about are ten in number; and they also give them the synonymous names of "arguments" and "positions." They are these: the first, based on the variety in animals; the second, on the differences in human beings; the third, on the different structures of the organs of sense; the fourth, on the circumstantial conditions; the fifth, on positions and intervals and locations; the sixth, on intermixtures; the seventh, on the quantities and formations of the underlying objects; the eighth, on the fact of relativity; the ninth, on the frequency or rarity of occurrence; the tenth, on the disciplines and customs and laws, the legendary beliefs and the dogmatic convictions. This order, however, we adopt without prejudice.

As superordinate to these there stand three Modes—that based on the subject who judges, that on the object judged, and that based on both. The first four of the ten Modes are subordinate to the Mode based on the subject (for the subject which judges is either an animal or a man or a sense, and existent in some condition): the seventh and tenth Modes are referred to that based on the object judged: the fifth, sixth, eighth, and ninth are referred to the Mode based on both subject and object. Furthermore, these three Modes are also referred to that of relation, so that the Mode of relation stands as the highest genus, and the three as species, and the ten as subordinate subspecies. We give this as the probable account of their numbers; and as to their argumentative force what we say is this:

The First argument (or Trope), as we said, is that which shows that the same impressions are not produced by the same objects owing to the differences in animals. This we infer both from the differences in their origins and from the variety of their bodily structures. Thus, as to origin, some animals are produced without sexual union, others by coition. And of those produced without coition, some come from fire, like the animalcules which appear in furnaces, others from putrid water, like gnats; others from wine when it turns sour, like ants; others from earth, like grasshoppers; others from marsh, like frogs; others from mud, like worms; others from asses, like beetles; others from greens, like caterpillars; others from fruits, like the gall-insects in wild figs; others from rotting animals, as bees from bulls and wasps from horses. Of the animals generated by coition, some—in fact the majority—come from homogeneous parents, others from heterogeneous parents, as do mules. Again, of animals in general, some are born alive, like men; others are born as eggs, like birds; and yet others as lumps of flesh, like bears. It is natural, then, that these dissimilar and variant modes of birth should produce much contrariety of sense affection, and that this is a source of its divergent, discordant, and conflicting character.

Moreover, the differences found in the most important parts of the body, and especially in those of which the natural function is judging and perceiving, are capable of producing a vast deal of divergence in the sense-impressions [owing to the variety in the animals]. Thus, sufferers from jaundice declare that objects which seem to us white are yellow, while those whose eyes are bloodshot call them blood-red. Since, then, some animals have eyes which are yellow, others bloodshot, others albino, others of other colors, they probably, I suppose, have different perceptions of color. Moreover, if we bend down over a book after having gazed long and fixedly at the sun, the letters seem to us to be golden in color and circling round. Since, then, some animals possess also a natural brilliance in their eyes and emit from them a fine and mobile stream of light, so that they can even see by night, we seem bound to suppose that they are differently affected from us by external objects. Jugglers, too, by means of smearing lamp wicks with the rust of copper or with the juice of the cuttlefish make the bystanders appear now copper-colored and now black—and that by just a small sprinkling of extra matter. Surely, then, we have much more reason to suppose that when different juices are intermingled in the vision of animals their impressions of the objects will become different. Again, when we press the eyeball at one side the forms, figures, and sizes of the objects appear oblong and narrow. So it is probable that all animals which have the pupil of the eye slanting and elongated such as goats, cats, and similar animals—have impressions of the objects which are different and unlike the notions formed of them by the animals which have round pupils. Mirrors, too, owing to differences in their construction, represent the external objects at one time as very small—as when the mirror is concave—at another time as elongated and narrow—as when the mirror is convex. Some mirrors, too, show the head of the figure reflected at the bottom and the feet at the top. Since, then, some organs of sight actually protrude beyond the face owing to their convexity, while others are quite concave, and others again lie in a level plane, on this account also it is probable that their impressions differ, and that the same objects, as seen by dogs, fishes, lions, men, and locusts, are neither equal in size nor similar in shape, but vary according to the image of each object created by the particular sight that receives the impression.

Of the other sense organs also the same account holds good. Thus, in respect of touch, how could one maintain that creatures covered with shells, with flesh, with prickles, with feathers, with scales, are all similarly affected? And as for the sense of hearing, how could we say that its perceptions are alike in animals with a very narrow auditory passage and those with a very wide one, or in animals with hairy ears and those with smooth ears? For, as regards this sense, even we ourselves find our hearing affected in one way when we have our ears plugged and in another way when we use them just as they are. Smell also will differ because of the variety in animals. For if we ourselves are affected in one way when we have a cold and our internal phlegm is excessive, and in another way when the parts about our head are filled with an excess of blood, feeling an aversion to smells which seem sweet to everyone else and regarding them as noxious, it is reasonable to suppose that animals too—since some are flaccid by nature and rich in phlegm, others rich in blood, others marked by a predominant excess of yellow or of black gall—are in each case impressed in different ways by the objects of smell. So too with the objects of taste; for some animals have rough and dry tongues, others extremely moist tongues. We ourselves, too, when our tongues are very dry, in cases of fever, think the food proffered us to be earthy and ill-flavored or bitter—an affection due to the variation in the predominating juices which we are said to contain. Since, then, animals also have organs of taste which differ and which have different juices in excess, in respect of taste also they will receive different impressions of the real objects. For just as the same food when digested becomes in one place a vein, in another an artery, in another a bone, in another a sinew, or some other piece of the body, displaying a different potency according to the difference in the parts which receive it;—and just as the same unblended water, when it is absorbed by trees, becomes in one place bark, in another branch, in another blossom, and so finally fig and quince and each of the other fruits;—and just as the single identical breath of a musician breathed into a flute becomes here a shrill note and there a deep note, and the same pressure of his hand on the lyre produces here a deep note and there a shrill note,—so likewise is it probable that the external objects appear different owing to differences in the structure of the animals which experience the sense-impressions.

But one may learn this more clearly from the preferences and aversions of animals. Thus, sweet oil seems very agreeable to men, but intolerable to beetles and bees; and olive oil is beneficial to men, but when poured on wasps and bees it destroys them; and seawater is a disagreeable and poisonous potion for men, but fish drink and enjoy it. Pigs, too, enjoy wallowing in the stinking mire rather than in clear and clean water. And whereas some animals eat grass, others eat shrubs, others feed in the woods, others live on seeds or flesh or milk; some of them, too, prefer their food high, others like it fresh, and while some prefer it raw, others like it cooked. And so generally, the things which are agreeable to some are to others disagreeable, distasteful, and deadly. Thus, quails are fattened by hemlock, and pigs by henbane; and pigs also enjoy eating salamanders, just as deer enjoy poisonous creatures, and swallows gnats. So, ants and wood lice, when swallowed by men, cause distress and griping, whereas the bear, whenever she falls sick, cures herself by licking them up. The mere touch of an oak twig paralyses the viper, and that of a plane leaf the bat. The elephant flees from the ram, the lion from the cock, sea monsters from the crackle of bursting beans, and the tiger from the sound of a drum. One might, indeed, cite many more examples, but—not to seem unduly prolix—if the same things are displeasing to some but pleasing to others, and pleasure and displeasure depend upon sense impression, then animals receive different impressions from the underlying objects.

But if the same things appear different owing to the variety in animals, we shall, indeed, be able to state our own impressions of the real object, but as to its essential nature we shall suspend judgment. For we cannot ourselves judge between our own impressions and those of other animals, since we ourselves are involved in the dispute and are, therefore, rather in need of a judge than competent to pass judgment ourselves. Besides, we are unable, either with or without proof, to prefer our own impressions to those of the irrational animals. For in addition to the probability that proof is, as we shall show, a nonentity, the so-called proof itself will be either apparent to us or non-apparent. If, then, it is non-apparent, we shall not accept it with confidence; while if it is apparent to us, inasmuch as what is apparent to animals is the point in question and the proof is apparent to us who are animals, it follows that we shall have to question the proof itself as to whether it is as true as it is apparent. It is, indeed, absurd to attempt to establish the matter in question by means of the matter in question, since in that case the same thing will be at once believed and disbelieved—believed in so far as it purports to prove but disbelieved in so far as it requires proof—which is impossible. Consequently we shall not possess a proof which enables us to give our own sense impressions the preference over those of the so-called irrational animals. If, then, owing to the variety in animals their sense impressions differ, and it is impossible to judge between them, we must necessarily suspend judgment regarding the external underlying objects.

By way of super-addition, too, we draw comparisons between mankind and the so-called irrational animals in respect of their sense impressions. For, after our solid arguments, we deem it quite proper to poke fun at those conceited braggarts, the Dogmatists. As a rule, our school compare the irrational animals in the mass with mankind, but since the Dogmatists captiously assert that the comparison is unequal, we—super-adding yet more—will carry our ridicule further and base our argument on one animal only, the dog for instance if you like, which is held to be the most worthless of animals. For even in this case we shall find that the animals we are discussing are no wise inferior to ourselves in respect of the credibility of their impressions.

Now it is allowed by the Dogmatists that this animal, the dog, excels us in point of sensation: as to smell it is more sensitive than we are, since by this sense it tracks beasts that it cannot see; and with its eyes it sees them more quickly than we do; and with its ears it is keen of perception. Next let us proceed with the reasoning faculty. Of reason one kind is internal, implanted in the soul, the other externally expressed. Let us consider first the internal reason. Now according to those Dogmatists who are, at present, our chief opponents—I mean the Stoics—internal reason is supposed to be occupied with the following matters: the choice of things congenial and the avoidance of things alien; the knowledge of the arts contributing thereto; the apprehension of the virtues pertaining to one's proper nature and of those relating to the passions. Now the dog—the animal upon which, by way of example, we have decided to base our argument—exercises choice of the congenial and avoidance of the harmful, in that it hunts after food and slinks away from a raised whip. Moreover, it possesses an art which supplies that which is congenial, namely hunting. Nor is it devoid even of virtue; for certainly if justice consists in rendering to each his due, the dog that welcomes and guards its friends and benefactors but drives off strangers and evildoers, cannot be lacking in justice. But if he possesses this virtue, then, since the virtues are interdependent, he possesses also all the other virtues; and these, say the philosophers, the majority of men do not possess. That the dog is also valiant we see by the way he repels attacks, and intelligent as well, as Homer too testified when he sang how Odysseus went unrecognized by all the people of his own household and was recognized only by the dog Argus, who neither was deceived by the bodily alterations of the hero nor had lost his original apprehensive impression, which indeed he evidently retained better than the men. And according to Chrysippus, who shows special interest in irrational animals, the dog even shares in the far-famed "Dialectic." This person, at any rate, declares that the dog makes use of the fifth complex indemonstrable syllogism when, arriving at a spot where three ways meet, after smelling at the two roads by which the quarry did not pass, he rushes off at once by the third without stopping to smell. For, says the old writer, the dog implicitly reasons thus: "The creature went either by this road, or by that, or by the other: but it did not go by this road or by that: therefore it went by the other." Moreover, the dog is capable of comprehending and assuaging his own sufferings; for when a thorn has got stuck in his foot he hastens to remove it by rubbing his foot on the ground and by using his teeth. And if he has a wound anywhere, because dirty wounds are hard to cure whereas clean ones heal easily, the dog gently licks off the pus that has gathered. Nay more, the dog admirably observes the prescription of Hippocrates: rest being what cures the foot, whenever he gets his foot hurt he lifts it up and keeps it as far as possible free from pressure. And when distressed by unwholesome humors he eats grass, by the help of which he vomits what is unwholesome and gets well again. If, then, it has been shown that the animal upon which, as an example, we have based our argument not only chooses the wholesome and avoids the noxious, but also possesses an art capable of supplying what is wholesome and is capable of comprehending and assuaging its own sufferings, and is not devoid of virtue, then—these being the things in which the perfection of internal reasons consists—the dog will be thus far perfect. And that, I suppose, is why certain of the professors of philosophy have adorned themselves with the title of this animal.

Concerning external reason, or speech, it is unnecessary for the present to inquire; for it has been rejected even by some of the Dogmatists as being a hindrance to the acquisition of virtue, for which reason they used to practice silence during the period of instruction; and besides, supposing that a man is dumb, no one will therefore call him irrational. But to pass over these cases, we certainly see animals—the subject of our argument—uttering quite human cries—jays, for instance, and others. And, leaving this point also aside, even if we do not understand the utterances of the so-called irrational animals, still it is not improbable that they converse although we fail to understand them; for in fact when we listen to the talk of barbarians we do not understand it, and it seems to us a kind of uniform chatter. Moreover, we hear dogs uttering one sound when they are driving people off, another when they are howling, and one sound when beaten, and a quite different sound when fawning. And so in general, in the case of all other animals as well as the dog, whoever examines the matter carefully will find a great variety of utterance according to the different circumstances, so that, in consequence, the so-called irrational animals may justly be said to participate in external reason. But if they neither fall short of mankind in the accuracy of their perceptions, nor in internal reason, nor yet (to go still further) in external reason, or speech, then they will deserve no less credence than ourselves in respect of their sense impressions. Probably, too, we may reach this conclusion by basing our argument on each single class of irrational animals. Thus, for example, who would deny that birds excel in quickness of wit or that they employ external reason? For they understand not only present events but future events as well, and these they foreshow to such as are able to comprehend them by means of prophetic cries as well as by other signs.

I have drawn this comparison (as I previously indicated) by way of super-addition, having already sufficiently proved, as I think, that we cannot prefer our own sense impressions to those of the irrational animals. If, however, the irrational animals are not less worthy of credence than we in regard to the value of sense impressions, and their impressions vary according to the variety of animal—then, although I shall be able to say what the nature of each of the underlying objects appears to me to be, I shall be compelled, for the reasons stated above, to suspend judgment as to its real nature.

Such, then, is the First of the Modes which induce suspense. ...

And thus by means of all the Ten Modes we are finally led to suspension of judgment.

QUESTIONS TO CONSIDER

- Is the Skeptic (as opposed to the Academic) sure about anything? What reasons does Sextus Empiricus supply to cast doubt upon things one might ordinarily say one knows?

- A real question arises as to the consistency of Sextus Empiricus' own view—is he not himself just dogmatizing? How does he argue that he is not? Is that argument itself not a mere dogmatization?

- If Sextus happens to be right, what is the implication for a philosophy of nature?

DAVID HUME—ENQUIRY

Skeptical Doubts Concerning the Operation of the Understanding—1

All the objects of human reason or enquiry may naturally be divided into two kinds, to wit, Relations of Ideas, and Matters of Fact. Of the first kind are the sciences of Geometry, Algebra, and Arithmetic; and in short, every affirmation which is either intuitively or demonstratively certain.

5   That the square of the hypotenuse is equal to the square of the two sides, is a proposition which expresses a relation between these figures.

> *"All our experimental conclusions proceed upon the supposition that the future will be conformable to the past."*

10 That three times five is equal to the half of thirty, expresses a relation between these numbers. Propositions of this kind are discoverable by the mere operation of thought, without dependence on what is anywhere existent in the universe. Though there never were a circle or triangle in nature, the truths demonstrated by Euclid would forever retain their
15 certainty and evidence.

Matters of fact, which are the second objects of human reason, are not ascertained in the same manner; nor is our evidence of their truth, however great, of a like nature with the foregoing. The contrary of every matter of fact is still possible; because it can never imply a contradiction
20 and is conceived by the mind with the same facility and distinctness, as if ever so conformable to reality. That the sun will not rise tomorrow is no less intelligible a proposition, and implies no more contradiction than the affirmation, that it will rise. We should in vain, therefore, attempt to demonstrate its falsehood. Were it demonstratively false, it would imply
25 a contradiction and could never be distinctly conceived by the mind.

It may, therefore, be a subject worthy of curiosity, to enquire what is the nature of that evidence which assures us of any real existence and matter of fact, beyond the present testimony of our senses, or the records of our memory. This part of philosophy, it is observable, has been little
30 cultivated, either by the ancients or moderns; and therefore our doubts and errors, in the prosecution of so important an enquiry, may be the more excusable, while we march through such difficult paths without any guide or direction. They may even prove useful, by exciting curiosity, and

destroying that implicit faith and security, which is the bane of all reasoning and free enquiry. The discovery of defects in the common philosophy, if any such there be, will not, I presume, be a discouragement, but rather an incitement, as is usual, to attempt something more full and satisfactory than has yet been proposed to the public.

All reasonings concerning matter of fact seem to be founded on the relation of Cause and Effect. By means of that relation alone we can go beyond the evidence of our memory and senses. If you were to ask a man, why he believes any matter of fact, which is absent; for instance, that his friend is in the country, or in France; he would give you a reason; and this reason would be some other fact; as a letter received from him, or the knowledge of his former resolutions and promises. A man finding a watch or any other machine in a desert island, would conclude that there had once been men in that island. All our reasonings concerning fact are of the same nature. And here it is constantly supposed that there is a connection between the present fact and that which is inferred from it. Were there nothing to bind them together, the inference would be entirely precarious. The hearing of an articulate voice and rational discourse in the dark assures us of the presence of some person: Why? because these are the effects of the human make and fabric, and closely connected with it. If we anatomize all the other reasonings of this nature, we shall find that they are founded on the relation of cause and effect, and that this relation is either near or remote, direct or collateral. Heat and light are collateral effects of fire, and the one effect may justly be inferred from the other.

If we would satisfy ourselves, therefore, concerning the nature of that evidence, which assures us of matters of fact, we must enquire how we arrive at the knowledge of cause and effect.

I shall venture to affirm, as a general proposition, which admits of no exception, that the knowledge of this relation is not, in any instance, attained by reasonings a priori; but arises entirely from experience, when we find that any particular objects are constantly conjoined with each other. Let an object be presented to a man of ever so strong natural reason and abilities; if that object be entirely new to him, he will not be able, by the most accurate examination of its sensible qualities, to discover any of its causes or effects. Adam, though his rational faculties be supposed, at the very first, entirely perfect, could not have inferred from the fluidity and transparency of water that it would suffocate him, or from the light and warmth of fire that it would consume him. No object ever discovers, by the qualities which appear to the senses, either the causes which produced it, or the effects which will arise from it; nor can our reason, unassisted by experience, ever draw any inference concerning real existence and matter of fact.

This proposition, that causes and effects are discoverable, not by reason but by experience, will readily be admitted with regard to such objects, as we remember to have once been altogether unknown to us; since we must be conscious of the utter inability, which we then lay under, of foretelling what would arise from them. Present two smooth pieces of marble to a man who has no tincture of natural philosophy; he will never discover that they will adhere together in such a manner as to require great force to separate them in a direct line, while they make so small a resistance to a lateral pressure. Such events, as bear little analogy to the common course of nature, are also readily confessed to be known only by experience; nor does any man imagine that the explosion of gunpowder, or the attraction of a lodestone, could ever be discovered by arguments a priori. In like manner, when an effect is supposed to depend upon an intricate machinery or secret structure of parts, we make no difficulty in attributing all our knowledge of it to experience. Who will assert that he can give the ultimate reason, why milk or bread is proper nourishment for a man, not for a lion or a tiger?

But the same truth may not appear, at first sight, to have the same evidence with regard to events, which have become familiar to us from our first appearance in the world, which bear a close analogy to the whole course of nature, and which are supposed to depend on the simple qualities of objects, without any secret structure of parts. We are apt to imagine that we could discover these effects by the mere operation of our reason, without experience. We fancy, that were we brought on a sudden into this world, we could at first have inferred that one billiard ball would communicate motion to another upon impulse; and that we needed not to have waited for the event, in order to pronounce with certainty concerning it. Such is the influence of custom, that, where it is strongest, it not only covers our natural ignorance, but even conceals itself, and seems not to take place, merely because it is found in the highest degree.

But to convince us that all the laws of nature, and all the operations of bodies without exception, are known only by experience, the following reflections may, perhaps, suffice. Were any object presented to us, and were we required to pronounce concerning the effect, which will result from it, without consulting past observation; after what manner, I beseech you, must the mind proceed in this operation? It must invent or imagine some event, which it ascribes to the object as its effect; and it is plain that this invention must be entirely arbitrary. The mind can never possibly find the effect in the supposed cause, by the most accurate scrutiny and examination. For the effect is totally different from the cause, and consequently can never be discovered in it. Motion in the second billiard ball is a quite distinct event from motion in the first; nor is there anything in the one to suggest the smallest hint of the other. A stone or piece of metal raised into the air, and left without any support, immediately falls: but to consider the matter a priori, is there anything we discover in this situation which can beget the idea of a downward, rather than an upward, or any other motion, in the stone or metal?

And as the first imagination or invention of a particular effect, in all natural operations, is arbitrary, where we consult not experience; so must we also esteem the supposed tie or connection between the cause and effect, which binds them together, and renders it impossible that any other effect could result from the operation of that cause. When I see, for instance, a billiard ball moving in a straight line towards another; even suppose motion in the second ball should by accident be suggested to me, as the result of their contact or impulse; may I not conceive, that a hundred different events might as well follow from that cause? May not both these balls remain at absolute rest? May not the first ball return in a straight line, or leap off from the second in any line or direction? All these suppositions are consistent and conceivable. Why then should we give the preference to one, which is no more consistent or conceivable than the rest? All our reasonings a priori will never be able to show us any foundation for this preference.

In a word, then, every effect is a distinct event from its cause. It could not, therefore, be discovered in the cause, and the first invention or conception of it, a priori, must be entirely arbitrary. And even after it is suggested, the conjunction of it with the cause must appear equally arbitrary; since there are always many other effects, which, to reason, must seem fully as consistent and natural. In vain, therefore, should we pretend to determine any single event, or infer any cause or effect, without the assistance of observation and experience.

Hence we may discover the reason why no philosopher, who is rational and modest, has ever pretended to assign the ultimate cause of any natural operation, or to show distinctly the action of that power, which produces any single effect in the universe. It is confessed, that the utmost effort of human reason is to reduce the principles, productive of natural phenomena, to a greater simplicity, and to resolve the many particular effects into a few general causes, by means of reasonings from analogy, experience, and observation. But as to the causes of these general causes, we should in vain attempt their discovery; nor shall we ever be able to satisfy ourselves, by any particular explication of them. These ultimate springs and principles are totally shut up from human curiosity and enquiry. Elasticity, gravity, cohesion of parts, communication of motion by impulse; these are probably the ultimate causes and principles which we shall ever discover in nature; and we may esteem ourselves sufficiently happy, if, by accurate enquiry and reasoning, we can trace up the particular phenomena to, or near to, these general principles. The most perfect philosophy of the natural kind only staves off our ignorance a little longer: as perhaps the most perfect philosophy of the moral or metaphysical kind serves only to discover larger portions of it. Thus, the observation of human blindness and weakness is the result of all philosophy, and meets us at every turn, in spite of our endeavors to elude or avoid it.

Nor is geometry, when taken into the assistance of natural philosophy, ever able to remedy this defect, or lead us into the knowledge of ultimate causes, by all that accuracy of reasoning for which it is so justly celebrated. Every part of mixed mathematics proceeds upon the supposition that certain laws are established by nature in her operations; and abstract reasonings are employed, either to assist experience in the discovery of these laws, or to determine their influence in particular instances, where it depends upon any precise degree of distance and quantity. Thus, it is a law of motion, discovered by experience, that the moment or force of any body in motion is in the compound ratio or proportion of its solid contents and its velocity; and consequently, that a small force may remove the greatest obstacle or raise the greatest weight, if, by any contrivance or machinery, we can increase the velocity of that force, so as to make it an overmatch for its antagonist. Geometry assists us in the application of this law, by giving us the just dimensions of all the parts and figures which can enter into any species of machine; but still the discovery of the law itself is owing merely to experience, and all the abstract reasonings in the world could never lead us one step towards the knowledge of it. When we reason a priori, and consider merely any object or cause, as it appears to the mind, independent of all observation, it never could suggest to us the notion of any distinct object, such as its effect; much less, show us the inseparable and inviolable connection between them. A man must be very sagacious who could discover by reasoning that crystal is the effect of heat, and ice of cold, without being previously acquainted with the operation of these qualities.

Skeptical Doubts Concerning the Operation of the Understanding—2

But we have not yet attained any tolerable satisfaction with regard to the question first proposed. Each solution still gives rise to a new question as difficult as the foregoing and leads us on to farther enquiries. When it is asked, what is the nature of all our reasonings concerning matter of fact? the proper answer seems to be, that they are founded on the relation of cause and effect. When again it is asked, what is the foundation of all our reasonings and conclusions concerning that relation? it may be replied in one word, Experience. But if we still carry on our sifting humor, and ask, what is the foundation of all conclusions from experience? this implies a new question, which may be of more difficult solution and explication. Philosophers, that give themselves airs of superior wisdom and sufficiency, have a hard task when they encounter persons of inquisitive dispositions, who push them from every corner to which they retreat, and who are sure at last to bring them to some dangerous dilemma. The best expedient to prevent this confusion, is to be modest in our pretensions; and even to discover the difficulty ourselves before it is objected to us. By this means, we may make a kind of merit of our very ignorance.

I shall content myself, in this section, with an easy task, and shall pretend only to give a negative answer to the question here proposed. I say then, that, even after we have experience of the operations of cause and effect, our conclusions from that experience are not founded on reasoning, or any process of the understanding. This answer we must endeavor both to explain and to defend.

It must certainly be allowed, that nature has kept us at a great distance from all her secrets and has afforded us only the knowledge of a few superficial qualities of objects; while she conceals from us those powers and principles on which the influence of those objects entirely depends. Our senses inform us of the color, weight, and consistence of bread; but neither sense nor reason can ever inform us of those qualities which fit it for the nourishment and support of a human body. Sight or feeling conveys an idea of the actual motion of bodies; but as to that wonderful force or power, which would carry on a moving body for ever in a continued change of place, and which bodies never lose but by communicating it to others; of this we cannot form the most distant conception. But notwithstanding this ignorance of natural powers and principles, we always presume, when we see like sensible qualities, that they have like secret powers, and expect that effects, similar to those which we have experienced, will follow from them. If a body of like color and consistence with that bread, which we have formerly eat, be presented to us, we make no scruple of repeating the experiment, and foresee, with certainty, like nourishment and support. Now this is a process of the mind or thought, of which I would willingly know the foundation. It is allowed on all hands that there is no known connection between the sensible qualities and the secret powers; and consequently, that the mind is not led to form such a conclusion concerning their constant and regular conjunction, by anything which it knows of their nature. As to past Experience, it can be allowed to give direct and certain information of those precise objects only, and that precise period of time, which fell under its cognizance: but why this experience should be extended to future times, and to other objects, which for aught we know, may be only in appearance similar; this is the main question on which I would insist. The bread, which I formerly eat, nourished me; that is, a body of such sensible qualities was, at that time, endued with such secret powers: but does it follow, that other bread must also nourish me at another time, and that like sensible qualities must always be attended with like secret powers? The consequence seems nowise necessary. At least, it must be acknowledged that there is here a consequence drawn by the mind; that there is a certain step taken; a process of thought, and an inference, which wants to be explained. These two propositions are far from being the same. I have found that such an object has always been attended with such an effect, and I foresee, that other objects, which are, in appearance, similar, will be attended with similar effects. I shall allow, if you please, that the one proposition may justly be inferred from the other: I know, in fact, that it always is inferred. But if you insist that the inference is made by a chain of reasoning, I desire you to produce that reasoning. The connection between these propositions is not intuitive.

5 There is required a medium, which may enable the mind to draw such an inference, if indeed it be drawn by reasoning and argument. What that medium is, I must confess, passes my comprehension; and it is incumbent on those to produce it, who assert that it really exists, and is the origin of all our conclusions concerning matter of fact.

10 This negative argument must certainly, in process of time, become altogether convincing, if many penetrating and able philosophers shall turn their enquiries this way and no one be ever able to discover any connecting proposition or intermediate step, which supports the understanding in this conclusion. But as the question is yet new, every

15 reader may not trust so far to his own penetration, as to conclude, because an argument escapes his enquiry, that therefore it does not really exist. For this reason it may be requisite to venture upon a more difficult task; and enumerating all the branches of human knowledge, endeavor to show that none of them can afford such an argument.

20 All reasonings may be divided into two kinds, namely, demonstrative reasoning, or that concerning relations of ideas, and moral reasoning, or that concerning matter of fact and existence. That there are no demonstrative arguments in the case seems evident; since it implies no contradiction that the course of nature may change, and that an object,

25 seemingly like those which we have experienced, may be attended with different or contrary effects. May I not clearly and distinctly conceive that a body, falling from the clouds, and which, in all other respects, resembles snow, has yet the taste of salt or feeling of fire? Is there any more intelligible proposition than to affirm, that all the trees will flourish in

30 December and January, and decay in May and June? Now whatever is intelligible, and can be distinctly conceived, implies no contradiction, and can never be proved false by any demonstrative argument or abstract reasoning a priori.

If we be, therefore, engaged by arguments to put trust in past experience,

35 and make it the standard of our future judgment, these arguments must be probable only, or such as regard matter of fact and real existence according to the division above mentioned. But that there is no argument

of this kind, must appear, if our explication of that species of reasoning be admitted as solid and satisfactory. We have said that all arguments concerning existence are founded on the relation of cause and effect; that our knowledge of that relation is derived entirely from experience; and that all our experimental conclusions proceed upon the supposition that the future will be conformable to the past. To endeavor, therefore, the proof of this last supposition by probable arguments, or arguments regarding existence, must be evidently going in a circle, and taking that for granted, which is the very point in question.

In reality, all arguments from experience are founded on the similarity which we discover among natural objects, and by which we are induced to expect effects similar to those which we have found to follow from such objects. And though none but a fool or madman will ever pretend to dispute the authority of experience, or to reject that great guide of human life, it may surely be allowed a philosopher to have so much curiosity at least as to examine the principle of human nature, which gives this mighty authority to experience, and makes us draw advantage from that similarity which nature has placed among different objects. From causes which appear similar we expect similar effects. This is the sum of all our experimental conclusions. Now it seems evident that, if this conclusion were formed by reason, it would be as perfect at first, and upon one instance, as after ever so long a course of experience. But the case is far otherwise. Nothing so like as eggs; yet no one, on account of this appearing similarity, expects the same taste and relish in all of them. It is only after a long course of uniform experiments in any kind, that we attain a firm reliance and security with regard to a particular event. Now where is that process of reasoning which, from one instance, draws a conclusion, so different from that which it infers from a hundred instances that are nowise different from that single one? This question I propose as much for the sake of information, as with an intention of raising difficulties. I cannot find, I cannot imagine any such reasoning. But I keep my mind still open to instruction, if anyone will vouchsafe to bestow it on me.

Should it be said that, from a number of uniform experiments, we infer a connection between the sensible qualities and the secret powers; this, I must confess, seems the same difficulty, couched in different terms. The question still recurs, on what process of argument this inference is founded? Where is the medium, the interposing ideas, which join propositions so very wide of each other? It is confessed that the color, consistence, and other sensible qualities of bread appear not, of themselves, to have any connection with the secret powers of nourishment and support. For otherwise we could infer these secret powers from the first appearance of these sensible qualities, without the aid of experience; contrary to the sentiment of all philosophers, and contrary to plain matter of fact. Here, then, is our natural state of ignorance with regard to the powers and influence of all objects. How is this remedied by experience? It only shows us a number of uniform effects, resulting from certain objects, and teaches us that those particular objects, at that particular time, were endowed with such powers and forces. When a new object, endowed with similar sensible qualities, is produced, we expect similar powers and forces, and look for a like effect. From a body of like color and consistence with bread we expect like nourishment and support. But this surely is a step or progress of the mind, which wants to be explained. When a man says, I have found, in all past instances, such sensible qualities conjoined with such secret powers: And when he says, Similar sensible qualities will always be conjoined with similar secret powers, he is not guilty of a tautology, nor are these propositions in any respect the same. You say that the one proposition is an inference from the other. But you must confess that the inference is not intuitive; neither is it demonstrative: Of what nature is it, then? To say it is experimental, is begging the question. For all inferences from experience suppose, as their foundation, that the future will resemble the past, and that similar powers will be conjoined with similar sensible qualities. If there be any suspicion that the course of nature may change, and that the past may be no rule for the future, all experience becomes useless, and can give rise to no inference or conclusion. It is impossible, therefore, that any arguments from experience can prove this resemblance of the past to the future, since all these arguments are founded on the supposition of that resemblance. Let the course of things be allowed hitherto ever so regular; that alone, without some new argument or inference, proves not that, for the future, it will continue so. In vain do you pretend to have learned the nature of bodies from your past experience. Their secret nature, and consequently all their effects and influence, may change, without any change in their sensible qualities. This happens sometimes, and with regard to some objects: Why may it not happen always, and with regard to all objects? What logic, what process or argument secures you against this supposition? My practice, you say, refutes my doubts. But you mistake the purport of my question. As an agent, I am quite satisfied in the point; but as a philosopher, who has some share of curiosity, I will not say skepticism, I want to learn the foundation of this inference. No reading, no enquiry has yet been able to remove my difficulty or give me satisfaction in a matter of such importance. Can I do better than propose the difficulty to the public, even though, perhaps, I have small hopes of obtaining a solution? We shall at least, by this means, be sensible of our ignorance, if we do not augment our knowledge.

I must confess that a man is guilty of unpardonable arrogance who concludes, because an argument has escaped his own investigation, that therefore it does not really exist. I must also confess that, though all the learned, for several ages, should have employed themselves in fruitless search upon any subject, it may still, perhaps, be rash to conclude positively that the subject must, therefore, pass all human comprehension. Even though we examine all the sources of our knowledge, and conclude them unfit for such a subject, there may still remain a suspicion, that the enumeration is not complete, or the examination not accurate. But with regard to the present subject, there are some considerations which seem to remove all this accusation of arrogance or suspicion of mistake.

It is certain that the most ignorant and stupid peasants—nay infants, nay even brute beasts—improve by experience, and learn the qualities of natural objects, by observing the effects which result from them. When a child has felt the sensation of pain from touching the flame of a candle, he will be careful not to put his hand near any candle; but will expect a similar effect from a cause which is similar in its sensible qualities and appearance. If you assert, therefore, that the understanding of the child is led into this conclusion by any process of argument or ratiocination, I may justly require you to produce that argument; nor have you any pretense to refuse so equitable a demand. You cannot say that the argument is abstruse and may possibly escape your enquiry; since you confess that it is obvious to the capacity of a mere infant. If you hesitate, therefore, a moment, or if, after reflection, you produce any intricate or profound argument, you, in a manner, give up the question, and confess that it is reasoning which engages us to suppose the past resembling the future, and to expect similar effects from causes which are, to appearance, similar. This is the proposition which I intended to enforce in the present section. If I be right, I pretend not to have made any mighty discovery. And if I be wrong, I must acknowledge myself to be indeed a very backward scholar; since I cannot now discover an argument which, it seems, was perfectly familiar to me long before I was out of my cradle.

Skeptical Solution of These Doubts—1

5 The passion for philosophy, like that for religion, seems liable to this inconvenience, that, though it aims at the correction of our manners, and extirpation of our vices, it may only serve, by imprudent management, to foster a predominant inclination, and push the mind, with more determined resolution, towards that side which already draws too much, 10 by the bias and propensity of the natural temper. It is certain that, while we aspire to the magnanimous firmness of the philosophic sage, and endeavor to confine our pleasures altogether within our own minds, we may, at last, render our philosophy like that of Epictetus, and other Stoics, only a more refined system of selfishness, and reason ourselves 15 out of all virtue as well as social enjoyment. While we study with attention the vanity of human life and turn all our thoughts towards the empty and transitory nature of riches and honors, we are, perhaps, all the while flattering our natural indolence, which, hating the bustle of the world, and drudgery of business, seeks a pretense of reason to give itself a full 20 and uncontrolled indulgence. There is, however, one species of philosophy which seems little liable to this inconvenience, and that because it strikes in with no disorderly passion of the human mind, nor can mingle itself with any natural affection or propensity; and that is the Academic or Skeptical philosophy. The academics always talk of doubt 25 and suspense of judgment, of danger in hasty determinations, of confining to very narrow bounds the enquiries of the understanding, and of renouncing all speculations which lie not within the limits of common life and practice. Nothing, therefore, can be more contrary than such a philosophy to the supine indolence of the mind, its rash arrogance, its 30 lofty pretensions, and its superstitious credulity. Every passion is mortified by it, except the love of truth; and that passion never is, nor can be, carried to too high a degree. It is surprising, therefore, that this philosophy, which, in almost every instance, must be harmless and innocent, should be the subject of so much groundless reproach and 35 obloquy. But, perhaps, the very circumstance which renders it so innocent is what chiefly exposes it to the public hatred and resentment. By flattering no irregular passion, it gains few partisans: By opposing so

many vices and follies, it raises to itself abundance of enemies, who stigmatize it as libertine, profane, and irreligious.

Nor need we fear that this philosophy, while it endeavors to limit our enquiries to common life, should ever undermine the reasonings of common life, and carry its doubts so far as to destroy all action, as well as speculation. Nature will always maintain her rights and prevail in the end over any abstract reasoning whatsoever. Though we should conclude, for instance, as in the foregoing section, that, in all reasonings from experience, there is a step taken by the mind which is not supported by any argument or process of the understanding; there is no danger that these reasonings, on which almost all knowledge depends, will ever be affected by such a discovery. If the mind be not engaged by argument to make this step, it must be induced by some other principle of equal weight and authority; and that principle will preserve its influence as long as human nature remains the same. What that principle is may well be worth the pains of enquiry.

Suppose a person, though endowed with the strongest faculties of reason and reflection, to be brought on a sudden into this world; he would, indeed, immediately observe a continual succession of objects, and one event following another; but he would not be able to discover anything farther. He would not, at first, by any reasoning, be able to reach the idea of cause and effect; since the particular powers, by which all natural operations are performed, never appear to the senses; nor is it reasonable to conclude, merely because one event, in one instance, precedes another, that therefore the one is the cause, the other the effect. Their conjunction may be arbitrary and casual. There may be no reason to infer the existence of one from the appearance of the other. And in a word, such a person, without more experience, could never employ his conjecture or reasoning concerning any matter of fact, or be assured of anything beyond what was immediately present to his memory and senses.

Suppose, again, that he has acquired more experience, and has lived so long in the world as to have observed familiar objects or events to be constantly conjoined together; what is the consequence of this experience? He immediately infers the existence of one object from the appearance of the other. Yet he has not, by all his experience, acquired any idea or knowledge of the secret power by which the one object produces the other; nor is it by any process of reasoning, he is engaged to draw this inference. But still he finds himself determined to draw it: and though he should be convinced that his understanding has no part in the operation, he would nevertheless continue in the same course of thinking. There is some other principle which determines him to form such a conclusion.

This principle is custom or habit. For wherever the repetition of any particular act or operation produces a propensity to renew the same act or operation, without being impelled by any reasoning or process of the understanding, we always say, that this propensity is the effect of Custom. By employing that word, we pretend not to have given the ultimate reason of such a propensity. We only point out a principle of human nature, which is universally acknowledged, and which is well known by its effects. Perhaps we can push our enquiries no farther or pretend to give the cause of this cause; but must rest contented with it as the ultimate principle, which we can assign, of all our conclusions from experience. It is sufficient satisfaction, that we can go so far, without repining at the narrowness of our faculties because they will carry us no farther. And it is certain we here advance a very intelligible proposition at least, if not a true one, when we assert that, after the constant conjunction of two objects—heat and flame, for instance, weight and solidity—we are determined by custom alone to expect the one from the appearance of the other. This hypothesis seems even the only one which explains the difficulty, why we draw, from a thousand instances, an inference which we are not able to draw from one instance, that is, in no respect, different from them. Reason is incapable of any such variation. The conclusions which it draws from considering one circle are the same which it would form upon surveying all the circles in the universe. But no man, having seen only one body move after being impelled by another, could infer that every other body will move after a like impulse. All inferences from experience, therefore, are effects of custom, not of reasoning.

Custom, then, is the great guide of human life. It is that principle alone which renders our experience useful to us, and makes us expect, for the future, a similar train of events with those which have appeared in the past. Without the influence of custom, we should be entirely ignorant of every matter of fact beyond what is immediately present to the memory and senses. We should never know how to adjust means to ends, or to employ our natural powers in the production of any effect. There would be an end at once of all action, as well as of the chief part of speculation.

But here it may be proper to remark, that though our conclusions from experience carry us beyond our memory and senses and assure us of matters of fact which happened in the most distant places and most remote ages, yet some fact must always be present to the senses or memory, from which we may first proceed in drawing these conclusions. A man, who should find in a desert country the remains of pompous buildings, would conclude that the country had, in ancient times, been cultivated by civilized inhabitants; but did nothing of this nature occur to him, he could never form such an inference. We learn the events of former ages from history; but then we must peruse the volumes in which this instruction is contained, and thence carry up our inferences from one testimony to another, till we arrive at the eyewitnesses and spectators of these distant events. In a word, if we proceed not upon some fact, present to the memory or senses, our reasonings would be merely hypothetical; and however the particular links might be connected with each other, the whole chain of inferences would have nothing to support it, nor could we ever, by its means, arrive at the knowledge of any real existence. If I ask why you believe any particular matter of fact, which you relate, you must tell me some reason; and this reason will be some other fact, connected with it. But as you cannot proceed after this manner, in infinitum, you must at last terminate in some fact, which is present to your memory or senses; or must allow that your belief is entirely without foundation.

What, then, is the conclusion of the whole matter? A simple one; though, it must be confessed, pretty remote from the common theories of philosophy. All belief of matter of fact or real existence is derived merely from some object, present to the memory or senses, and a customary conjunction between that and some other object. Or in other words; having found, in many instances, that any two kinds of objects—flame and heat, snow and cold—have always been conjoined together; if flame or snow be presented anew to the senses, the mind is carried by custom to expect heat or cold, and to believe that such a quality does exist, and will discover itself upon a nearer approach. This belief is the necessary result of placing the mind in such circumstances. It is an operation of the soul, when we are so situated, as unavoidable as to feel the passion of love, when we receive benefits; or hatred, when we meet with injuries. All these operations are a species of natural instincts, which no reasoning or process of the thought and understanding is able either to produce or to prevent.

At this point, it would be very allowable for us to stop our philosophical researches. In most questions we can never make a single step farther; and in all questions we must terminate here at last, after our most restless and curious enquiries. But still our curiosity will be pardonable, perhaps commendable, if it carry us on to still farther researches, and make us examine more accurately the nature of this belief, and of the customary conjunction, whence it is derived. By this means we may meet with some explications and analogies that will give satisfaction; at least to such as love the abstract sciences, and can be entertained with speculations, which, however accurate, may still retain a degree of doubt and uncertainty. As to readers of a different taste, the remaining part of this section is not calculated for them, and the following enquiries may well be understood, though it be neglected.

Skeptical Solution of These Doubts—2

Nothing is more free than the imagination of man; and though it cannot exceed that original stock of ideas furnished by the internal and external senses, it has unlimited power of mixing, compounding, separating, and dividing these ideas, in all the varieties of fiction and vision. It can feign a train of events, with all the appearance of reality, ascribe to them a particular time and place, conceive them as existent, and paint them out to itself with every circumstance, that belongs to any historical fact, which it believes with the greatest certainty. Wherein, therefore, consists the difference between such a fiction and belief? It lies not merely in any peculiar idea, which is annexed to such a conception as commands our assent, and which is wanting to every known fiction. For as the mind has authority over all its ideas, it could voluntarily annex this particular idea to any fiction, and consequently be able to believe whatever it pleases; contrary to what we find by daily experience. We can, in our conception, join the head of a man to the body of a horse; but it is not in our power to believe that such an animal has ever really existed.

It follows, therefore, that the difference between fiction and belief lies in some sentiment or feeling, which is annexed to the latter, not to the former, and which depends not on the will, nor can be commanded at pleasure. It must be excited by nature, like all other sentiments; and must arise from the particular situation, in which the mind is placed at any particular juncture. Whenever any object is presented to the memory or senses, it immediately, by the force of custom, carries the imagination to conceive that object, which is usually conjoined to it; and this conception is attended with a feeling or sentiment, different from the loose reveries of the fancy. In this consists the whole nature of belief. For as there is no matter of fact which we believe so firmly that we cannot conceive the contrary, there would be no difference between the conception assented to and that which is rejected, were it not for some sentiment which distinguishes the one from the other. If I see a billiard ball moving toward another, on a smooth table, I can easily conceive it to stop upon contact. This conception implies no contradiction; but still it feels very differently from that conception by which I represent to myself the impulse and the communication of motion from one ball to another.

Were we to attempt a definition of this sentiment, we should, perhaps, find it a very difficult, if not an impossible task; in the same manner as if we should endeavor to define the feeling of cold or passion of anger, to a creature who never had any experience of these sentiments. Belief is the true and proper name of this feeling; and no one is ever at a loss to know the meaning of that term; because every man is every moment conscious of the sentiment represented by it. It may not, however, be improper to attempt a description of this sentiment; in hopes we may, by that means, arrive at some analogies, which may afford a more perfect explication of it. I say, then, that belief is nothing but a more vivid, lively, forcible, firm, steady conception of an object, than what the imagination alone is ever able to attain. This variety of terms, which may seem so unphilosophical, is intended only to express that act of the mind, which renders realities, or what is taken for such, more present to us than fictions, causes them to weigh more in the thought, and gives them a superior influence on the passions and imagination. Provided we agree about the thing, it is needless to dispute about the terms. The imagination has the command over all its ideas, and can join and mix and vary them, in all the ways possible. It may conceive fictitious objects with all the circumstances of place and time. It may set them, in a manner, before our eyes, in their true colors, just as they might have existed. But as it is impossible that this faculty of imagination can ever, of itself, reach belief, it is evident that belief consists not in the peculiar nature or order of ideas, but in the manner of their conception, and in their feeling to the mind. I confess, that it is impossible perfectly to explain this feeling or manner of conception. We may make use of words which express something near it. But its true and proper name, as we observed before, is belief, which is a term that everyone sufficiently understands in common life. And in philosophy, we can go no farther than assert, that belief is something felt by the mind, which distinguishes the ideas of the judgment from the fictions of the imagination. It gives them more weight and influence; makes them appear of greater importance; enforces them in the mind; and renders them the governing principle of our actions. I hear at present, for instance, a person's voice, with whom I am acquainted; and the sound comes as from the next room. This impression of my senses immediately conveys my thought to the person, together with all the surrounding objects. I paint them out to myself as existing at present, with the same qualities and relations, of which I formerly knew them possessed. These ideas take faster hold of my mind than ideas of an enchanted castle. They are very different to the feeling, and have a much greater influence of every kind, either to give pleasure or pain, joy or sorrow.

Let us, then, take in the whole compass of this doctrine, and allow, that the sentiment of belief is nothing but a conception more intense and steady than what attends the mere fictions of the imagination, and that this manner of conception arises from a customary conjunction of the object with something present to the memory or senses: I believe that it will not be difficult, upon these suppositions, to find other operations of the mind analogous to it, and to trace up these phenomena to principles still more general.

We have already observed that nature has established connections among particular ideas, and that no sooner one idea occurs to our thoughts than it introduces its correlative, and carries our attention towards it, by a gentle and insensible movement. These principles of connection or association we have reduced to three, namely, resemblance, contiguity and causation, which are the only bonds that unite our thoughts together, and beget that regular train of reflection or discourse, which, in a greater or less degree, takes place among all mankind. Now here arises a question, on which the solution of the present difficulty will depend. Does it happen, in all these relations, that, when one of the objects is presented to the senses or memory, the mind is not only carried to the conception of the correlative, but reaches a steadier and stronger conception of it than what otherwise it would have been able to attain? This seems to be the case with that belief which arises from the relation of cause and effect. And if the case be the same with the other relations or principles of associations, this may be established as a general law, which takes place in all the operations of the mind.

We may, therefore, observe, as the first experiment to our present purpose, that, upon the appearance of the picture of an absent friend, our idea of him is evidently enlivened by the resemblance, and that every passion, which that idea occasions, whether of joy or sorrow, acquires new force and vigor. In producing this effect, there concur both a relation and a present impression. Where the picture bears him no resemblance, at least was not intended for him, it never so much as conveys our thought to him: and where it is absent, as well as the person, though the mind may pass from the thought of the one to that of the other, it feels its idea to be rather weakened than enlivened by that transition. We take a pleasure in viewing the picture of a friend, when it is set before us; but when it is removed, rather choose to consider him directly than by reflection in an image, which is equally distant and obscure.

The ceremonies of the Roman Catholic religion may be considered as instances of the same nature. The devotees of that superstition usually plead in excuse for the mummeries, with which they are upbraided, that they feel the good effect of those external motions, and postures, and actions, in enlivening their devotion and quickening their fervor, which otherwise would decay, if directed entirely to distant and immaterial objects. We shadow out the objects of our faith, say they, in sensible types and images, and render them more present to us by the immediate presence of these types, than it is possible for us to do merely by an intellectual view and contemplation. Sensible objects have always a greater influence on the fancy than any other; and this influence they readily convey to those ideas to which they are related, and which they resemble. I shall only infer from these practices, and this reasoning, that the effect of resemblance in enlivening the ideas is very common; and as in every case a resemblance and a present impression must concur, we are abundantly supplied with experiments to prove the reality of the foregoing principle.

We may add force to these experiments by others of a different kind, in considering the effects of contiguity as well as of resemblance. It is certain

DO WE HAVE IT ALL WRONG?

that distance diminishes the force of every idea, and that, upon our approach to any object; though it does not discover itself to our senses; it operates upon the mind with an influence, which imitates an immediate impression. The thinking on any object readily transports the mind to what is contiguous; but it is only the actual presence of an object, that transports it with a superior vivacity. When I am a few miles from home, whatever relates to it touches me more nearly than when I am two hundred leagues distant, though even at that distance the reflecting on anything in the neighborhood of my friends or family naturally produces an idea of them. But as in this latter case, both the objects of the mind are ideas; notwithstanding there is an easy transition between them; that transition alone is not able to give a superior vivacity to any of the ideas, for want of some immediate impression.

No one can doubt but causation has the same influence as the other two relations of resemblance and contiguity. Superstitious people are fond of the relics of saints and holy men, for the same reason, that they seek after types or images, in order to enliven their devotion, and give them a more intimate and strong conception of those exemplary lives, which they desire to imitate. Now it is evident, that one of the best relics, which a devotee could procure, would be the handiwork of a saint; and if his cloths and furniture are ever to be considered in this light, it is because they were once at his disposal, and were moved and affected by him; in which respect they are to be considered as imperfect effects, and as connected with him by a shorter chain of consequences than any of those, by which we learn the reality of his existence.

Suppose that the son of a friend, who had been long dead or absent, were presented to us; it is evident, that this object would instantly revive its correlative idea, and recall to our thoughts all past intimacies and familiarities, in more lively colors than they would otherwise have appeared to us. This is another phenomenon, which seems to prove the principle above mentioned.

We may observe, that, in these phenomena, the belief of the correlative object is always presupposed; without which the relation could have no effect. The influence of the picture supposes that we believe our friend to have once existed. Contiguity to home can never excite our ideas of home, unless we believe that it really exists. Now I assert, that this belief, where it reaches beyond the memory or senses, is of a similar nature, and

35

arises from similar causes, with the transition of thought and vivacity of conception here explained. When I throw a piece of dry wood into a fire, my mind is immediately carried to conceive, that it augments, not extinguishes the flame. This transition of thought from the cause to the effect proceeds not from reason. It derives its origin altogether from custom and experience. And as it first begins from an object, present to the senses, it renders the idea or conception of flame more strong and lively than any loose, floating reverie of the imagination. That idea arises immediately. The thought moves instantly towards it, and conveys to it all that force of conception, which is derived from the impression present to the senses. When a sword is leveled at my breast, does not the idea of wound and pain strike me more strongly, than when a glass of wine is presented to me, even though by accident this idea should occur after the appearance of the latter object? But what is there in this whole matter to cause such a strong conception, except only a present object and a customary transition of the idea of another object, which we have been accustomed to conjoin with the former? This is the whole operation of the mind, in all our conclusions concerning matter of fact and existence; and it is a satisfaction to find some analogies, by which it may be explained. The transition from a present object does in all cases give strength and solidity to the related idea.

Here, then, is a kind of pre-established harmony between the course of nature and the succession of our ideas; and though the powers and forces, by which the former is governed, be wholly unknown to us; yet our thoughts and conceptions have still, we find, gone on in the same train with the other works of nature. Custom is that principle, by which this correspondence has been effected, so necessary to the subsistence of our species, and the regulation of our conduct, in every circumstance and occurrence of human life. Had not the presence of an object, instantly excited the idea of those objects, commonly conjoined with it, all our knowledge must have been limited to the narrow sphere of our memory and senses; and we should never have been able to adjust means to ends, or employ our natural powers, either to the producing of good, or avoiding of evil. Those, who delight in the discovery and contemplation of final causes, have here ample subject to employ their wonder and admiration.

I shall add, for a further confirmation of the foregoing theory, that, as this operation of the mind, by which we infer like effects from like causes, and vice versa, is so essential to the subsistence of all human creatures, it is not probable, that it could be trusted to the fallacious deductions of our reason, which is slow in its operations; appears not, in any degree, during the first years of infancy; and at best is, in every age and period of human life, extremely liable to error and mistake. It is more conformable to the ordinary wisdom of nature to secure so necessary an act of the mind, by some instinct or mechanical tendency, which may be infallible in its operations, may discover itself at the first appearance of life and thought, and may be independent of all the labored deductions of the understanding. As nature has taught us the use of our limbs, without giving us the knowledge of the muscles and nerves, by which they are actuated; so has she implanted in us an instinct, which carries forward the thought in a correspondent course to that which she has established among external objects; though we are ignorant of those powers and forces, on which this regular course and succession of objects totally depends.

QUESTIONS TO CONSIDER

- How do the two types of knowledge, matters of fact and relation between ideas, differ? With which type does Hume seem primarily concerned?

- What is the skeptical problem Hume presents to us when it comes to knowing matters of fact? Consider his examples carefully. Is he right, that experience alone could not assure us that a billiard ball striking another will always have the usual effect? Before we experience it, could we possibly predict what would happen if we were to ignite gunpowder or bring a magnet (lodestone) near ferrous metal?

- Is the claim that, in nature, the future will always be like the past, provable by experience?

- If Hume happened to be right, what would be the implication for a philosophy of nature?

- What solution does Hume propose to the skeptical problem he has raised? What difference does he draw out between knowledge such as is found in relations between ideas and *belief*? Is a belief rooted in evidence? If not, then in what?

UNITY | IDENTITY | ORIGINS

2

EARLY MATERIALISM

Materialism took hold during the early Greek and classical Roman eras. The philosophers whom we shall first look at are called Presocratics, not only because they lived before Socrates, but because their philosophical interests differed sharply from his. We will consider them in four groups. The first two contain philosophers who emphasize the unity of natural things (so-called monists), the third, philosophers who, in contrast, believe that an explanation is needed for the great diversity of natural things (pluralists), and the fourth philosophers who, though also pluralists, have recourse to natural explanations in terms of indivisible material parts, a view known today as classical atomism.

MATERIALISTIC MONISM

THALES

All things come from water.

The earth rests on water.

A magnet has a soul, since it moves iron. All things are full of gods.

The wet nature, easily reformed into each thing, is shaped in various ways: for [the part] of it which turns into vapor becomes like air, and what is thinned out of the air becomes ether, and, as water settles and changes into mud, it becomes earth. Therefore Thales claimed that, among the four elements, water was the element, as being more of a cause [than the others].

ANAXIMANDER

Anaximander of Miletus, son of Praxiades, a fellow-citizen and associate of Thales, said that the material cause and first element of things was the Infinite, he being the first to introduce this name of the material cause. He says that it is neither water nor any other of what are now called the elements, but a substance different from them which is infinite, from which arise all the heavens and the worlds within them.

He says that this is eternal and ageless, and that it encompasses all the worlds.

And into that from which things take their rise they pass away once more, "as is ordained; for they make reparation and satisfaction to one another for their injustice according to the appointed," as he says in these somewhat poetical terms.

And besides this, there was an eternal motion, in which was brought about the origin of the worlds.

He did not ascribe the origin of things to any alteration in matter, but said that the oppositions in the substratum, which was a boundless body, were separated out.

[He holds] that this (i.e., a body over and above the elements) is what is infinite, and not air or water, in order that the other things may not be destroyed by their infinity. They are in opposition to one another—air is cold, water moist, and fire hot—and therefore if any one of them were infinite, the rest would have ceased to be by this time. Accordingly [he says] that what is infinite is something other than the elements, and that from it the elements arise.

ANAXIMENES

Anaximenes of Miletus, son of Eurystratos, who had been an associate of Anaximander, said, like him, that the underlying substance was one and infinite. He did not, however, say it was indeterminate, like Anaximander, but determinate; for he said it was Air.

From it, he said, the things that are, and have been, and shall be, the gods and things divine, took their rise, while other things come from its offspring.

"Just as," he said, "our soul, being air, holds us together, so do breath and air encompass the whole world."

And the form of the air is as follows. Where it is most even, it is invisible to our sight; but cold and heat, moisture and motion, make it visible. It is always in motion; for, if it were not, it would not change so much as it does.

It differs in different substances in virtue of its rarefaction and condensation.

When it is dilated so as to be rarer, it becomes fire; while winds, on the other hand, are condensed Air. Cloud is formed from air by compression; and this, still further condensed, becomes water. Water, condensed still more, turns to earth; and when condensed as much as it can be, to stones.

QUESTIONS TO CONSIDER

- For Thales, Anaximander, and Anaximenes, is being one, or many? What, for each, is the principle of all things? In your judgment, is this claim plausible in any way?
- Do these philosophers admit any sort of change? If so, what kind?
- What kind of a principle is water, for Thales, the Infinite, for Anaximander, or air, for Anaximenes? That is, does it bring about change in some way, or is it merely required in order for change to occur?
- Would it be fair to each philosopher to assert that each element and other things are different kinds of thing?
- Why, claims Anaximander, can the principle of all things not be earth, or air, or fire, or water?

ELEATIC MONISM

PARMENIDES OF ELEA

The Way of Truth

Come now, I will tell you—and do you hearken to my saying and carry it away—the only two ways of search that can be thought of. The first, namely, that It is, and that it is impossible for anything not to be, is the way of conviction, for truth is its companion. The other, namely, that It
5   is not, and that something must not be—that, I tell you, is a wholly untrustworthy path. For you cannot know what is not—that is impossible—nor utter it; for it is the same thing that can be thought and that can be.

It must be that what can be thought and spoken of is; for it is possible
10 for it to be, and it is not possible for what is nothing to be. This is what I bid you ponder. I hold you back from this first way of inquiry, and from this other **"This shall never be proved, that the things that are not, are."** also, upon which mortals knowing nothing wander in two minds; for
15 hesitation guides the wandering thought in their breasts, so that they are borne along stupefied like men deaf and blind.

Undiscerning crowds, in whose eyes the same thing and not the same is and is not, and all things travel in opposite directions!

For this shall never be proved, that the things that are not, are; and do
20 you restrain your thought from this way of inquiry.

One path only is left for us to speak of, namely, that It is. In it are very many tokens that what is, is uncreated and indestructible, alone, complete, immovable and without end. Nor was it ever, nor will it be; for now it is, all at once, a continuous one. For what kind of origin for it will
25 you look for? In what way and from what source could it have drawn its increase? I shall not let you say nor think that it came from what is not; for it can neither be thought nor uttered that what is not is. And, if it came from nothing, what need could have made it arise later rather than sooner? Therefore, must it either be altogether or be not at all. Nor will

---

the force of truth suffer anything to arise besides itself from that which in any way is. Wherefore, Justice does not loose her fetters and let anything come into being or pass away but holds it fast.

"Is it or is it not?" Surely it is judged, as it must be, that we are to set aside
5 the one way as unthinkable and nameless (for it is no true way), and that the other path is real and true. How, then, can what is be going to be in the future? Or how could it come into being? If it came into being, it is not; nor is it if it is going to be in the future. Thus is becoming extinguished and passing away not to be heard of.

10 Nor is it divisible, since it is all alike, and there is no more of it in one place than in another, to hinder it from holding together, nor less of it, but everything is full of what is. Wherefore all holds together; for what is, is in contact with what is.

Moreover, it is immovable in the bonds of mighty chains, without
15 beginning and without end; since coming into being and passing away have been driven afar, and true belief has cast them away. It is the same, and it rests in the self-same place, abiding in itself. And thus it remains constant in its place; for hard necessity keeps it in the bonds of the limit that holds it fast on every side. Wherefore it is not permitted to what is
20 to be infinite; for it is in need of nothing; while, if it were infinite, it would stand in need of everything.

Look steadfastly with your mind at things afar as though they were at hand. You cannot cut off what anywhere is from holding fast to what is anywhere; neither is it scattered abroad throughout the universe, nor
25 does it come together.

It is the same thing that can be thought and for the sake of which the thought exists; for you cannot find thought without something that is, to which it is betrothed. And there is not, and never shall be, any time other than that which is present, since fate has chained it so as to be whole and
30 immovable. Wherefore all these things are but the names which mortals have given, believing them to be true—coming into being and passing away, being and not being, change of place and alteration of bright color.

Where, then, it has a farthest boundary, it is complete on every side, equally poised from the center in every direction, like the mass of a

rounded sphere; for it cannot be greater or smaller in one place than in another. For there is nothing which is not that could keep it from reaching out equally, nor is it possible that there should be more of what is in this place and less in that, since it is all inviolable. For, since it is equal
5   in all directions, it is equally confined within limits.

The Way of Opinion

Here shall I close my trustworthy speech and thought about the truth. Henceforward learn the opinions of mortals, giving ear to the deceptive ordering of my words...

Thus, according to men's opinions, did things come into being, and thus
10   they are now. In time (they think) they will grow up and pass away. To each of these things men have assigned a fixed name.

QUESTIONS TO CONSIDER

- What is Parmenides' overall conclusion? How does he support it? Does he attempt to explain nature as we know it? For example, do things even come into being and cease to be, for him?
- According to Parmenides, what "shall never be proved"? Does this make sense? How does he describe being itself (that which is)?
- What do the words 'coming into being' and 'alteration' mean, for Parmenides?

MELISSUS OF SAMOS

If nothing is, what can be said of it as of something real?

What was, was ever, and ever will be. For, if it had come into being, it needs must have been nothing before it came into being. Now, if it were
15   nothing, in no wise could anything have arisen out of nothing.

Since, then, it has not come into being, and since it is, was ever, and ever shall be, it has no beginning or end, but is without limit. For, if it had come into being, it would have had a beginning (for it would have begun to come into being at some time or other) and an end (for it would have
20   ceased to come into being at some time or other); but, if it neither began

44

nor ended, and ever was and ever will be, it has no beginning or end; for it is not possible for anything to be ever without all being.

Further, just as it ever is, so it must ever be infinite in magnitude.

But nothing which has a beginning or end is either eternal or infinite.

5   If it were not one, it would be bounded by something else.

For if it is infinite, it must be one; for if it were two, it could not be infinite; for then they would be bounded by one another.

And, since it is one, it is alike throughout; for if it were unlike, it would be many and not one.

10   So then it is eternal and infinite and one and all alike. And it cannot perish nor become greater, nor does it suffer pain or grief. For, if any of these things happened to it, it would no longer be one. *"What was, was ever, and ever will be."* For if it is altered, then the real must needs not be all alike, but what was

15   before must pass away, and what was not must come into being. Now, if it changed by so much as a single hair in ten thousand years, it would all perish in the whole of time...

This argument, then, is the greatest proof that it is one alone; but the following are proofs of it also. If there were a many, these would have to

20   be of the same kind as I say that the one is. For if there is earth and water, and air and iron, and gold and fire, and if one thing is living and another dead, and if things are black and white and all that people say they really are—if that is so, and if we see and hear aright, each one of these must be such as we first decided, and they cannot be changed or altered, but

25   each must be just as it is. But, as it is, we say that we see and hear and understand aright, and yet we believe that what is warm becomes cold, and what is cold warm; that what is hard turns soft, and what is soft hard; that what is living dies, and that things are born from what lives not; and that all those things are changed, and that what they were and what they

30   are now are in no way alike. We think that iron, which is hard, is rubbed away by contact with the finger; and so with gold and stone and everything which we fancy to be strong, and that earth and stone are made out of water; so that it turns out that we neither see nor know

realities. Now these things do not agree with one another. We said that there were many things that were eternal and had forms and strength of their own, and yet we fancy that they all suffer alteration, and that they change from what we see each time. It is clear, then, that we did not see rightly after all, nor are we right in believing that all these things are many. They would not change if they were real, but each thing would be just what we believed it to be; for nothing is stronger than true reality. But if it has changed, what was has passed away, and what was not is come into being. So then, if there were many things, they would have to be just of the same nature as the one.

Now, if it were to exist, it must needs be one; but if it is one, it cannot have body; for, if it had body it would have parts, and would no longer be one.

QUESTIONS TO CONSIDER

- For Melissus, what are the characteristics of what exists? Compare his position with that of Parmenides. To what extent are the positions similar? To what extent are they dissimilar?
- According to Melissus, is any sort of change possible? If so, what sort is possible? If not, why not?
- Analyze Melissus' argument that things cannot come into being or cease to exist. What is his conclusion, and what reasons does he give in support of this conclusion? Is this a good argument?

ZENO OF ELEA

You cannot traverse an infinite number of points in a finite time. You must traverse the half of any given distance before you traverse the whole, and the half of that again before you can traverse it. This goes on *ad infinitum*, so that there are an infinite number in any given space, and it cannot be traversed in a finite time.

A   C   D   E   B

MATERIALISTIC PLURALISM

EMPEDOCLES OF ACRAGAS

Fools!—for they have no far-reaching thoughts—who think that what before was not comes into being, or that anything can perish and be utterly destroyed. For it cannot be that anything can arise from what in no way is, and it is impossible and unheard of that what is should perish; for it will always be, wherever one may keep putting it.

A man who is wise in such matters would never surmise in his heart that, as long as mortals live what men choose to call their life, [so long] they are, and suffer good and ill; while before they were formed and after they have been dissolved they are, it seems, nothing at all.

There is no coming into being of anything that perishes, nor any end for it in baneful death.; but only mingling and separation of what has been mingled. 'Coming into being' is but a name given to these by men.

But, when the elements have been mingled in the fashion of a man and come to the light of day, or in the fashion of the

race of wild beasts or plants or birds, then men say that these come into being and when they are separated, they call that, as is the custom, woeful death. I too follow the custom and call it so myself.

Come, I shall now tell you first of all the beginning of the sun, and the sources from which have sprung all the things we now behold, the earth and the billowy sea, the damp mist and the Titan air that binds his circle fast round all things.

Hear first the four roots of all things: shining Zeus [fire], life-bringing Hera [air], Aidoneus [earth], and Nestis [water] dripping with tears, the well-spring of mortals.

Behold the sun, everywhere bright and warm, and all the immortal things that are bathed in its heat and bright radiance. Behold the rain, everywhere dark and cold; and from the earth issue forth things close-pressed and solid. When they are in strife all these are different in form and separated; but they come together in love and are desired by one another.

For out of these have sprung all things that were and are and shall be—trees and men and women, beasts and birds and the fishes that dwell in
5   the waters, yes, and the gods that live long lives and are exalted in honor.

For these things are what they are; but, running through one another, they take different shapes—so much does mixture change them.

Just as when painters are elaborating temple-offerings, men whom Metus has well-taught their art—they, when they have taken pigments of many
10   colors with their hands, mix them in a harmony, more of some and less of others, and from them produce shapes like all things, making trees and men and women, beasts
15   and fishes that dwell in the waters, yes, and gods, that live long lives, and are *"There is no coming-into-being of anything that perishes, nor any end for it in baneful death, but only mingling and separation of what has been mingled."* exalted in honor—so let not the error prevail over your mind, that there is any other source of all the perishable creatures that appear in countless
20   numbers. Know this for sure, for you have heard the tale from a goddess.

And the kindly earth in its well-wrought ovens received two parts of shining Nestis out of the eight, and four of Hephaistos; and they became white bones, divinely fitted together by the cements of Harmony.

And the earth meets with these in nearly equal proportions, with
25   Hephaistos and Water and shining Air, anchoring in the perfect havens of Kypris—either a little more of it, or less of it and more of them. From these did blood arise and the various forms of flesh.

At one time things grew together to be one only out of many, at another they parted asunder so as to be many instead of one—Fire and Water
30   and Earth and the mighty height of Air, dread Strife, too, apart from these, and balancing every one of them, and Love among them, their equal in length and breadth. Contemplate her with your mind, nor sit with dazed eyes. It is she that is thought to be implanted in the frame of

mortals. It is she that makes them have kindly thoughts and work the works of peace. They call her by the names of Joy and Aphrodite.

For all these are equal and alike in age, yet each has a different prerogative and its own peculiar nature. And nothing comes into being besides these, nor do they pass away; for, if they had been passing away continually, they would not be now.

Nor is any part of the whole empty. From where, then, could anything come to increase it? Where, too, could these things perish, since no place is empty of them? They are what they are, but, running through one another, different things continually come into being from different sources, yet ever alike.

I shall you a twofold tale. At one time things grew to be one only out of many; at another, that divided up to be many instead of one. There is a double becoming of perishable things and a double passing away. The coming together of all things brings one generation into being and destroys it; the other grows up and is scattered as things become divided. And these things never cease, continually changing places, at one time all uniting in one through Love, at another each carried in different directions by the repulsion of Strife. Thus, as far as it is their nature to grow into one out of many, and to become many once more when the one is parted asunder, so far they come into being and their life abides not. But, inasmuch as they never cease changing their places continually, so far they are immovably as they go round the circle of existence.

But, as divinity was mingled still further with divinity, these things joined together as each might chance, and many other things beside them continually arose.

QUESTIONS TO CONSIDER

- What do fools think, and why is it foolish? Does Empedocles have the same sort of principle as the Milesians? What are his principles?
- For Empedocles, can there be more than four kinds of thing? (For example, would he agree that horses, trees, bone, blood, and so on, even exist?) If so, how? If not, why not?

- Does Empedocles have any principles other than the four elements? If so, what are these principles? If not, how does he explain motion and change?

- Are love and hatred a different sort of principle from those we have already seen? If so, how do they differ? If not, how are they related to change?

- Are coming-to-be and passing away real, for Empedocles?

- How would Empedocles explain regularity in nature, for example, that cattle normally have the heads of cattle and men the heads of men? Is there any reason why things should be as they are, for Empedocles?

- In your judgment, is it probable in any way that things are made up of earth, air, fire, and water? Is his explanation of how compounds are formed altogether unreasonable, or does it even resemble a current view?

- Are earth, air, fire, and water destructible, by Empedocles' account?

- Is change real, for Empedocles? Is his account of change (leaving aside, for the moment, his choice of elements) an unreasonable one?

ANAXAGORAS OF CLAZOMENAE

All things were together, infinite both in number and in smallness—for the small too was infinite. And, when all things were together, none of them could be distinguished because of their smallness. For air and ether prevailed over all things, being both of them infinite; for among all things 5 these are the greatest both in quantity and size.

Nor is there a least of what is small, but there is always a smaller; for it is impossible that what is should cease to be by being divided. But there is always something greater than what is great, and it is equal to the small in amount, and, 10 compared with itself, each thing is both great and small.

"How can hair come from not-hair, or flesh from not-flesh?"

And since these things are so, we must suppose that there are contained many things and of all sorts in all (the things) that are brought together, seeds of all things, with all sorts of shapes and colors and flavors.

But before they were separated off, when all things were together, not 15 even was any color distinguishable; for the mixture of all things prevented it—of the moist and the dry, and the warm and the cold, and the light and the dark [and much earth being in it], and of a multitude of innumerable seeds in no way like each other. For none of the other things 20 either is like any other.

For how can hair come from not-hair, or flesh from not-flesh?

And since the portions of the great and of the small are equal in amount, for this reason, too, all things will be in everything; nor is it possible for them to be apart, but all things have a portion of everything. Since it is impossible for there to be a least thing, they cannot be separated, nor come to be by themselves; but they must be now, just as they were in the beginning, all together. And in all things many things are contained, and an equal number both in the greater and in the smaller of the things that are separated off.

Nor are the things that are in one world divided nor cut off from one another with a hatchet, neither the warm from the cold nor the cold from the warm.

And when those things are being distinguished in this way, we must know that all of them are neither more nor less; for it is not possible for them to be more than all, and all are always equal.

The Hellenes are wrong in using the expressions 'coming into being' and 'passing away'; for nothing comes into being or passes away, but there is a mingling and separation of the things that are. So they would be right to call coming into being 'mixture' and passing away 'separation'.

Because of the weakness of our senses, we cannot judge the truth.

In everything there is a portion of everything except Nous [Mind], and there are some things in which there is Nous also.

And when Nous began to move things, separating off took place from all that was moved, and so far as Nous set in motion all was separated. And as things were set in motion and separated, the revolution caused them to be separated much more.

[Things] revolve and are separated off by the force and speed. And the speed makes the force. And their speed is not like the speed of any of the things that are now among men, but in every way many times as quick.

The dense and the moist and the cold and the dark came together where the earth is now, while the rare and the warm and the dry [and the bright] went out towards the further part of the ether.

From these as they are separated off earth is solidified; for from mists water is separated off, and from water earth. From the earth stones are
5   solidified by the cold, and these rush outwards more than water.

All other things partake in a portion of everything, while Nous is infinite and self-ruled, and is mixed with nothing, but is alone, itself by itself. For if it were not by itself, but were mixed with anything else, it would partake in all things if it were mixed with any; for in everything there is a portion
10   of everything, as has been said by me in what went before, and the things mixed with it would hinder it, so that it would have power over nothing in the same way that it has now being alone by itself. For it is the thinnest of all things and the purest, and it has all knowledge about everything and the greatest strength; and Nous has power over all things, both greater
15   and smaller, that have life. And Nous had power over the whole revolution, so that it began to revolve in the beginning. And it began to revolve first from a small beginning; but the revolution now extends over a larger space and will extend over a larger still. And all the things that are mingled together and separated off and distinguished are known by
20   Nous. And Nous set in order all things that were to be and that were, and all things that are not now and that are, and this revolution in which now revolve the stars and the sun and the moon, and the air and the ether that are separated off. And this revolution caused the separating off, and the rare is separated off from the dense, the warm from the cold, the light
25   from the dark, and the dry from the moist. And there are many portions in many things. But nothing is altogether separated off nor distinguished from everything else except Nous. And all Nous is alike, both the greater and the smaller; while nothing else is like anything else, but each single thing is and was most manifestly those things of which it has most in it.

QUESTIONS TO CONSIDER

- Anaxagoras' position is unlike any we have encountered so far. How does he propose to explain change, for example, how, according to him, is it possible for wood to become fire when it burns?
- Does Anaxagoras' view really explain change? If so, what sort of change? If not, why not? Is there anything in Anaxagoras' explanation of change

which is similar to Empedocles' own notion? If so, where is the similarity? If not, how does change come about for Anaxagoras?

- Given that everything is in everything, how does Anaxagoras ex-plain the differences among things, for example, what would make calcium different from iron, assuming that each contains infinitely small parts of everything?

- What is the basic argument that all things must be in all things? With what basic data does this argument begin? Is this argument reasonable in light of the other positions we have considered?

- What is the point of the fifth paragraph?

- What is Nous, and what function does it have in a change?

EARLY ATOMISM

DEMOCRITUS OF ABDERA

The elements [of all things] are the full and the empty—being and non-being; being is full and solid, non-being is empty and rare: being exists no

"It is impossible that many things come from one or one from many."

⁵ more than non-being, because the void exists [no less] than body: and these are the causes of things as matter.

[These] principles are infinite in number—and they are atoms, undivided bodies, which are unchangeable due to their solidity, and which have no void within them.

¹⁰ It is impossible that many things come from one or one from many.

Things are divisible because of the void in them.

The differences [among the atoms] are the causes of other things—and there are three such differences: shape, arrangement, and position... for A differs from N in shape, AN from NA in arrangement, I from H in

¹⁵ position.

The number of shapes [of atoms] is infinite, since there is no reason why they should be one shape rather than another.

The atoms move in the infinite void, and are separate from one another, and they differ in shape, size, position, and arrangement. Overtaking one another, they come together, and some are cast away in a chance direction, while others, having become intertwined with each other on account of the symmetry of their shapes, sizes, positions, and arrangement, hold fast, and in this way compound bodies come into being.

And [the atoms] cling to one another and stay together until such time as a stronger necessity from the outside shakes them and scatters them apart.

The first bodies are always in motion in the infinite void.

[Atoms] move in the infinite void as the result of mutual impact.

Sweet and bitter exist by convention, hot and cold exist by convention, color exists by convention—but in reality only atoms and void. (It is thought and imagined that the things we sense do exist, but there is no such thing as it is sensed—only atoms and the void.)

Bitter taste comes from small, smooth, round [atoms], which have a winding surface, so they are sticky and viscous; salt taste comes from large [atoms which are] not round, but sometimes uneven.

Nothing occurs by chance, but all happens for a reason and of necessity.

Necessity is the resistance and motion and impact of matter.

In compound bodies, the lighter is what has more void, while the heavier is what has less void.

QUESTIONS TO CONSIDER

- What is Democritus' first basic point? Of the Pre-Socratics, who would agree with this point and who would disagree?
- Democritus says, "it is impossible that one thing come from two or two things from one." Does his explanation of the world support this? Would Empedocles agree? Would Anaxagoras?

- How does Democritus explain color, taste, and, in general, all the sensible qualities?

- Do the atoms themselves have any characteristics? If so, describe them. If not, why not?

- Does Democritus have anything in his explanation of nature or change which is similar to Empedocles' love and hatred and to Anaxagoras' mind? If so, what is it? If not, how does change come about?

- Do the atoms differ from one another in any way? If so, how?

- Would Democritus admit that a cactus differs essentially from a pig? If he would, how would they differ? If he would not, what follows with respect to our knowledge of the world?

- In your judgment, is Democritus more, or less, consistent with common experience than Empedocles, Anaxagoras, or the Milesians?

- What are Democritus' first principles? What is it which makes the motion of the atoms even possible?

- Why do the atoms combine in various ways?

- Why is empty space needed for change to occur? Given this, what sort of change does Democritus admit? Does he admit any other sorts of change?

- Are colors and flavors real, by Democritus' account? If the atoms have no color or flavor, then how might one explain these things?

- Given Democritus' system, why is it impossible for one thing to come from two or two from one?

EPICURUS AND LUCRETIUS

After the conquests of Alexander the Great, the Hellenistic era of philosophy began, producing two prominent philosophical views: stoicism and epicureanism. Of the two, the philosophy of Epicurus ("epicureanism") represents a development of Pre-Socratic thought (his basic assumptions are those of Democritus.) Lucretius was a later, Roman proponent of epicureanism. His own contribution to Epicurus' view, On the Nature of Things, is a philosophical poem dealing with physical theory and ethics. Though Lucretius was born 300 years after the death of Socrates, the Pre-Socratic way of looking at nature remains strong.

EPICURUS—LETTER TO HERODOTUS

Nothing is created out of that which does not exist: for if it were, everything would be created out of everything with no need of seeds. And again, if that which disappears were destroyed into that which did not exist, all things would have perished, since that into which they were dissolved would not exist.

Furthermore, the universe always was such as it is now, and always will be the same. For there is nothing into which it changes: for outside the universe there is nothing which could come into it and bring about the change.

Moreover, the universe is bodies and space: for that bodies exist, sense itself witnesses in the experience of all men, and in accordance with the evidence of sense we must of necessity judge of the imperceptible by reasoning, as I have already said. And if there were not that which we term void and place and intangible existence, bodies would have nowhere to exist and nothing through which to move, as they are seen to move.

And besides these two nothing can even be thought of either by conception or on the analogy of things conceivable such as could be grasped as whole existences and not spoken of as the accidents or properties of such existences. Furthermore, among bodies some are compounds, and others those of which compounds are formed. And these latter are indivisible and unalterable (if, that is, all things are not to be destroyed into the non-existent, but something permanent is to remain behind at the dissolution of compounds): they are completely solid in nature and can by no means be dissolved in any part. So it must needs be that the first beginnings are indivisible corporeal existences...

> *"The atoms move continuously for all time, some of them falling straight down, others swerving, and others recoiling from their collisions."*

And the atoms move continuously for all time, some of them falling straight down, others swerving, and others recoiling from their collisions. And of the latter, some are borne on, separating to a long distance from one another, while others again recoil and recoil, whenever they chance to be checked by the interlacing with others, or else shut in by atoms interlaced around them. For on the one hand the nature of the void which separates each atom by itself brings this about, as it is not able to afford resistance, and on the other hand the hardness which belongs to the atoms makes them recoil after collision to as great a distance as the interlacing permits separation after the collision. And these motions have no beginning, since the atoms and the void are the cause.

QUESTIONS TO CONSIDER

- With whose philosophical position is Epicurus most in agreement?

- What two basic principles does Epicurus enunciate at the outset? Have we seen them before? Apart from their differences, would the Pre-Socratics agree with these principles?

- Epicurus gives arguments for the existence of atoms and void. What would Parmenides say of his argument for the existence of bodies? What type of argument (categorical, conditional) does he offer for the existence of void?

- How does Epicurus argue that the universe is boundless?

- In what condition are the atoms throughout all of time? What sorts of motion do they undergo?

- What are the characteristics of the atoms (speed, direction, composition, divisibility, size) and the space (void) they exist in?

LUCRETIUS—ON THE NATURE OF THINGS

5   First-beginnings [atoms] therefore are of solid singleness, massed together and cohering closely by means of least parts, not compounded out of a union of those parts, but, rather, strong in everlasting singleness. From them nature allows nothing to be torn, nothing further to be worn away, reserving them as seeds for things.

10 This point too herein we wish you to apprehend—when bodies are borne downwards sheer through void by their own weights, at quite uncertain times and uncertain spots they push themselves a little from their course: you just and 15 only just can call it a change of inclination. If they were not used to swerve, they would all fall down, like drops of rain, through the deep void, and no clashing would have been begotten nor blow produced among the first beginnings: thus nature never would have produced anything.

"Again and again I say, bodies must swerve a little."

But if perhaps someone believes that heavier bodies, as they are carried more quickly sheer through space, can fall from above on the lighter and so beget blows able to produce begetting motions, he goes most widely astray from true reason. For whenever bodies fall through water and thin air, they must quicken their descents in proportion to their weights, because the body of water and subtle nature of air cannot retard everything in equal degree, but more readily give way, overpowered by the heavier: on the other hand empty void cannot offer resistance to anything in any direction at any time, but must, as its nature craves, continually give way; and for this reason all things must be moved and borne along with equal velocity though of unequal weights through the unresisting void. Therefore heavier things will never be able to fall from above on lighter nor of themselves to beget blows sufficient to produce the varied motions by which nature carries on things. Wherefore again and again I say bodies must swerve a little; and yet not more than the least possible; lest we be found to be imagining oblique motions and this the reality should refute. For this we see to be plain and evident, that weights, so far as in them is, cannot travel obliquely, when they fall from above, at least so far as you can perceive; but that nothing swerves in any case from the straight course, who is there that can perceive?

QUESTIONS TO CONSIDER

- Here Lucretius famously introduces the swerve. Why must atoms swerve, and what does it mean for an atom to do this?

3

ARISTOTELIAN AND THOMISTIC HYLOMORPHISM

Aristotle was born in Stagira some fifteen years after the death of Socrates. The range of his philosophical writing is very impressive, including works in biology, astronomy, logic, philosophical psychology, ethics, politics, natural philosophy, and metaphysics. His Physics was the starting point for a study of the natural world, which account was adopted and developed by Thomas Aquinas in his philosophical and theological works As will become clear, taking matter and form as principles of all natural things has implications for psychology, ethics, and natural theology, as well as various branches of study within these areas..

ARISTOTLE—PHYSICS

I—1

Since understanding and scientific knowledge come about from a knowledge of principles, causes, and elements in all inquiries in which there are such things, (for we think that we know a thing when we know
5   its first causes and first principles, all the way down to its primary elements), it is clear that we should first try to define those things which concern the principles in the science of nature also.

The natural way to proceed is from things which are more known and clearer to us to things which are clearer and more known by nature: for
10   what is known to us and what is known simply [by nature] are not the same. And so it is necessary to proceed in this way, from things which are less clear by nature (but which are clearer to us) to things which are clearer and more known by nature.

But what are at first clear and evident to us are things that are more confused: later, the elements and principles become known from these by dividing them. And so one ought to proceed from universals to singulars: for the whole is more known according to the senses, and the universal is a kind of whole: for it includes many things as parts within itself. Names also have a similar relation to a definition: for they signify some whole in an indefinite way, (for example, 'circle',) whereas the definition distinguishes it into particulars. Also, children at first call all men fathers and all women mothers, but later identify each of them.

QUESTIONS TO CONSIDER

- As one would expect, the first chapter of Aristotle's Physics is an introduction to the general study of natural things. Here Aristotle tells us where we ought to begin in this science and why we must begin there.

- What is the conclusion of the first paragraph in this chapter? What evidence does Aristotle give to support this conclusion?

- What is the "natural way to proceed" in learning? Does Aristotle take this method to apply to all learning, or merely to learning in this science?

- Aristotle gives three examples to support his claim thatwe naturally proceed from what is more known to us to what is more known by nature. Given this, what sorts of thing, generally, are more known to us?

I—7

We, therefore, shall speak as follows: first discussing generation as a whole: for it is according to nature first to consider what is common and then what is proper to each species.

Now we say that one thing comes from another, and one sort of thing from another sort, in speaking either of simple things, or of those which are composite. My meaning is this. A man may become a musician, or what is not musical may become a musician, or a man who is not musical may become a musical man. Now I call what is becoming [something,] man, and what is not musical, simple, and what is coming about, the musical, I also call simple. But [I call] composite both what is becoming [something] and what is

"Whatever comes into being is always something composite."

coming about, as when we say that a man who is not musical becomes a musical man.

Now of these, one is not only said to have become this, but also to have come from this, as for example, the musical from what is not musical, but the reverse is not said of all things: for a musician does not come from a man, whereas a man becomes a musician.

Some of the simple things which become [something,] however, remain, while others do not remain, for the man remains, and is a man still in becoming a musician, but what is not musical and the unmusical do not remain, whether simply or in a composite way.

Now these things being set out, from every thing which comes about this may be concluded by anyone who directs his attention to it, that there must always be something which is the subject of generation, as we have said. And this, though it is one in number, yet is not one in form: (for by one in form, I mean the same thing as one in definition: for to be a man and to be unmusical are not the same.) And one [principle,] indeed, remains, but the other does not remain: what is not opposed remains, for man remains, but the musical and the unmusical do not remain. Nor does that which is composed of the two remain, as, for example, an unmusical man.

Now that a thing should come from something, rather than that a thing becomes another, is said more of things which do not remain, as, for example, the musical is said to come about from the unmusical, but not from man. Even so, this is sometimes said of things which remain: for we say that a statue comes from bronze and not that the bronze becomes a statue. The coming about from the opposite, which does not remain, however, is described in both ways, namely: this thing is said to come from that, and that thing is said to become this: for the musical comes from the unmusical, and the unmusical becomes musical. The like also takes place with the composite: for both one becomes musical from being an unmusical man, and an unmusical man is said to have become musical.

Since, however, the term 'coming to be' is said in many ways, some things are said not to come about simply, but to become this, and to come about simply belongs only to substances.

Now with things other [than substance,] there clearly must be something which is the subject of what is coming about: for quantity, quality, relation, when, and where come about through a subject, for substance alone is said of no other subject, whereas all other things are said of
5   substance.

But that substances, and other simple things, come about from a subject will become clear to one who considers the matter. For there is always some subject from which the thing produced comes about, as, for example, plants and animals from seed.

10   But of the simple things which come into being, some come about by a change of shape, as a statue from bronze, some by addition, as things which are increased, some by separation, as Mercury from a stone, others by composition, as a house, and still others by a change in quality, as things which are changed according to their matter.

15   Clearly, then, all the things which come into being come about from an underlying subject. From what has been said, then, it is clear that whatever comes into being is always something composite.

And there is something, indeed, which comes about, but there is also something which becomes this thing, and this is twofold: for it is either
20   the subject or the opposite. I mean, for example, that the unmusical is the opposite, and that man is the subject, or that the lack of shape, form, or order, are opposites, and that the bronze, the stone, or the gold, are underlying subjects.

Clearly, therefore, if natural things have causes and principles from which
25   primarily they are and come to be, not accidentally, but what each is said to be according to its essence: then every thing comes about from subject and form: for a musical man is composed, in a certain way, from man and the musical: for you resolve the definition [of musical man] into the definitions of these things. Clearly, then, things which come about come
30   from these [subject and form.]

The subject, however, is one in number, but two in kind: (for man and gold, and in short matter, can be numbered: for it is more a 'this', and what comes about is not generated from it according to accident, whereas the privation, or contrary, is accidental:) and form, however, is one principle, as, for example, order, or music, or one of other things which are predicated in this way.

And so, in one way there are two principles, but in another there are three, and in one way the contraries are the principles as if someone should speak of the musical and the unmusical, or of the hot and the cold, or the harmonized and the unharmonized, whereas in another way they are not contraries: for it is impossible for contraries to be acted upon by each other. This [problem], however, is solved because the subject is something [entirely] different: for it is not a contrary. So that, in a way, the principles are no more than the contraries, but two in number, as it were, nor again are they simply two, because their essence is different, but three: for the essence of man differs from the essence of the unmusical, and also the essence of shapelessness differs from that of bronze.

We have declared how many are the principles of natural things which are concerned with coming into being and how they are just so many. It is also clear that something must subsist as a subject to the contraries and that the contraries are two; yet in a way this is not necessary: for one of the contraries is sufficient to produce change by its absence and presence.

And the underlying nature may be scientifically known by analogy. For just as the bronze is to the statue, or the wood to the bed, or matter (before it receives form) and the lack of form to anything which has form, so is this subject nature to substance, or to a 'this', or to a being.

This, then, is one of the principles, though it is not one, nor a being, in the same way as a 'this', another principle is form, and, further, there is what is contrary [to form,] the privation.

Now how there are two principles, and how there are more than two, has been declared above. First, then, it was said that the principles are contraries only, then, that something else must be admitted as a subject and that there are three principles. Yet, from what we have just said, it is evident how the contraries differ, how the principles are related to each other, and what their subject is. It is not yet clear, however, whether the form, or the subject, is the essence of a thing. But that the principles are three, and how they are three, and what the mode is of their existence, is clear.

How many principles there are, then, and what they are, can be seen from what has been said.

QUESTIONS TO CONSIDER

- Why does Aristotle consider generation (coming into being) in general before he considers each type of generation in detail?

- Explain the distinction between a simple thing and a composite thing using an original example. Taking our example of food becoming hot, what is the simple thing which persists throughout this change? What simple thing does not persist throughout the change? Is what persists one of the contraries? Is what does not persist one of the contraries?

- What, then, are the three kinds of principle involved in any change? Is there anything in our language which reflects this distinction among principles?

- What are the two types of generation (or becoming) to which Aristotle refers? In the case of something becoming this (e.g., food becoming hot), is it obvious what the underlying subject is? Suppose, however, we consider the change involved in digesting the food. Whereas before, we could say the food changed from being cold to being hot, is it apparent what the underlying subject is in the food becoming part of an animal? According to Aristotle, is there an underlying principle in this second type of change?

- How does Aristotle show that what is involved in a change must be a composite thing? What does Aristotle call the underlying principle? What does he call that principle which is no longer present at the end of the change?

- In what manner are we aware of the underlying principle in a change in substance (as in the case of digesting food?) What names does Aristotle give to the three types of principle involved in change?

II—1

Of things that exist, some exist by nature, and others through other causes. Animals and their parts, as well as plants and simple bodies, such as earth and fire, air and water, exist by nature: for we say that these and similar things exist by nature—yet all these things seem to differ from those which do not exist by nature. For each of them has within itself a principle of motion and rest, whether according to place, or according to increase and decrease, or according to alteration [change in quality], whereas a bed, a garment, and any other thing of this sort, insofar as they receive these names, and insofar as they are produced by art, have no innate tendency to change. Yet, insofar as such things happen to be made of stone or earth, or a mixture of these, to that extent they do have [such a principle]. So that nature is a certain principle and cause of motion and rest in that to which it primarily belongs essentially, not accidentally (and I say not accidentally, because a man being a doctor, might be a cause of his own health: yet it is not insofar as he is healed that he possesses [the art of] medicine, rather it happens that the physician and the one healed are the same: it is also the case that these are sometimes separated from each other.) And so it is with everything else which is made: for none of them has in itself a principle of [its own] making, rather for some this principle] is in other things external to themselves, for example, a house, and everything else which is made by hand, while others have it in themselves, yet not essentially—such things as are causes of themselves accidentally. 'Nature', then, is what we have said.

Those things 'have a nature' which have this sort of principle. And these are all substances: for [a substance] is a subject, and nature always exists in a subject. These [substances] are also 'according to nature', as well as those things which are found in them in virtue of what they are, as that fire tends upwards: for this [property] is not 'a nature,' nor does it 'have a nature', rather it is 'by nature' or 'according to nature'. What nature is, then, and what 'by nature' and 'according to nature' [mean], has been stated. And to try to prove that nature exists would be absurd: for it is clear that there are many such things, but to show things which are clear through such as are unclear is characteristic of one who cannot distinguish between what is known through itself and what is not known through itself (and it is clear that this could happen: for one who was blind from birth might reason about colors), so that for such men the discussion would be about mere words, and they would understand nothing.

Now to some, the nature and substance of things which exist by nature seems to be the first constituent of a thing and what is essentially without order. For example, wood is the nature of a bed, and brass of a statue.

A sign of this, says Antiphon, is that if someone were to bury a bed, and the rotted wood acquired the power to germinate, it would not be a bed that would come up, but wood, so that the arrangement, according to rule and art, belonged to it [only] accidentally, whereas the substance is what remains, which is continually acted upon. And if each of these is related to something else in the same way (as, for example, brass and gold to water, or bones and wood to earth, and so on,) that thing, then, would be their nature and substance. And so some say that fire, others earth, others air, others water, others some of these, and still others all of them, is the nature of things. For whatever one of them thought to be of this kind, whether one or many, this, or these, they said, is the whole of substance, and all other things are the passions, habits, and dispositions of these, and any one of them is eternal (since there is no change among themselves,) whereas other things are generated and corrupted over and over again.

In one way, then, nature is said to be the first subject matter in everything which has in itself a principle of motion and change. Yet in another way it is said to be the shape or form which is according to the definition. For just as what is according to art or artistic is called 'art', so also that which is according to nature or natural is called 'nature'. We should not say that something exists by art if it is a bed (for example) only in potency and does not have the form of a bed yet, nor should we say that it is a work of art. The same holds true for things which exist by nature: for what is flesh or bone in potency does not have its own nature, nor does it exist by nature, until it receives the form which is according to the definition, and it is in defining this that we say what flesh is, or bone. So that, in another way, the nature of things which contain in themselves a principle of motion is the form or species, which is separable [from the thing] only in definition. (And what is composed of these, for example, a man, is not a nature, but is natural.)

And this [form] is the nature [of a thing] more than matter: for a thing is said to exist more when it is actual than when it is potential.

Further: man is generated from man, but a bed is not generated from a bed: and so they say that it is not the arrangement that is the nature [of that thing], but the wood, since, if it were to germinate, it would not become a bed, but wood. If, then, this [matter] is art, form is also nature: for man is generated from man.

Again, nature, when considered as the process of coming into being, is said to be the way to nature [as a form]. For it is not the same as healing, which is said to be the way not to the art of medicine but to health: for healing must come from the art of medicine, and not lead to it. Nature [as the process of generation], however, is not related to nature [as form] in this way, rather that which is born proceeds or grows from something to something. Into what, then, does it grow? Not into that from which [it came], but into that to which [it tends]. Form, then, is also nature. But form and nature are said in two ways: for the privation is also a form, in some way. And whether there is a privation or a contrary [involved] in simple generation or not will be taken up later.

QUESTIONS TO CONSIDER

- According to Aristotle, in what two ways do things exist? What seems to be common to those things which exist by nature?

- How do artifacts differ from natural things? Given this preliminary difference, how does Aristotle define nature?

- Why does Aristotle add the qualification 'but not accidentally' to his definition of nature? What does accidentally mean in this context? What examples does Aristotle give of accidental things?

- In trying to render the definition of nature more precise, Aristotle refers to matter—one of the principles of change mentioned in the first book of the *Physics*. What evidence is there that the nature of a thing is its matter?

- To what principle does Aristotle next make reference in rendering his definition of nature more specific? Have we seen this principle before? If so, where? Why might someone think that the nature of something is its form? Is the form of a thing something existing separately from it?

- Is what is composed of matter and form a nature? If so, why? If not, why not? Can a principle exist by itself?

- Of the two, matter and form, which is more the nature of something? Why?

- Summarize the third sense of nature which Aristotle gives here. If matter and form are nature, in some way, what of privation? Is privation the nature of a thing in any way?

1—What are matter and form?

Since some things are able to be, even though they are not yet, and some things already are, that which is able both to be and not to be is said to be in potency, while that which already is, is said to be in act. Being, however, is twofold: namely, essential being (or the substantial being of some thing, for example, that a man exists, and this is being simply) and accidental being (for example, that a man is white, and this is being in a qualified way.)

Now something is in potency with respect to each of these [types of being.] For something is in potency to a man, (as the sperm and the egg,) and another thing is in potency to being white, for example, a man. And both that which is in potency to substantial being and that which is in potency to accidental being can be called matter, as the sperm is the matter of man and man is the matter of whiteness. But these [types of matter] differ, since

"In order that there be generation, then, three things are required: namely, being in potency, which is matter; and nonbeing in act, which is privation; and that through which something comes to be in act, which is form."

that which is in potency to substantial being is called the matter from which, while that which is in potency to accidental being is called the matter in which.

Likewise, properly speaking, that which is in potency to substantial being is called prime matter, while what is in potency to accidental being is called a subject: for the subject gives being to the accident, namely, to the one already existing, since the accident has no being except through its subject, whence it is said that the accidental form is in a subject, while it is not said that the substantial form is in a subject. And [prime] matter differs from a subject in this way, for the subject is what does not have being because something comes to it, rather, it exists through itself, and has complete being, just as a man does not have being [simply] through being white. But that is called [prime] matter which has being because something comes to it, since, of itself, it is incomplete; rather, it has no being, as Averroes says in the second book of his Commentary on the De Anima. Hence, simply speaking, form gives being to matter, but an accident does not give being to its subject, rather, the subject [gives being] to the accident, although sometimes 'matter' is used for 'subject,' and vice-versa.

Now, just as everything which is in potency is able to be called matter, thus everything from which something has being (whether it be substantial being or accidental being) can be called form; just as a man, when he is white in potency, becomes white in act through whiteness, and the sperm, when it is potentially a man, becomes actually a man through the soul. And because the form produces being in act, form is called act. Nevertheless, what makes substantial being in act is called substantial form, while what makes accidental being in act is called accidental form.

Since generation is a motion to form, to the two sorts of form there correspond two sorts of generation: to the substantial form there corresponds simple generation, to the accidental form there corresponds generation in a qualified way. For when a substantial form is introduced, it is said that something has come to be simply, for example: a man has come to be, or: a man has been generated. But when an accidental form has been introduced, it is not said that something has come to be simply, but that it has come to be this [such;] as when a man becomes white, we do not say that a man has come to be or that a man has been generated simply, but that he has come to be white [of such a color.]

And to this two-fold generation there is opposed a two-fold corruption, namely, [corruption] simply, and [corruption] in a qualified way. Simple generation and corruption are found in the genus of substance; but qualified generation and corruption are found in all other genera. And since generation is a certain change from non-being to being, while corruption, on the contrary, is from being to non-being, nevertheless generation does not come about from just any non-being, but from that non-being which is a being in potency; just as a statue [comes about] from bronze, which is a statue in potency and not in act.

In order that there be generation, then, three things are required: namely, being in potency, which is matter; and nonbeing in act, which is privation; and that through which something comes to be in act, which is form.

Just as when a statue is made out of bronze, the bronze, which is in potency to the form of the statue, is the matter; that which is unshaped or indisposed is the privation; and the shape, by reason of which it is called a statue, is the form. Yet it is not a substantial form, since the bronze, before the coming of the shape, already has being in act, and its being does not depend upon that shape, rather, it is an accidental form. (For all artificial forms are accidental forms.) For art only works upon what is already formed in a being perfected by nature.

5

QUESTIONS TO CONSIDER

- How does Aquinas define "being in potency", "being in act", "essential being", and "accidental being"?

- How do the two different types of matter differ? What are the two types of form?

- What is generation, and what are the two types of generation? What is corruption, and what are the two types of corruption?

- What sort of non-being is involved in a change? What, finally, are Aquinas' three principles of change?

2—How are matter, form, and privation related?

There are, then, three principles of nature: namely, matter, form, and privation, of which one, the form, is that for the sake of which there is a generation; while the other two [matter and privation] are on the part of that from which there is a generation. Hence, matter and privation are the same in subject but differ in definition. For bronze and 'the unshaped' are the same before the coming of the form: yet it is called bronze for one reason and unshaped for another. Hence, privation is not said to be a principle *per se*, but *per accidens*, since it coincides with the matter; just as we say that it is accidental that the doctor builds: for it is not because he is a doctor, but because he is a builder, which coincides with the doctor in the same subject.

10

15

Yet there are two kinds of accident: namely, necessary, which is not separated from the thing, (as the risible from man,) and non-necessary, which is separated, as white from a man. Hence, although privation is a principle accidentally, nevertheless it does not follow that it is not necessary for generation, since matter is never completely without privation: for insofar as it has one form, it has the privation of another,

20

25

and vice-versa, as in fire there is the privation of air, and in air there is the privation of fire.

It must also be noted that, though generation is from nonbeing, we do not say that negation is the principle, but privation, since negation does not determine a subject to itself. For not to see is able to be said even of non-beings, as 'the chimera does not see' and also of beings which do not naturally have sight, as of stones. But a privation is said only of a certain subject, in which it is natural for the positive state to come to be, just as blindness is only said of things which can see by nature. And since generation is not from non-being simply but from a non-being which is in some subject, and not in just any subject, but in a certain one (since fire does not come to be from just any non-fire, but from a certain non-fire in which the form of fire naturally comes to be,) therefore it is said that privation is the principle and not negation.

But privation differs from the matter and form insofar as they are principles both in being and in coming to be. For in order for a statue to come to be, it is necessary that there be bronze and that finally there be the shape of the statue; and also, when the statue already exists, these two must be there. But privation is a principle in coming to be and not in being, for while the statue is coming to be it is necessary that there be no statue (yet). For if it already were, it could not come to be, since whatever comes to be does not (yet) exist (except in successive things, as in motion and time.) But since the statue already exists, the privation of statue is not there, since affirmation and negation are not found together, nor are privation and its positive state. Further, privation is a *per accidens* principle, as was explained above, while the others are *per se* principles.

From what has been said, therefore, it is clear that matter differs from form and from privation according to its notion [definition]. For matter is that in which form and privation are understood, as in the bronze is understood the shaped and the 'unshaped'. Nevertheless, sometimes matter is named with privation, at other times [it is named] without privation: just as bronze, when it is the matter of a statue, does not [of itself] imply a privation, since from this [alone], that I say 'bronze', the indisposed or 'unshaped' is not understood; but flour, since it is the matter with respect to bread, implies in itself a privation of the form of bread, since from this, that I say 'flour', there is signified an indisposition or lack of order opposed to the form of bread. And since the matter or the subject remains in generation, but not privation, nor the composite of matter and privation, therefore the matter which does not imply privation is the one which remains: while [the matter] which does [imply privation] passes away.

It should also be noted that some matter has [itself] a composition of form: for example, bronze, although it is matter with respect to a statue, is nevertheless itself composed of matter and form; and therefore bronze is not called prime matter, since it has a form. But that matter which is understood without any form or privation whatsoever, but is subject to form and privation, is called prime matter, since there is not another matter before it.

Now since every definition and all understanding is through a form, therefore prime matter can be neither defined nor known, except through a comparison to form; for example, it might be said that prime matter is that which is related to all forms and privations as bronze to the statue and to 'the shapeless'. And this matter is called prime simply.

It must also be noted that prime matter and form are neither generated nor corrupted, since every generation is from some thing to some thing. Now that from which there is a generation is matter, while that to which there is a generation is form. Therefore, if matter and form themselves were generated, there would be matter of matter and form of form, and so on ad infinitum. Hence, properly speaking, there is generation only of the composite [of matter and form].

Note also that, though prime matter has no form or privation in its definition, (as in the definition of bronze itself there is neither 'shaped' nor 'shapeless',) nevertheless matter never exists without form and privation, for it is sometimes under one form and sometimes under another. Furthermore, it is never able to exist through itself, because it is not able to be in act (since it has no form in its definition, and since to be in act is only through a form,) rather, it is only in potency. And thus whatever is in act cannot be called prime matter.

- Which principles are that from which a change takes place?
- Is privation absolutely necessary for a change to occur? Why can
- negation (as opposed to privation) not be a principle of change? Which make a thing the kind of thing that it is?
- Which matter is itself made up of matter and form? Which is not?
- If neither prime matter nor form can come into being or be destroyed, what can?

THOMAS AQUINAS—THE MIXTURE OF ELEMENTS

Many have difficulty with how elements are in a mixture. It seemed to some that, with the active and passive qualities of the elements drawn
5 together to a mean in some way through alteration, the substantial forms of the elements must remain, for if they did not remain, it would seem to be a corruption of the elements, and not a mixture.

Further, if the substantial form of a mixed body [mixture] is the act of a matter which does not already have the forms of the simple bodies, then
10 the simple bodies would lose the notion of elements. For an element is that out of which a thing is first made, and which is in that thing, and

"The forms of the elements are in mixed bodies, not actually, but virtually."

which is indivisible in species; for with the substantial forms removed, a
15 mixed body would not be made up of simple bodies such that they would remain in it.

But it is impossible that it be so; for it is impossible for matter to receive the diverse forms of the elements in the same way. Therefore, if the substantial forms of the elements were to be preserved in a mixed body,
20 it would be necessary that they be in different parts of the matter. But matter can have different parts only if quantity is already understood to be present; for with quantity removed, substance remains indivisible, as is clear in the first book of the Physics. But a physical body is made up of matter, existing with a certain quantity, and the substantial form which
25 comes [to it]. Therefore the different parts of the matter subsisting under the forms of the elements take on the notion of many bodies. But it is

impossible for many bodies to be in a single place. Therefore, the elements will not be in every part of the mixed body; and thus it will not be a true mixture, but [only] according to the senses, as happens in a collection of invisible or insensible bodies, on account of their smallness.

5 Further, every substantial form requires a proper disposition in matter, without which it cannot exist—whence, alteration is the way to generation and corruption. But it is impossible for the proper disposition which is required for the form of fire and that which is required for the form of water to come together in the same thing, since fire and water 10 are contraries in virtue of such dispositions. And it is impossible for contraries to be together in the same thing equally. Therefore, it is impossible for the substantial forms of fire and water to be in the same part of the mixed body. If, therefore, a mixed body comes to be, with the substantial forms of the simple bodies remaining, it follows that it is not 15 a true mixture, but only according to the senses, with the insensible parts placed next to each other, as it were, on account of their smallness.

Now others, wishing to avoid both these arguments, fell into an even greater difficulty. For, in order that the mixtures of the elements might be distinguished from their corruption, they said that the substantial 20 forms of the elements do remain in the mixed body in some way; but lest they be compelled to say that the mixture is [merely] according to the senses and not according to the truth, they put it forth that the forms of the elements do not remain in the mixed body in their completeness, but are reduced to a certain mean; for they said that the forms of the elements 25 admit of more and less and are contrary to one another.

Now because this is clearly against common opinion and the words of the Philosopher who says, in the Categories, that nothing is contrary to substance and that it does not admit of more and less, they continued, and said that the forms of the elements are the most imperfect, as they 30 are closer to prime matter: whence they are means between substantial forms and accidental forms; and thus, insofar as they approach to the nature of an accidental form, they are able to admit of more and less, given that they may be contrary to one another.

But this position is improbable in many ways. First, because it is 35 altogether impossible that there be a mean between substance and accidents: for there would [then also] be a mean between affirmation and negation. For it is proper to an accident to exist in a subject, but [it is proper] to a substance not to be in a subject. Substantial forms are in matter, indeed, but not in a subject: for a subject is some individual thing; but the substantial form is what makes the subject some individual thing, it does not presuppose it.

Likewise it is ridiculous to say that there is a mean between those things which are not of one kind; since it is necessary that the mean and the extremes be of one kind, as is proved in the tenth book of the Metaphysics. Therefore, nothing can be a mean between substance and accident.

Therefore it is necessary to find another way, in which the truth of the mixture will be preserved and in which the elements will not be wholly corrupted but may remain in the mixed body in some way. Therefore, we must consider that the active and passive qualities of the elements are contrary to each other and admit of more and less. But from contrary qualities admitting of more and less a mean quality can be constituted, which has the 'taste' of the nature of each extreme, as gray between white and black and warm between hot and cold. Therefore, with the extremes of the qualities of the elements removed, there is constituted from them a certain mean quality, which is the proper quality of a mixed body, differing, nevertheless, in different ways according to the diverse proportion of the mixture: and this quality is, indeed, the proper disposition to the form of a mixed body, just as a simple quality is to the form of a simple body. Therefore, just as the extremes are found in the mean, which participates in the nature of each, so the qualities of the simple bodies are found in the proper quality of a mixed body. But the quality of a simple body is, indeed, other than its substantial form, however, it acts in virtue of the substantial form; otherwise heat alone would heat, yet the substantial form would not become actual through its [the quality's] power, since nothing acts outside its own species.

In this way, therefore, the powers of the substantial forms of the simple bodies are preserved in mixed bodies. Thus the forms of the elements are in mixed bodies, not actually, but virtually: and this is what the Philosopher says in the first book of On Generation and Corruption: "therefore the elements do not remain in the mixed body in act, as body and white, nor is one or both either corrupted or altered; for their power is preserved."

- In Aquinas' terms, do the substantial forms of the elements remain in a true mixture? What evidence does he offer to show that they must remain?

- Yet there are also reasons to think that the substantial forms do not remain. Let us suppose that we shall produce salt from sodium and chlorine. Can the matter (which will receive the forms of sodium and chlorine) have the forms of both simultaneously? How might it?

- Aquinas' solution is to say that, rather than reducing the substantial forms of the elements to a mean, he constructs a mean from the proper qualities of these same elements. So, just as fire requires a hot body in order to come about, and a liquid requires a (relatively) cooler one, their combination (if possible,) which would be a true mixture, would require a warm body: the mean between hot and cold.

IMPLICATIONS

4

NATURAL PHILOSOPHY AND HUMAN KNOWLEDGE

Can we know? If so, what can we know? Earlier, we saw an answer given to this question in the reasonings of Sextus Empiricus and David Hume, yet there are other answers—these are questions philosophers have asked themselves from the very beginning. What bearing does a materialistic outlook have upon the nature and limits of human knowing? What does a hylomorphist have to say about the matter? Are there other positions, and what are their implications? Through a consideration of philosophers from ancient to recent times, we will work our way through some of the basic answers that have been given to these fundamental questions.

We begin this section by revisiting Parmenides' view and juxtaposing it to another early view, that of Heraclitus. Recall how eager Parmenides is to justify his own way as the Way of Truth. Another Pre-Socratic thinker, Heraclitus, seems more comfortable with the possibility of error—especially given the way nature has been put together.

PARMENIDES AND HERACLITUS

PARMENIDES

The Way of Truth

Come now, I will tell you—and do you hearken to my saying and carry it away—the only two ways of search that can be thought of. The first, namely, that It is, and that it is impossible for anything not to be, is the way of conviction, for truth is its companion. The other, namely, that It is not, and that something must not be—that, I tell you, is a wholly untrustworthy path. For you cannot know what is not—that is

5

impossible—nor utter it; for it is the same thing that can be thought and that can be.

QUESTIONS TO CONSIDER

- [Review the reading from Parmenides, above, as needed.]
- What is Parmenides' overall conclusion? How does he support it? Does he attempt to explain nature as we know it? For example, do things even come into being and cease to be, for him?
- According to Parmenides, what "shall never be proved"? Does this make sense? How does he describe being itself (that which is)?
- What do the words 'coming into being' and 'alteration' mean, for Parmenides?

HERACLITUS OF EPHESUS

It is wise to hearken not to me but to my argument, and to confess that all things are one.

5   This order, which is the same in all things, no one of gods or men has made; but it was ever, is now, and ever shall be an ever-living Fire, fixed measures of it kindling and fixed measures going out.

You cannot step twice into the same rivers.

10 The transformations of Fire are, first of all, sea (and half of the sea is earth, half fiery storm-cloud).

All things are exchanged for Fire, and Fire for all things, as wares are exchanged for gold and gold for wares.

Fire is want and satiety.

15 Fire lives the death of earth, and air lives the death of fire; water lives the death of air, earth that of water.

The sun is new every day.

Hesiod is most men's teacher. Men think he knew very many things, a man who did not know day and night! They are one.

It is cold things that become warm, and what is warm that cools; what is wet dries, and the parched is moistened.

5 You cannot step twice into the same rivers; for fresh waters are ever flowing in upon you.

Homer was wrong in saying: "Would that strife might perish from among gods and men!" He did not see that he was praying for the destruction of the universe; for, if his prayer were heard, all things would
10 pass away.

War is the father of all and the king of all; and some he has made gods and some men, some bond and some free.

Men do not know how that which is drawn in different directions harmonizes with itself. The harmonious structure of the world depends
15 upon opposite tension, like that of the bow and lyre.

It is opposition that brings things together. Good and ill are the same.

You must couple together things whole and things not whole, what is drawn together and what is drawn asunder, the harmonious and the discordant. The one is made up of all things, and all things issue from the
20 one.

We must know that war is the common and justice is strife, and that all things come into being and pass away through strife.

The way up and the way down is one and the same.

The quick and the dead, the waking and the sleeping, the young and the
25 old, are the same; the former are changed and become the latter, and the latter are changed into the former.

We step and do not step into the same rivers; we are and are not.

It finds rest in change.

It is not good for men to get all they wish to get. It is disease that makes health pleasant and good; hunger, plenty and weariness, rest.

One day is equal to another.

- What are your rough impressions of Heraclitus' philosophical position? If we were to speak of the basic 'stuff' out of which all things are made, what would this be, for Heraclitus?

- Parmenides and Zeno tended to emphasize the unity and immovability of what exists. Would Heraclitus be inclined to agree with them?

- One of Heraclitus' most famous remarks is what he says about stepping into the same river twice. What is Heraclitus getting at here?

- Note what Heraclitus says when he speaks of the river a second. Strictly speaking, how do these two claims relate to one another?

- Consider what place the many contrasts Heraclitus includes in his account of nature have in his overall argument. (Such contrasts are, for example, life and death, day and night, good and evil, up and down, and so on.)

MATERIALISM

THOMAS HOBBES—LEVIATHAN

Of Man—Introduction

[1] Nature (the art whereby God has made and governs the world) is by the art of man, as in many other things, so in this also imitated, that it can make an artificial animal. For seeing life is but a motion of limbs, the beginning of which is in some principal part within, why may we not say that all automata (engines that move themselves by springs and wheels as does a watch) have an artificial life? For what is the heart, but a spring; and the nerves, but so many strings; and the joints, but so many wheels, giving motion to the whole body, such as was intended by the Artificer?

—Of Sense

[1] Concerning the thoughts of man, I will consider them first singly, and afterwards in train or dependence upon one another. Singly, they are every one a representation or appearance of some quality, or other accident of a body without us, which is commonly called an object. Which object works on the eyes, ears, and other parts of man's body, and by diversity of working produces diversity of appearances.

[2] The original of them all is that which we call sense, (for there is no conception in a man's mind which has not at first, totally or by parts, been begotten upon the organs of sense). The rest are derived from that original.

[3] To know the natural cause of sense is not very necessary to the business now in hand; and I have elsewhere written of the same at large. Nevertheless, to fill each part of my present method, I will briefly deliver the same in this place.

[4] The cause of sense is the external body, or object, which presses the organ proper to each sense, either immediately, as in the taste and touch; or mediately, as in seeing, hearing, and smelling, which pressure, by the mediation of nerves and other strings and membranes of the body, continued inwards to the brain and heart, causes there a resistance, or counterpressure, or endeavor of the heart to deliver itself: which endeavor, because outward, *"Life is but a motion of limbs."* seems to be some matter without. And this seeming, or fancy, is that which men call sense; and consists, as to the eye, in a light, or color figured; to the ear, in a sound; to the nostril, in an odor; to the tongue and palate, in a savor; and to the rest of the body, in heat, cold, hardness, softness, and such other qualities as we discern by feeling. All which qualities called sensible are in the object that causes them but so many several motions of the matter, by which it presses our organs diversely. Neither in us that are pressed are they anything else but diverse motions (for motion produces nothing but motion). But their appearance to us is fancy, the same waking that dreaming. And as pressing, rubbing, or striking the eye makes us fancy a light, and pressing the ear produces a din; so do the bodies also we see, or hear, produce the same by their strong, though unobserved action. For if those colors and sounds were in the bodies or objects that cause

them, they could not be severed from them, as by glasses and in echoes by reflection we see they are, where we know the thing we see is in one place, the appearance, in another. And though at some certain distance

the real and very object seem invested with the fancy it begets in us; yet still the object is one thing, the image or fancy is another. So that sense in all cases is nothing else but original fancy caused (as I have said) by the pressure that is, by the motion of external things upon our eyes, ears, and other organs, thereunto ordained.

[5] But the philosophy schools, through all the universities of Christendom, grounded upon certain texts of Aristotle, teach another doctrine; and say, for the cause of vision, that the thing seen sends forth on every side a visible species, (in English) a visible show, apparition, or aspect, or a being seen; the receiving of which into the eye is seeing. And for the cause of hearing, that the thing heard sends forth an audible species, that is, an audible aspect, or audible being seen, which, entering at the ear, makes hearing. Nay, for the cause of understanding also, they say the thing understood sends forth an intelligible species, that is, an intelligible being seen, which, coming into the understanding, makes us understand. I say not this, as disapproving the use of universities: but because I am to speak hereafter of their office in a Commonwealth, I must let you see on all occasions by the way what things would be amended in them; amongst which the frequency of insignificant speech is one.

—Of Imagination

[1] That when a thing lies still, unless somewhat else stir it, it will lie still forever, is a truth that no man doubts of. But that when a thing is in motion, it will eternally be in motion, unless somewhat else stay it, though the reason be the same (namely, that nothing can change itself), is not so easily assented to. For men measure, not only other men, but all other things, by themselves: and because they find themselves subject after motion to pain and lassitude, think everything else grows weary of motion, and seeks repose of its own accord; little considering whether it be not some other motion wherein that desire of rest they find in themselves consists. From hence it is that the schools say, heavy bodies fall downwards out of an appetite to rest, and to conserve their nature in that place which is most proper for them; ascribing appetite, and

knowledge of what is good for their conservation (which is more than man has), to things inanimate, absurdly.

[2] When a body is once in motion, it moves (unless something else hinder it) eternally; and whatsoever hinders it, cannot in an instant, but in time, and by degrees, quite extinguish it: and as we see in the water, though the wind cease, the waves give not over rolling for a long time after; so also it happens in that motion which is made in the internal parts of a man, then, when he sees, dreams, etc. For after the object is removed, or the eye shut, we still retain an image of the thing seen, though more obscure than when we see it. And this is it the Latins call imagination, from the image made in seeing, and apply the same, though improperly, to all the other senses. But the Greeks call it fancy, which signifies appearance, and is as proper to one sense as to another. Imagination, therefore, is nothing but decaying sense; and is found in men and many other living creatures, as well sleeping as waking.

[3] The decay of sense in men waking is not the decay of the motion made in sense, but an obscuring of it, in such manner as the light of the sun obscures the light of the stars, which stars do no less exercise their virtue by which they are visible in the day than in the night. But because amongst many strokes which our eyes, ears, and other organs receive from external bodies, the predominant only is sensible; therefore the light of the sun being predominant, we are not affected with the action of the stars. And any object being removed from our eyes, though the impression it made in us remain, yet other objects more present succeeding, and working on us, the imagination of the past is obscured and made weak, as the voice of a man is in the noise of the day.

From whence it follows that the longer the time is, after the sight or sense of any object, the weaker is the imagination.

For the continual change of man's body destroys in time the parts which in sense were moved: so that distance of time, and of place, has one and the same effect in us. For as at a great distance of place that which we look at appears dim, and without distinction of the smaller parts, and as voices grow weak and inarticulate: so also after great distance of time our imagination of the past is weak; and we lose, for example, of cities we have seen, many particular streets; and of actions, many particular circumstances. This decaying sense, when we would express the thing itself (I mean fancy itself), we call imagination, as I said before. But when we would express the decay, and signify that the sense is fading, old, and past, it is called memory. So that imagination and memory are but one thing, which for diverse considerations has diverse names.

[4] Much memory, or memory of many things, is called experience. Again, imagination being only of those things which have been formerly perceived by sense, either all at once, or by parts at several times; the former (which is the imagining the whole object, as it was presented to the sense) is simple imagination, as when one imagines a man, or horse, which he has seen before. The other is compounded, when from the sight of a man at one time, and of a horse at another, we conceive in our mind a centaur. So when a man compounds the image of his own person with the image of the actions of another man, as when a man imagines himself a Hercules or an Alexander (which happens often to them that are much taken with reading of romances), it is a compound imagination, and properly but a fiction of the mind. There be also other imaginations that rise in men, though waking, from the great impression made in sense: as from gazing upon the sun, the impression leaves an image of the sun before our eyes a long time after; and from being long and vehemently attendant upon geometrical figures, a man shall in the dark, though awake, have the images of lines and angles before his eyes; which kind of fancy has no particular name, as being a thing that does not commonly fall into men's discourse.

[5] The imaginations of them that sleep are those we call dreams. And these also (as all other imaginations) have been before, either totally or by parcels, in the sense. And because in sense, the brain and nerves, which are the necessary organs of sense, are so benumbed in sleep as not easily to be moved by the action of external objects, there can happen in sleep no imagination, and therefore no dream, but what proceeds from the agitation of the inward parts of man's body; which inward parts, for the connection they have with the brain and other organs, when they be distempered do keep the same in motion; whereby the imaginations there formerly made, appear as if a man were waking; saving that the organs of sense being now benumbed, so as there is no new object which can master and obscure them with a more vigorous impression, a dream must needs be more clear, in this silence of sense, than are our waking thoughts. And hence it cometh to pass that it is a hard matter, and by many thought impossible, to distinguish exactly between sense and

dreaming. For my part, when I consider that in dreams I do not often nor constantly think of the same persons, places, objects, and actions that I do waking, nor remember so long a train of coherent thoughts dreaming as at other times; and because waking I often observe the absurdity of dreams, but never dream of the absurdities of my waking thoughts, I am well satisfied that, being awake, I know I dream not; though when I dream, I think myself awake.

[6] And seeing dreams are caused by the distemper of some of the inward parts of the body, diverse distempers must needs cause different dreams. And hence it is that lying cold breeds dreams of fear and raises the thought and image of some fearful object, the motion from the brain to the inner parts, and from the inner parts to the brain being reciprocal; and that as anger causes heat in some parts of the body when we are awake, so when we sleep the overheating of the same parts causes anger and raises up in the brain the imagination of an enemy. In the same manner, as natural kindness when we are awake causes desire, and desire makes heat in certain other parts of the body; so also too much heat in those parts, while we sleep, raises in the brain an imagination of some kindness shown. In sum, our dreams are the reverse of our waking imaginations; the motion when we are awake beginning at one end, and when we dream, at another.

QUESTIONS TO CONSIDER

- To what does Hobbes compare human beings, in his Introduction? How does he define life?

- What is the origin (original) of all human thought? Are our sensations in things as we sense them, by Hobbes' account? What is the implication of this for human knowledge?

- What does Hobbes call the images we hold in our imaginations? What principle explain why they are "fainter" than our sensations? What would follow about our thoughts, which arise from images in our imagination?

BERTRAND RUSSELL—WHAT I BELIEVE

God and immortality, the central dogmas of the Christian religion, find no support in science. It cannot be said that either doctrine is essential to religion, since neither is found in Buddhism. (With regard to immortality, this statement in an unqualified form might be misleading, but it is correct in the last analysis.) But we in the West have come to think of them as the irreducible minimum of theology. No doubt people will continue to entertain these beliefs, because they are pleasant, just as it is pleasant to think ourselves virtuous and our enemies wicked. But for my part I cannot see any ground for either. I do not pretend to be able to prove that there is no God. I equally cannot prove that Satan is a fiction. The Christian God may exist; so may the Gods of Olympus, or of ancient Egypt, or of Babylon. But no one of these hypotheses is more probable than any other: they lie outside the region of even probable knowledge, and therefore there is no reason to consider any of them. I shall not enlarge upon this question, as I have dealt with it elsewhere.

QUESTIONS TO CONSIDER

- Does Russell think he can show that there is no God, does he think he can show that there is a God, or does he think he can show neither?
- What is Russell's view regarding human knowledge: what can we know, and how far does our knowledge extend?

STEVEN PINKER—IS SCIENCE KILLING THE SOUL?

Many of our faculties evolved to mesh with real things in the world. We have a complicated system of depth perception and shape recognition that prevents us from bumping into trees and falling off cliffs. The fact that our ability to recognize an object comes from complicated circuitry of the brain does not mean that there aren't real objects out there. Indeed, the brain evolved in order to give us as accurate a representation as possible of what is objectively out in the world.

- Why should we have evolved as *knowers* rather than not?

PLATONIC FORMALISM

Plato was one of the greatest philosophers who ever lived. A student of Socrates, he was 28 years old when Socrates was brought up on charges of impiety and corrupting the youth (399 B.C.) As we discover through Plato's own works, his teacher was convicted and sentenced to death by drinking poison.

Most of Plato's writings have come to us in the form of dialogues, many with Socrates as the main speaker. Through the medium of his teacher, Plato addressed many important and vexing questions which confront us even to this day.

Although Socrates (and Plato) tended to shy away from discussions about nature and our understanding of it, there is one dialogue which takes up such questions in detail: the Timaeus. An account of the creation of the natural world, this work exerted a tremendous influence upon the thinkers of those times and later ones. Along with passages from the Timaeus we have included key selections from Plato's most famous dialogue, the Republic, in which Plato elaborates upon his doctrine of Forms.

PLATO—THE CRATYLUS

There is a matter, master Cratylus, about which I often dream, and should like to ask your opinion: Tell me whether there is, or is not, any absolute beauty or good, or any other absolute existence?

Certainly, Socrates, I think that there is.

5   Then let us seek the true beauty: not asking whether a face is fair, or anything of that sort, or whether all this is in a flux; but let us ask whether the true beauty is not always beautiful.

Certainly.

And can we rightly speak of a beauty which is always passing away, and is first this and then that; must not the same thing be born and retire and vanish while the word is in our mouths?

Undoubtedly.

5 Then how can that be a real thing which is never in the same state? for obviously things which are the same cannot change while they remain the same; and if they are always in the same state and the same, then, without losing their original form, they can never change or be moved.

Certainly, they cannot.

10 Nor yet can they be known by anyone; for at the moment that the observer approaches, then they become other and of another nature, so that you cannot get any further in knowing their nature and state, for you cannot know that which has no state.

That is true.

15 Nor can we reasonably say, Cratylus, that there is knowledge at all, if everything is in a state of transition and there is nothing abiding; for if knowledge did not change or cease to be knowledge, then knowledge would ever abide and exist. But if the very nature of knowledge changes, at the time when the change occurs, there will be no knowledge; and if 20 the transition is always going on, there will always be no knowledge, and, according to this view, there will be no one to know and nothing to be known: but if that which knows and that which is known exists ever, and

"Can we rightly speak of a beauty which is always passing away?"

25 the beautiful and the good and every other thing also exist, then I do not think that they can be like a flux or progress, as we were just now supposing. Whether there is this eternal nature in things, or whether the truth is what Heraclitus and his followers and many others say, is a question hard to determine; and no man of sense will like to put himself 30 or the education of his mind in the power of names; neither will he so far trust names or the givers of names as to be confident in any knowledge which condemns himself and other existences to an unhealthy state of unreality; he will not believe that everything is in a flux like leaky vessels, or that the world is a sick man who has a running at the nose. This

doctrine, Cratylus, may indeed, perhaps, be true, but is also very likely to be untrue; and therefore I would have you reflect well and manfully, and not allow yourself to be too easily persuaded now in the days of our youth, which is the time of learning; but search, and when you have found the truth, come and tell me.

I will do as you say, though I can assure you, Socrates, that I have been considering the matter already, and the result of a great deal of trouble and consideration is that I incline to Heraclitus.

QUESTIONS TO CONSIDER

- Historically, Cratylus was a student of Heraclitus. Does Cratylus initially support his teacher's view of things? Does he ultimately do so?
- What problem does Socrates discover when placing the view that all things change up against absolute beauty, goodness, and so on?
- What position does Socrates favor by the end of this selection: that there are absolutes, or that all things constantly change? What about Cratylus?

PLATO—THE TIMAEUS

Let me make another attempt to explain my meaning more clearly. Suppose a person to make all kinds of figures of gold and to be always remodeling each form into all the rest; somebody points to one of them and asks what it is. By far the safest and truest answer is, that is gold, and not to call the triangle or any other figures which are formed in the gold these, as though they had existence, since they are in process of change while he is making the assertion, but if the questioner be willing to take the safe and the indefinite expression, such, we should be satisfied. And the same argument applies to the universal nature which receives all bodies—that must be always called the same, for, inasmuch as she always receives all things, she never departs at all from her own nature and never, in any way or at any time, assumes a form like that of any of the things which enter into her; she is the natural recipient of all impressions, and is stirred and informed by them, and appears different from time to time by reason of them. But

"One kind of being is the form which is always the same, uncreated and indestructible."

the forms which enter into and go out of her are the likenesses of eternal realities modeled after their patterns in a wonderful and mysterious manner, which we will hereafter investigate.

Wherefore also we must acknowledge that one kind of being is the form which is always the same, uncreated and indestructible, never receiving anything into itself from without, nor itself going out to any other, but invisible and imperceptible by any sense, and of which the contemplation is granted to intelligence only. And there is another nature of the same name with it, and like to it, perceived by sense, created, always in motion, becoming in place and again vanishing out of place, which is apprehended by opinion jointly with sense. And there is a third nature, which is space and is eternal, and admits not of destruction and provides a home for all created things, and is apprehended, when all sense is absent, by a kind of spurious reason, and is hardly real—which we, beholding as in a dream, say of all existence that it must of necessity be in some place and occupy a space, but that what is neither in heaven nor in earth has no existence.

QUESTIONS TO CONSIDER

- Bearing in mind the discussion found in the Cratylus, why would Plato insist that there must be a "form which is always the same, uncreated and indestructible"? Could such a thing be found in the world of matter?
- What is the function of the forms which are constantly changing? What is their relation to the "eternal" principle?

PLATO—THE REPUBLIC

And now, I said, let me show in a figure how far our nature is enlightened or unenlightened—Behold! human beings living in an underground den, which has a mouth open towards the light and reaching all along the den; here they have been from their childhood, and have their legs and necks chained so that they cannot move, and can only see before them, being prevented by the chains from turning round their heads. Above and behind them a fire is blazing at a distance, and between the fire and the prisoners there is a raised way, like the screen which marionette players have in from of them, over which they show the puppets.

I see.

And do you see, I said, men passing along the wall carrying all sorts of vessels, and statues and figures of animals made of wood and stone and various materials, which appear over the wall? Some of them are talking, others silent.

You have shown me a strange image, and they are strange prisoners.

Like ourselves, I replied, and they see only their own shadows, or the shadows of one another, which the fire throws on the opposite wall of the cave?

True, he said; how could they see anything but the shadows if they were never allowed to move their heads?

And of the objects which are being carried in like manner they would only see the shadows?

Yes, he said.

And if they were able to converse with one another, would they not suppose that they were naming what was actually before them?

Very true.

And suppose further that the prison had an echo which came from the other side, would they not be sure to fancy when one of the passers-by spoke that the voice which they heard came from the passing shadow?

No question, he replied.

To them, I said, the truth would be literally nothing but the shadows of the images.

That is certain.

And now look again and see what will naturally follow if the prisoners are released and disabused of their error. At first, when any of them is liberated and compelled suddenly to stand up and turn his neck round and walk and look towards the light, he will suffer sharp pains; the glare will distress him, and he will be unable to see the realities of which in his former state he had seen the shadows; and then conceive someone saying to him, that what he saw before was an illusion, but that now, when he is approaching nearer *"Behold! Human beings living in an underground den."* to being and his eye is turned towards more real existence, he has a clearer vision,—what will be his reply? And you may further imagine that his instructor is pointing to the objects as they pass and requiring him to name them—will he not be perplexed? Will he not fancy that the shadows which he formerly saw are truer than the objects which are now shown to him?

Far truer.

And if he is compelled to look straight at the light, will he not have a pain in his eyes which will make him turn away to take refuge in the objects of vision which he can see, and which he will conceive to be in reality clearer than the things which are now being shown to him?

True, he said.

And suppose once more that he is reluctantly dragged up a steep and rugged ascent, and held fast until he is forced into the presence of the sun himself, is he not likely to be pained and irritated? When he approaches the light his eyes will be dazzled, and he will not be able to see anything at all of what are now called realities.

Not all in a moment, he said.

He will require to grow accustomed to the sight of the upper world. And first he will see the shadows best, next the reflections of men and other objects in the water, and then the objects themselves; then he will gaze upon the light of the moon and the stars and the spangled heaven; and he will see the sky and the stars by night better than the sun or the light of the sun by day?

Certainly.

Last of all he will be able to see the sun, and not mere reflections of him in the water, but he will see him in his own proper place, and not in another; and he will contemplate him as he is.

Certainly.

5   He will then proceed to argue that this is he who gives the season and the years, and is the guardian of all that is in the visible world, and in a certain way the cause of all things which he and his fellows have been accustomed to behold?

Clearly, he said, he would first see the use and then reason about him.

10   And when he remembered his old habitation, and the wisdom of the den and his fellow-prisoners, do you not suppose that he would felicitate himself on the change, and pity them?

Certainly, he would.

And if they were in the habit of conferring honors among themselves on 15   those who were quickest to observe the passing shadows and to remark which of them went before, and which followed after, and which were together; and who were therefore best able to draw conclusions as to the future, do you think that he would care for such honors and glories, or envy the possessors of them? Would he not say with Homer "better to 20   be the poor servant of a poor master," and to endure anything, rather than think as they do and live after their manner?

Yes, he said, I think that he would rather suffer anything than entertain these false notions and live in this miserable manner.

Imagine once more, I said, such an one coming suddenly out of the sun 25   to be replaced in his old situation; would he not be certain to have his eyes full of darkness?

To be sure, he said.

And if there were a contest, and he had to compete in measuring the shadows with the prisoners who had never moved out of the den, while 30   his sight was still weak, and before his eyes had become steady (and the time which would be needed to acquire this new habit of sight might be very considerable), would he not be ridiculous? Men would say of him that up he went and down he came without his eyes; and that it was better not even to think of ascending; and if anyone tried to release another and lead him up to the light, let them only catch the offender, and they would put him to death.

No question, he said.

This entire allegory, I said, you may now append, dear Glaucon, to the previous argument; the prison-house is the world of sight, the light of the fire is the sun, and you will not misapprehend me if you interpret the journey upwards to be the ascent of the soul your desire, I have expressed—whether rightly or wrongly God knows. But, whether true or false, my opinion is that in the world of knowledge the idea of good appears last of all, and is seen only with an effort; and, when seen is also inferred to be the universal author of all things beautiful and right, parent of light and of the lord of light in this visible world, and the immediate source of reason and truth in the intellectual; and that this is the power upon which he who would act rationally either in public or private life must have his eye fixed.

I agree, he said, as far as I am able to understand you.

Moreover, I said, you must not wonder that those who attain to this beatific vision are unwilling to descend to human affairs; for their souls are ever hastening into the upper world where they desire to dwell; which desire of theirs is very natural, if our allegory may be trusted.

Yes, very natural.

And is there anything surprising in one who passes from divine contemplations to the evil state of man, misbehaving himself in a ridiculous manner; if, while his eyes are blinking and before he has become accustomed to the surrounding darkness, he is compelled to fight in courts of law, or in other places, about the images or the shadows of images of justice, and is endeavoring to meet the conceptions of those who have never yet seen absolute justice?

Anything but surprising, he replied.

Anyone who has common sense will remember that the bewilderments of the eyes are of two kinds, and arise from two causes, either from coming out of the light or from going into the light, which is true of the mind's eye, quite as much as of the bodily eye; and he who remembers this when he sees any one whose vision is perplexed and weak, will not be too ready to laugh; he will first ask whether that soul of man has come out of the brighter life, and is unable to see because unaccustomed to the dark, or having turned form darkness to the day is dazzled by excess of light. And he will count the one happy in his condition and state of being, and he will pity the other; or, if he have a mind to laugh at the soul which comes from below into the light, there will be more reason in this than in the laugh which greets him who returns from above out of the light into the den.

QUESTIONS TO CONSIDER

- Describe Plato's cave. Who do the cave's prisoners represent? What is the function of the fire burning within the cave, compared to that of the sun, burning outside it?

- What would the passage from the cave correspond to, in our lives? What would existence outside the cave signify, then?

- If the cave signifies the state of human ignorance, our present life, then why would a freed prisoner ever want to return? Through what successive stages would such a person go in their journey? Do you think Plato (who wrote the dialogue) has anyone especially in mind when he says, "Men would say of him [the returning prisoner] that up he went and down he came without his eyes; and that it was better not even to think of ascending; and if anyone tried to release another and lead him up to the light, let them only catch the offender, and they would put him to death"?

CARTESIAN DUALISM

RENÉ DESCARTES—MEDITATIONS

I—Of the Things of Which We May Doubt

1. Several years have now elapsed since I first became aware that I had accepted, even from my youth, many false opinions for true, and that consequently what I afterward based on such principles was highly doubtful; and from that time I was convinced of the necessity of undertaking once in my life to rid myself of all the opinions I had adopted, and of commencing anew the work of building from the foundation, if I desired to establish a firm and abiding *"Suppose that we are dreaming."* superstructure in the sciences. But as this enterprise appeared to me to be one of great magnitude, I waited until I had attained an age so mature as to leave me no hope that at any stage of life more advanced I should be better able to execute my design. On this account, I have delayed so long that I should henceforth consider I was doing wrong were I still to consume in deliberation any of the time that now remains for action. Today, then, since I have opportunely freed my mind from all cares and am happily disturbed by no passions], and since I am in the secure possession of leisure in a peaceable retirement, I will at length apply myself earnestly and freely to the general overthrow of all my former opinions.

2. But, to this end, it will not be necessary for me to show that the whole of these are false—a point, perhaps, which I shall never reach; but as even now my reason convinces me that I ought not the less carefully to withhold belief from what is not entirely certain and indubitable, than from what is manifestly false, it will be sufficient to justify the rejection of the whole if I shall find in each some ground for doubt. Nor for this purpose will it be necessary even to deal with each belief individually, which would be truly an endless labor; but, as the removal from below of the foundation necessarily involves the downfall of the whole edifice, I will at once approach the criticism of the principles on which all my former beliefs rested.

3. All that I have, up to this moment, accepted as possessed of the highest truth and certainty, I received either from or through the senses. I observed, however, that these sometimes misled us; and it is the part of prudence not to place absolute confidence in that by which we have even once been deceived.

4. But it may be said, perhaps, that, although the senses occasionally mislead us respecting minute objects, and such as are so far removed from us as to be beyond the reach of close observation, there are yet many other of their informations (presentations), of the truth of which it is manifestly impossible to doubt; as for example, that I am in this place, seated by the fire, clothed in a winter dressing gown, that I hold in my hands this piece of paper, with other intimations of the same nature. But how could I deny that I possess these hands and this body, and withal escape being classed with persons in a state of insanity, whose brains are so disordered and clouded by dark bilious vapors as to cause them pertinaciously to assert that they are monarchs when they are in the greatest poverty; or clothed in gold] and purple when destitute of any covering; or that their head is made of clay, their body of glass, or that they are gourds? I should certainly be not less insane than they, were I to regulate my procedure according to examples so extravagant.

5. Though this be true, I must nevertheless here consider that I am a man, and that, consequently, I am in the habit of sleeping, and representing to myself in dreams those same things, or even sometimes others less probable, which the insane think are presented to them in their waking moments. How often have I dreamt that I was in these familiar circumstances, that I was dressed, and occupied this place by the fire, when I was lying undressed in bed? At the present moment, however, I certainly look upon this paper with eyes wide awake; the head which I now move is not asleep; I extend this hand consciously and with express purpose, and I perceive it; the occurrences in sleep are not so distinct as all this. But I cannot forget that, at other times I have been deceived in sleep by similar illusions; and, attentively considering those cases, I perceive so clearly that there exist no certain marks by which the state of waking can ever be distinguished from sleep, that I feel greatly astonished; and in amazement I almost persuade myself that I am now dreaming.

6. Let us suppose, then, that we are dreaming, and that all these particulars—namely, the opening of the eyes, the motion of the head, the forthputting of the hands—are merely illusions; and even that we really possess neither an entire body nor hands such as we see. Nevertheless it must be admitted at least that the objects which appear to us in sleep are, as it were, painted representations which could not have been formed unless in the likeness of realities; and, therefore, that those general objects, at all events, namely, eyes, a head, hands, and an entire body, are not simply imaginary, but really existent. For, in truth, painters themselves, even when they study to represent sirens and satyrs by forms the most fantastic and extraordinary, cannot bestow upon them natures absolutely new, but can only make a certain medley of the members of different animals; or if they chance to imagine something so novel that nothing at all similar has ever been seen before, and such as is, therefore, purely fictitious and absolutely false, it is at least certain that the colors of which this is composed are real. And on the same principle, although these general objects, viz. a body, eyes, a head, hands, and the like, be imaginary, we are nevertheless absolutely necessitated to admit the reality at least of some other objects still more simple and universal than these, of which, just as of certain real colors, all those images of things, whether true and real, or false and fantastic, that are found in our consciousness (*cogitatio*) are formed.

7. To this class of objects seem to belong corporeal nature in general and its extension; the figure of extended things, their quantity or magnitude, and their number, as also the place in, and the time during, which they exist, and other things of the same sort.

8. We will not, therefore, perhaps reason illegitimately if we conclude from this that Physics, Astronomy, Medicine, and all the other sciences that have for their end the consideration of composite objects, are indeed of a doubtful character; but that Arithmetic, Geometry, and the other sciences of the same class, which regard merely the simplest and most general objects, and scarcely inquire whether or not these are really existent, contain somewhat that is certain and indubitable: for whether I am awake or dreaming, it remains true that two and three make five, and that a square has but four sides; nor does it seem possible that truths so apparent can ever fall under a suspicion of falsity or incertitude].

9. Nevertheless, the belief that there is a God who is all powerful, and who created me, such as I am, has, for a long time, obtained steady possession of my mind. How, then, do I know that he has not arranged that there should be neither earth, nor sky, nor any extended thing, nor figure, nor magnitude, nor place, providing at the same time, however, for the rise in me of the perceptions of all these objects, and] the persuasion that these do not exist otherwise than as I perceive them? And further, as I sometimes think that others are in error respecting matters of which they believe themselves to possess a perfect knowledge, how do I know that I am not also deceived each time I add together two and three, or number the sides of a square, or form some judgment still more simple, if more simple indeed can be imagined? But perhaps Deity has not been willing that I should be thus deceived, for he is said to be supremely good. If, however, it were repugnant to the goodness of Deity to have created me subject to constant deception, it would seem likewise to be contrary to his goodness to allow me to be occasionally deceived; and yet it is clear that this is permitted.

10. Some, indeed, might perhaps be found who would be disposed rather to deny the existence of a Being so powerful than to believe that there is nothing certain. But let us for the present refrain from opposing this opinion, and grant that all which is here said of a Deity is fabulous: nevertheless, in whatever way it be supposed that I reach the state in which I exist, whether by fate, or chance, or by an endless series of antecedents and consequents, or by any other means, it is clear (since to be deceived and to err is a certain defect) that the probability of my being so imperfect as to be the constant victim of deception, will be increased exactly in proportion as the power possessed by the cause, to which they assign my origin, is lessened. To these reasonings I have assuredly nothing to reply but am constrained at last to avow that there is nothing of all that I formerly believed to be true of which it is impossible to doubt, and that not through thoughtlessness or levity, but from cogent and maturely considered reasons; so that henceforward, if I desire to discover anything certain, I ought not the less carefully to refrain from assenting to those same opinions than to what might be shown to be manifestly false.

11. But it is not sufficient to have made these observations; care must be taken likewise to keep them in remembrance. For those old and customary opinions perpetually recur—long and familiar usage giving

them the right of occupying my mind, even almost against my will, and subduing my belief; nor will I lose the habit of deferring to them and confiding in them so long as I shall consider them to be what in truth they are, viz, opinions to some extent doubtful, as I have already shown, but still highly probable, and such as it is much more reasonable to believe than deny. It is for this reason I am persuaded that I shall not be doing wrong, if, taking an opposite judgment of deliberate design, I become my own deceiver, by supposing, for a time, that all those opinions are entirely false and imaginary, until at length, having thus balanced my old by my new prejudices, my judgment shall no longer be turned aside by perverted usage from the path that may conduct to the perception of truth. For I am assured that, meanwhile, there will arise neither peril nor error from this course, and that I cannot for the present yield too much to distrust, since the end I now seek is not action but knowledge.

12. I will suppose, then, not that Deity, who is sovereignly good and the fountain of truth, but that some malignant demon, who is at once exceedingly potent and deceitful, has employed all his artifice to deceive me; I will suppose that the sky, the air, the earth, colors, figures, sounds, and all external things, are nothing better than the illusions of dreams, by means of which this being has laid snares for my credulity; I will consider myself as without hands, eyes, flesh, blood, or any of the senses, and as falsely believing that I am possessed of these; I will continue resolutely fixed in this belief, and if indeed by this means it be not in my power to arrive at the knowledge of truth, I shall at least do what is in my power, viz, suspend my judgment], and guard with settled purpose against giving my assent to what is false, and being imposed upon by this deceiver, whatever be his power and artifice. But this undertaking is arduous, and a certain indolence insensibly leads me back to my ordinary course of life; and just as the captive, who, perchance, was enjoying in his dreams an imaginary liberty, when he begins to suspect that it is but a vision, dreads awakening, and conspires with the agreeable illusions that the deception may be prolonged; so I, of my own accord, fall back into the train of my former beliefs, and fear to arouse myself from my slumber, lest the time of laborious wakefulness that would succeed this quiet rest, in place of bringing any light of day, should prove inadequate to dispel the darkness that will arise from the difficulties that have now been raised.

- In the course of the first Meditation, does Descartes reject his earlier views outright (that is, does he insist that they are false?) What does he mean by doubt, in this context?

- Does Descartes doubt, or deny, what his senses tell him? What's the difference?

- What about the truths of mathematics: is Descartes saying that 2 + 3 does not equal 5? What has the possible existence of a malignant demon have to do with this Meditation?

V—Of the Essence of Material Things; and Again of God: That He Exists

14. For although I am of such a nature as to be unable, while I possess a very clear and distinct apprehension of a matter, to resist the conviction of its truth, yet because my constitution is also such as to incapacitate me from keeping my mind continually fixed on the same object, and as I frequently recollect a past judgment without at the same time being able to recall the grounds of it, it may happen meanwhile that other reasons are presented to me which would readily cause me to change my opinion, if I did not know that God existed; and thus I should possess no true and certain knowledge, but merely vague and vacillating opinions. Thus, for example, when I consider the nature of the rectilinear] triangle, it most clearly appears to me, who have been instructed in the principles of geometry, that its three angles are equal to two right angles, and I find it impossible to believe otherwise, while I apply my mind to the demonstration; but as soon as I cease from attending to the process of proof, although I still remember that I had a clear comprehension of it, yet I may readily come to doubt of the truth demonstrated, if I do not know that there is a God: for I may persuade myself that I have been so constituted by nature as to be sometimes deceived, even in matters which I think I apprehend with the greatest evidence and certitude, especially when I recollect that I frequently considered many things to be true and certain which other reasons afterward constrained me to reckon as wholly false.

15. But after I have discovered that God exists, seeing I also at the same time observed that all things depend on him, and that he is no deceiver,

and thence inferred that all which I clearly and distinctly perceive is of necessity true: although I no longer attend to the grounds of a judgment, no opposite reason can be alleged sufficient to lead me to doubt of its truth, provided only I remember that I once possessed a clear and distinct comprehension of it. My knowledge of it thus becomes true and certain. And this same knowledge extends likewise to whatever I remember to have formerly demonstrated, as the truths of geometry and the like: for what can be alleged against them to lead me to doubt of them? Will it be that my nature is such that I may be frequently deceived? But I already know that I cannot be deceived in judgments of the grounds of which I possess a clear knowledge. Will it be that I formerly deemed things to be true and certain which I afterward discovered to be false? But I had no clear and distinct knowledge of any of those things, and, being as yet ignorant of the rule by which I am assured of the truth of a judgment, I was led to give my assent to them on grounds which I afterward discovered were less strong than at the time I imagined them to be. What further objection, then, is there? Will it be said that perhaps I am dreaming (an objection I lately myself raised), or that all the thoughts of which I am now conscious have no more truth than the reveries of my dreams? But although, in truth, I should be dreaming, the rule still holds that all which is clearly presented to my intellect is indisputably true.

16. And thus I very clearly see that the certitude and truth of all science depends on the knowledge alone of the true God, insomuch that, before I knew him, I could have no perfect knowledge of any other thing. And now that I know him, I possess the means of acquiring a perfect knowledge respecting innumerable matters, as well relative to God himself and other intellectual objects as to corporeal nature, in so far as it is the object of pure mathematics which do not consider whether it exists or not.

QUESTIONS TO CONSIDER

- What has the existence of God to do with human knowledge, by Descartes' account in this Meditation?

VI—Of the Existence of Material Things and the Real Distinction Between the Mind and Body of Man

1. There now only remains the inquiry as to whether material things exist. With regard to this question, I at least know with certainty that such things may exist, in as far as they constitute the object of the pure mathematics, since, regarding them in this aspect, I can conceive them clearly and distinctly. For there can be no doubt that God possesses the power of producing all the objects I am able distinctly to conceive, and I never considered anything impossible to him, unless when I experienced a contradiction in the attempt to conceive it aright. Further, the faculty of imagination which I possess, and of which I am conscious that I make use when I apply myself to the consideration of material things, is sufficient to persuade me of their existence: for, when I attentively consider what imagination is, I find that it is simply a certain application of the cognitive faculty (*facultas cognoscitiva*) to a body which is immediately present to it, and which therefore exists.

2. And to render this quite clear, I remark, in the first place, the difference that subsists between imagination and pure intellection or conception]. For example, when I imagine a triangle I not only conceive (*intelligo*) that it is a figure comprehended by three lines, but at the same time also I look upon (*intueor*) these three lines as present by the power and internal application of my mind (*acie mentis*), and this is what I call imagining. But if I desire to think of a chiliagon, I indeed rightly conceive that it is a figure composed of a thousand sides, as easily as I conceive that a triangle is a figure composed of only three sides; but I cannot imagine the thousand sides of a chiliagon as I do the three sides of a triangle, nor, so to speak, view them as present with the eyes of my mind].

And although, in accordance with the habit I have of always imagining something when I think of corporeal things, it may happen that, in conceiving a chiliagon, I confusedly represent some figure to myself, yet it is quite evident that this is not a chiliagon, since it in no wise differs from that which I would represent to myself, if I were to think of a myriagon, or any other figure of many sides; nor would this representation be of any use in discovering and unfolding the properties that constitute the difference between a chiliagon and other polygons. But if the question turns on a pentagon, it is quite true that I can conceive its figure, as well as that of a chiliagon, without the aid of imagination;

but I can likewise imagine it by applying the attention of my mind to its five sides, and at the same time to the area which they contain. Thus I observe that a special effort of mind is necessary to the act of imagination, which is not required to conceiving or understanding (*ad intelligendum*); and this special exertion of mind clearly shows the difference between imagination and pure intellection (*imaginatio* et *intellectio pura*).

3. I remark, besides, that this power of imagination which I possess, in as far as it differs from the power of conceiving, is in no way necessary to my nature or] essence, that is, to the essence of my mind; for although I did not possess it, I should still remain the same that I now am, from which it seems we may conclude that it depends on something different from the mind. And I easily understand that, if some body exists, with which my mind is so conjoined and united as to be able, as it were, to consider it when it chooses, it may thus imagine corporeal objects; so that this mode of thinking differs from pure intellection only in this respect, that the mind in conceiving turns in some way upon itself, and considers some one of the ideas it possesses within itself; but in imagining it turns toward the body, and contemplates in it some object conformed to the idea which it either of itself conceived or apprehended by sense. I easily understand, I say, that imagination may be thus formed, if it is true that there are bodies; and because I find no other obvious mode of explaining it, I thence, with probability, conjecture that they exist, but only with probability; and although I carefully examine all things, nevertheless I do not find that, from the distinct idea of corporeal nature I have in my imagination, I can necessarily infer the existence of any body.

4. But I am accustomed to imagine many other objects besides that corporeal nature which is the object of the pure mathematics, as, for example, colors, sounds, tastes, pain, and the like, although with less distinctness; and, inasmuch as I perceive these objects much better by the senses, through the medium of which and of memory, they seem to have reached the imagination, I believe that, in order the more advantageously to examine them, it is proper I should at the same time examine what sense-perception is, and inquire whether from those ideas that are apprehended by this mode of thinking (consciousness), I cannot obtain a certain proof of the existence of corporeal objects.

5. And, in the first place, I will recall to my mind the things I have hitherto held as true, because perceived by the senses, and the foundations upon which my belief in their truth rested; I will, in the second place, examine the reasons that afterward constrained me to doubt of them; and, finally, I will consider what of them I ought now to believe.

6. Firstly, then, I perceived that I had a head, hands, feet and other members composing that body which I considered as part, or perhaps even as the whole, of myself. I perceived further that that body was placed among many others, by which it was capable of being affected in diverse ways, both beneficial and hurtful; and what was beneficial I remarked by a certain sensation of pleasure, and what was hurtful by a sensation of pain. And besides this pleasure and pain, I was likewise conscious of hunger, thirst, and other appetites, as well as certain corporeal inclinations toward joy, sadness, anger, and similar passions. And, out of myself, besides the extension, figure, and motions of bodies, I likewise perceived in them hardness, heat, and the other tactile qualities, and, in addition, light, colors, odors, tastes, and sounds, the variety of which gave me the means of distinguishing the sky, the earth, the sea, and generally all the other bodies, from one another. And certainly, considering the ideas of all these qualities, which were presented to my mind, and which alone I properly and immediately perceived, it was not without reason that I thought I perceived certain objects wholly different from my thought, namely, bodies from which those ideas proceeded; for I was conscious that the ideas were presented to me without my consent being required, so that I could not perceive any object, however desirous I might be, unless it were present to the organ of sense; and it was wholly out of my power not to perceive it when it was thus present. And because the ideas I perceived by the senses were much more lively and clear, and even, in their own way, more distinct than any of those I could of myself frame by meditation, or which I found impressed on my memory, it seemed that they could not have proceeded from myself, and must therefore have been caused in me by some other objects; and as of those objects I had no knowledge beyond what the ideas themselves gave me, nothing was so likely to occur to my mind as the supposition that the objects were similar to the ideas which they caused. And because I recollected also that I had formerly trusted to the senses, rather than to reason, and that the ideas which I myself formed were not so clear as those I perceived by sense, and that they were even for the most part composed of parts of the latter, I was readily persuaded that I had no

idea in my intellect which had not formerly passed through the senses. Nor was I altogether wrong in likewise believing that that body which, by a special right, I called my own, pertained to me more properly and strictly than any of the others; for in truth, I could never be separated from it as from other bodies; I felt in it and on account of it all my appetites and affections, and in fine I was affected in its parts by pain and the titillation of pleasure, and not in the parts of the other bodies that were separated from it. But when I inquired into the reason why, from this I know not what sensation of pain, sadness of mind should follow, and why from the sensation of pleasure, joy should arise, or why this indescribable twitching of the stomach, which I call hunger, should put me in mind of taking food, and the parchedness of the throat of drink, and so in other cases, I was unable to give any explanation, unless that I was so taught by nature; for there is assuredly no affinity, at least none that I am able to comprehend, between this irritation of the stomach and the desire of food, any more than between the perception of an object that causes pain and the consciousness of sadness which springs from the perception. And in the same way it seemed to me that all the other judgments I had formed regarding the objects of sense, were dictates of nature; because I remarked that those judgments were formed in me, before I had leisure to weigh and consider the reasons that might constrain me to form them.

7. But, afterward, a wide experience by degrees sapped the faith I had reposed in my senses; for I frequently observed that towers, which at a distance seemed round, appeared square, when more closely viewed, and that colossal figures, raised on the summits of these towers, looked like small statues, when viewed from the bottom of them; and, in other instances without number, I also discovered error in judgments founded on the external senses; and not only in those founded on the external, but even in those that rested on the internal senses; for is there aught more internal than pain? And yet I have sometimes been informed by parties whose arm or leg had been amputated, that they still occasionally seemed to feel pain in that part of the body which they had lost,—a circumstance that led me to think that I could not be quite certain even that any one of my members was affected when I felt pain in it. And to these grounds of doubt I shortly afterward also added two others of very wide generality: the first of them was that I believed I never perceived anything when awake which I could not occasionally think I also perceived when asleep, and as I do not believe that the ideas I seem to

perceive in my sleep proceed from objects external to me, I did not any more observe any ground for believing this of such as I seem to perceive when awake; the second was that since I was as yet ignorant of the author of my being or at least supposed myself to be so, I saw nothing to prevent my having been so constituted by nature as that I should be deceived even in matters that appeared to me to possess the greatest truth. And, with respect to the grounds on which I had before been persuaded of the existence of sensible objects, I had no great difficulty in finding suitable answers to them; for as nature seemed to incline me to many things from which reason made me averse, I thought that I ought not to confide much in its teachings. And although the perceptions of the senses were not dependent on my will, I did not think that I ought on that ground to conclude that they proceeded from things different from myself, since perhaps there might be found in me some faculty, though hitherto unknown to me, which produced them.

8. But now that I begin to know myself better, and to discover more clearly the author of my being, I do not, indeed, think that I ought rashly to admit all which the senses seem to teach, nor, on the other hand, is it my conviction that I ought to doubt in general of their teachings.

9. And, firstly, because I know that all which I clearly and distinctly conceive can be produced by God exactly as I conceive it, it is sufficient that I am able clearly and distinctly to conceive one thing apart from another, in order to be certain that the one is different from the other, seeing they may at least be made to exist separately, by the omnipotence of God; and it matters not by what power this separation is made, in order to be compelled to judge them different; and, therefore, merely because I know with certitude that I exist, and because, in the meantime, I do not observe that aught necessarily belongs to my nature or essence beyond my being a thinking thing, I rightly conclude that my essence consists only in my being a thinking thing or a substance whose whole essence or nature is merely thinking]. And although I may, or rather, as I will shortly say, although I certainly do possess a body with which I am very closely conjoined; nevertheless, because, on the one hand, I have a clear and distinct idea of myself, in as far as I am only a thinking and unextended thing, and as, on the other hand, I possess a distinct idea of body, in as far as it is only an extended and unthinking thing, it is certain that I, that is, my mind, by which I am what I am], is entirely and truly distinct from my body, and may exist without it.

10. Moreover, I find in myself diverse faculties of thinking that have each their special mode: for example, I find I possess the faculties of imagining and perceiving, without which I can indeed clearly and distinctly conceive myself as entire, but I cannot reciprocally conceive them without conceiving myself, that is to say, without an intelligent substance in which they reside, for in the notion we have of them, or to use the terms of the schools] in their formal concept, they comprise some sort of intellection; whence I perceive that they are distinct from myself as modes are from things. I remark likewise certain other faculties, as the power of changing place, of assuming diverse figures, and the like, that cannot be conceived and cannot therefore exist, any more than the preceding, apart from a substance in which they inhere. It is very evident, however, that these faculties, if they really exist, must belong to some corporeal or extended substance, since in their clear and distinct concept there is contained some sort of extension, but no intellection at all. Further, I cannot doubt but that there is in me a certain passive faculty of perception, that is, of receiving and taking knowledge of the ideas of sensible things; but this would be useless to me, if there did not also exist in me, or in some other thing, another active faculty capable of forming and producing those ideas. But this active faculty cannot be in me in as far as I am but a thinking thing], seeing that it does not presuppose thought, and also that those ideas are frequently produced in my mind without my contributing to it in any way, and even frequently contrary to my will. This faculty must therefore exist in some substance different from me, in which all the objective reality of the ideas that are produced by this faculty is contained formally or eminently, as I before remarked; and this substance is either a body, that is to say, a corporeal nature in which is contained formally and in effect] all that is objectively and by representation] in those ideas; or it is God himself, or some other creature, of a rank superior to body, in which the same is contained eminently. But as God is no deceiver, it is manifest that he does not of himself and immediately communicate those ideas to me, nor even by the intervention of any creature in which their objective reality is not formally, but only eminently, contained. For as he has given me no faculty whereby I can discover this to be the case, but, on the contrary, a very strong inclination to believe that those ideas arise from corporeal objects, I do not see how he could be vindicated from the charge of deceit, if in truth they proceeded from any other source, or were produced by other causes than corporeal things: and accordingly it must be concluded, that corporeal objects exist. Nevertheless, they are not perhaps exactly such as we

perceive by the senses, for their comprehension by the senses is, in many instances, very obscure and confused; but it is at least necessary to admit that all which I clearly and distinctly conceive as in them, that is, generally speaking all that is comprehended in the object of speculative geometry, really exists external to me.

11. But with respect to other things which are either only particular, as, for example, that the sun is of such a size and figure, etc., or are conceived with less clearness and distinctness, as light, sound, pain, and the like, although they are highly dubious and uncertain, nevertheless on the ground alone that God is no deceiver, and that consequently he has permitted no falsity in my opinions which he has not likewise given me a faculty of correcting, I think I may with safety conclude that I possess in myself the means of arriving at the truth. And, in the first place, it cannot be doubted that in each of the dictates of nature there is some truth: for by nature, considered in general, I now understand nothing more than God himself, or the order and disposition established by God in created things; and by my nature in particular I understand the assemblage of all that God has given me.

12. But there is nothing which that nature teaches me more expressly or more sensibly than that I have a body which is ill affected when I feel pain, and stands in need of food and drink when I experience the sensations of hunger and thirst, etc. And therefore I ought not to doubt but that there is some truth in these informations.

QUESTIONS TO CONSIDER

- We started off with Descartes in doubt over whether there is a material world outside his mind, and even whether he has a body. What does he say now? As it turns out, are Descartes' sense reliable?

IV—8

In view of these distinctions it is obvious that the one-sided theories which some people express about all things cannot be valid—on the one hand the theory that nothing is true (for, say they, there is nothing to prevent every statement from being like the statement 'the diagonal of a square is commensurate with the side'), on the other hand the theory that everything is true. These views are practically the same as that of Heraclitus; for he who says that all things are *"All such views are exposed to the often-expressed objection, that they destroy themselves."* true and all are false also makes each of these statements separately, so that since they are impossible, the double statement must be impossible too.

Again, there are obviously contradictories which cannot be at the same time true—nor on the other hand can all statements be false; yet this would seem more possible in the light of what has been said.—But against all such views we must postulate, as we said above,' not that something is or is not, but that something has a meaning, so that we must argue from a definition, viz. by assuming what falsity or truth means. If that which it is true to affirm is nothing other than that which it is false to deny, it is impossible that all statements should be false; for one side of the contradiction must be true. Again, if it is necessary with regard to everything either to assert or to deny it, it is impossible that both should be false; for it is one side of the contradiction that is false.—Therefore all such views are also exposed to the often-expressed objection, that they destroy themselves. For he who says that everything is true makes even the statement contrary to his own true, and therefore his own not true (for the contrary statement denies that it is true), while he who says everything is false makes himself also false.—And if the former person excepts the contrary statement, saying it alone is not true, while the latter excepts his own as being not false, none the less they are driven to postulate the truth or falsity of an infinite number of statements; for that which says the true statement is true is true, and this process will go on to infinity.

Evidently, again, those who say all things are at rest are not right, nor are those who say all things are in movement. For if all things are at rest, the same statements will always be true and the same always false—but this obviously changes; for he who makes a statement, himself at one time was not and again will not be. And if all things are in motion, nothing will be true; everything therefore will be false. But it has been shown that this is impossible. Again, it must be that which is that changes; for change is from something to something. But again it is not the case that all things are at rest or in motion sometimes, and nothing for ever; for there is something which always moves the things that are in motion, and the first mover is itself unmoved.

QUESTIONS TO CONSIDER

- Two different sets of 'one-sided theories' are addressed. What are they, and how does each refute itself?

- Which of the Pre-Socratics holds the position that all things are at rest? That all things are in movement? How does Aristotle argue against each of these positions?. What is the only remaining possibility, then? What sort of thing is Aristotle talking about when he says, 'the first mover is itself unmoved'?

THOMAS AQUINAS—SUMMA THEOLOGIAE

84 1—Does the soul know bodies through the intellect?

Objection 3. Further, the intellect is concerned with things that are necessary and unchangeable. But all bodies are mobile and changeable. Therefore the soul cannot know bodies through the intellect.

On the contrary, Science is in the intellect. If, therefore, the intellect does not know bodies, it follows that there is no science of bodies; and thus perishes natural science, which treats of mobile bodies.

I answer that, it should be said in order to elucidate this question, that the early philosophers, who inquired into the natures of things, thought there was nothing in the world save bodies. And because they observed that all bodies are mobile and considered them to be ever in a state of flux, they were of opinion that we can have no certain knowledge of the true nature of things. For what is in a continual state of flux, cannot be grasped with any degree of certitude, for it passes away ere the mind can form a judgment thereon: according to the saying of Heraclitus, that "it is not possible twice to touch a drop of water in a passing torrent," as the Philosopher relates (Metaph. iv, Did. iii, 5).

After these came Plato, who, wishing to save the certitude of our knowledge of truth through the intellect, maintained that, besides these things corporeal, there is another genus of beings, separate from matter and movement, which beings he called "species" or "ideas," by participation of

"The received is in the receiver after the mode of the receiver."

which each one of these singular and sensible things is said to be either a man, or a horse, or the like. Wherefore he said that sciences and definitions, and whatever appertains to the act of the intellect, are not referred to these sensible bodies, but to those beings immaterial and separate: so that according to this the soul does not understand these corporeal things, but the separate species thereof.

Now this may be shown to be false for two reasons.

First, because, since those species are immaterial and immovable, knowledge of movement and matter would be excluded from science (which knowledge is proper to natural science), and likewise all demonstration through moving and material causes.

Secondly, because it seems ridiculous, when we seek for knowledge of things which are to us manifest, to introduce other beings, which cannot be the substance of those others, since they differ from them essentially: so that granted that we have a knowledge of those separate substances, we cannot for that reason claim to form a judgment concerning these sensible things.

Now it seems that Plato strayed from the truth because, having observed that all knowledge takes place through some kind of similitude, he thought that the form of the thing known must of necessity be in the knower in the same manner as in the thing known. Then he observed that the form of the thing understood is in the intellect under conditions of universality, immateriality, and immobility: which is apparent from the very operation of the intellect, whose act of understanding has a universal extension, and is subject to a certain amount of necessity: for the mode of action corresponds to the mode of the agent's form. Wherefore he concluded that the things which we understand must have in themselves an existence under the same conditions of immateriality and immobility.

But there is no necessity for this. For even in sensible things it is to be observed that the form is otherwise in one sensible than in another: for instance, whiteness may be of great intensity in one, and of a less intensity in another: in one we find whiteness with sweetness, in another without sweetness. In the same way the sensible form is conditioned differently in the thing which is external to the soul, and in the senses which receive the forms of sensible things without receiving matter, such as the color of gold without receiving gold. So also the intellect, according to its own mode, receives under conditions of immateriality and immobility, the species of material and mobile bodies: for the received is in the receiver according to the mode of the receiver. We must conclude, therefore, that through the intellect the soul knows bodies by a knowledge which is immaterial, universal, and necessary.

Reply to Objection 3. Every movement presupposes something immovable: for when a change of quality occurs, the substance remains unmoved; and when there is a change of substantial form, matter remains unmoved. Moreover, the various conditions of mutable things are themselves immovable; for instance, though Socrates be not always sitting, yet it is an immovable truth that whenever he does sit he remains in one place. For this reason, there is nothing to hinder our having an immovable science of movable things.

84 2—Does the soul understand corporeal things through its essence?

I answer that, the ancient philosophers held that the soul knows bodies through its essence. For it was universally admitted that "like is known by like." But they thought that the form of the thing known is in the knower in the same mode as in the thing known. The Platonists however were of a contrary opinion. For Plato, having observed that the intellectual soul has an immaterial nature, and an immaterial mode of knowledge, held that the forms of things known subsist immaterially. While the earlier natural philosophers, observing that things known are corporeal and material, held that things known must exist materially even in the soul that knows them. And therefore, in order to ascribe to the soul a knowledge of all things, they held that it has the same nature in common with all. And because the nature of a result is determined by its principles, they ascribed to the soul the nature of a principle; so that those who thought fire to be the principle of all, held that the soul had the nature of fire; and in like manner as to air and water. Lastly, Empedocles, who held the existence of our four material elements and two principles of movement, said that the soul was composed of these. Consequently, since they held that things exist in the soul materially, they maintained that all the soul's knowledge is material, thus failing to discern intellect from sense.

But this opinion will not hold. First, because in the material principle of which they spoke, the various results do not exist save in potentiality. But a thing is not known according as it is in potentiality, but only according as it is in act, as is shown Metaph. ix (Did. viii, 9): wherefore neither is a power known except through its act. It is therefore insufficient to ascribe to the soul the nature of the principles in order to explain the fact that it knows all, unless we further admit in the soul natures and forms of each individual result, for instance, of bone, flesh, and the like; thus does Aristotle argue against Empedocles (De Anima i, 5). Secondly, because if it were necessary for the thing known to exist materially in the knower, there would be no reason why things which have a material existence outside the soul should be devoid of knowledge; why, for instance, if by fire the soul knows fire, that fire also which is outside the soul should not have knowledge of fire.

We must conclude, therefore, that material things known must needs exist in the knower, not materially, but immaterially. The reason of this is, because the act of knowledge extends to things outside the knower: for we know things even that are external to us. Now by matter the form of a thing is determined to some one thing. Wherefore it is clear that knowledge is in inverse ratio of materiality. And consequently, things that are not receptive of forms save materially, have no power of knowledge whatever—such as plants, as the Philosopher says (De Anima ii, 12). But the more immaterially a thing receives the form of the thing known, the more perfect is its knowledge. Therefore the intellect which abstracts the species not only from matter, but also from the individuating conditions of matter, has more perfect knowledge than the senses, which receive the form of the thing known, without matter indeed, but subject to material conditions. Moreover, among the senses, sight has the most perfect knowledge, because it is the least material, as we have remarked above (Question 78, Article 3): while among intellects the more perfect is the more immaterial.

It is therefore clear from the foregoing, that if there be an intellect which knows all things by its essence, then its essence must needs have all things in itself immaterially; thus the early philosophers held that the essence of the soul, that it may know all things, must be actually composed of the principles of all material things. Now this is proper to God, that His Essence comprise all things immaterially as effects pre-exist virtually in their cause. God alone, therefore, understands all things through His Essence: but neither the human soul nor the angels can do so.

84 3—Does the soul understand all things through innate species?

On the contrary, The Philosopher, speaking of the intellect, says (De Anima iii, 4) that it is like "a tablet on which nothing is written."

I answer that, since form is the principle of action, a thing must be related to the form which is the principle of an action, as it is to that action: for instance, if upward motion is from lightness, then that which only potentially moves upwards must needs be only potentially light, but that which actually moves upwards must needs be actually light. Now we observe that man sometimes is only a potential knower, both as to sense and as to intellect. And he is reduced from such potentiality to act— through the action of sensible objects on his senses, to the act of sensation—by instruction or discovery, to the act of understanding. Wherefore we must say that the cognitive soul is in potentiality both to the images which are the principles of sensing, and to those which are the principles of understanding. For this reason Aristotle (De Anima iii, 4) held that the intellect by which the soul understands has no innate species but is at first in potentiality to all such species.

But since that which has a form actually, is sometimes unable to act according to that form on account of some hindrance, as a light thing may be hindered from moving upwards; for this reason did Plato hold that naturally man's intellect is filled with all intelligible species, but that, by being united to the body, it is hindered from the realization of its act. But this seems to be unreasonable.

First, because, if the soul has a natural knowledge of all things, it seems impossible for the soul so far to forget the existence of such knowledge as not to know itself to be possessed thereof: for no man forgets what he knows naturally; that, for instance, the whole is larger than the part, and such like. And especially unreasonable does this seem if we suppose that it is natural to the soul to be united to the body, as we have established above (76, 1): for it is unreasonable that the natural operation of a thing be totally hindered by that which belongs to it naturally.

Secondly, the falseness of this opinion is clearly proved from the fact that if a sense be wanting, the knowledge of what is apprehended through that sense is wanting also: for instance, a man who is born blind can have no knowledge of colors. This would not be the case if the soul had innate images of all intelligible things. We must therefore conclude that the soul does not know corporeal things through innate species.

QUESTIONS TO CONSIDER

- In what way is Aquinas' account of knowledge different from those of the materialists and Plato? What about René Descartes?
- The view taken by Aristotle and Thomas Aquinas are often called 'middle views'. Is that the case here?

5

NATURAL PHILOSOPHY, FREEDOM, AND RIGHT ACTION

A separate question from our discussion of the possibility of human knowledge is whether we are free: that is, whether we make free choices. As before, the position one takes about what nature is, in general, has a bearing upon what constitutes human nature, including human freedom. A further implication, in this case, brings us to another question: if we can (or cannot) be said to be free, what of moral responsibility? After all, if we are not free to choose or not to choose, how can we be held responsible for right (or wrong) actions? And if we cannot be held responsible, how is ethics even possible? Much lies in the balance, then, when we consider the implications of natural philosophy for human life.

EARLY MATERIALISM

EPICURUS—LETTER TO MENOECEUS

Fate, which some introduce as sovereign over all things, he [the wise man] scorns, affirming rather that some things happen of necessity, others by chance, others through our own agency. For he sees that necessity destroys responsibility and that chance is inconstant; whereas our own actions are autonomous, and it is to them that praise and blame naturally attach. It were better, indeed, to accept the legends of the gods than to bow beneath that yoke of destiny

> *"Better to accept the legends of the gods than to bow beneath that yoke of destiny which the natural philosophers have imposed."*

which the natural philosophers have imposed. The one holds out some faint hope that we may escape if we

118

honor the gods, while the necessity of the naturalists is deaf to all entreaties. Nor does he hold chance to be a god, as the world in general does, for in the acts of a god there is no disorder; nor to be a cause, though an uncertain one, for he believes that no good or evil is dispensed by chance to men so as to make life blessed, though it supplies the starting point of great good and great evil. He believes that the misfortune of the wise is better than the prosperity of the fool. It is better, in short, that what is well judged in action should not owe its successful issue to the aid of chance.

LUCRETIUS—ON THE NATURE OF THINGS

This terror and darkness of mind must be dispelled, not by the rays of the sun and glittering shafts of day, but by the aspect and the law of nature, the warp of whose design we shall begin with this first principle, nothing is ever gotten out of nothing by divine power. Fear, in truth, holds in check all mortals in this way, because they see many operations go on in earth and heaven, the causes of which they can in no way understand, believing them therefore to be done by divine power. For these reasons, when we shall have seen that nothing can be produced from nothing, we shall then more correctly ascertain that which we are seeking, both the elements out of which everything can be produced and the manner in which all things are done without the hand of the gods.

This point too herein we wish you to apprehend: when bodies are borne downwards sheer through void by their own weights, at quite uncertain times and uncertain spots they push themselves a little from their course: you just and only just can call it a change of inclination. *"Besides blows and weights there is another cause of motions, from which this power of free action has been begotten in us."* If they were not used to swerve, they would all fall down, like drops of rain, through the deep void, and no clashing would have been begotten nor blow produced among the first beginnings: thus nature never would have produced anything.

But if perhaps someone believes that heavier bodies, as they are carried more quickly sheer through space, can fall from above on the lighter and so beget blows able to produce begetting motions, he goes most widely astray from true reason. For whenever bodies fall through water and thin air, they must quicken their descents in proportion to their weights, because the body of water and subtle nature of air cannot retard everything in equal degree, but more readily give way, overpowered by the heavier: on the other hand empty void cannot offer resistance to anything in any direction at anytime, but must, as its nature craves, continually give way; and for this reason all things must be moved and borne along with equal velocity though of unequal weights through the unresisting void. Therefore heavier things will never be able to fall from above on lighter nor of themselves to beget blows sufficient to produce the varied motions by which nature carries on things. Wherefore again and again I say bodies must swerve a little; and yet not more than the least possible; lest we be found to be imagining oblique motions and this the reality should refute. For this we see to be plain and evident, that weights, so far as in them is, cannot travel obliquely, when they fall from above, at least so far as you can perceive; but that nothing swerves in any case from the straight course, who is there that can perceive?

Again if all motion is ever linked together and a new motion ever springs from another in a fixed order and first-beginnings do not by swerving make some commencement of motion to break through the decrees of fate, that cause follow not cause from everlasting, whence have all living creatures here on earth, whence, I ask, has been wrested from the fates the power by which we go forward whither the will leads each, by which likewise we change the direction of our motions neither at a fixed time nor fixed place; but when and where the minditself has prompted? For beyond a doubt in these things his own will makes for each a beginning and from this beginning motions are welled through the limbs. See you not too, when the barriers are thrown open at a given moment, that yet the eager powers of the horses cannot start forward so instantaneously as the mind itself desires? The whole store of matter through the whole body must be sought out, in order that stirred up through all the frame it may follow with undivided effort the bent of the mind; so that you see the beginning of motion is born from the heart, and the action first commences in the will of the mind and next is transmitted through the whole body and frame. Quite different is the case when we move on propelled by a stroke inflicted by the strong might and strong compulsion of another; for then it is quite clear that all the matter of the whole body moves and is hurried on against our inclination, until the will has reined it in throughout the limbs. Do you see then in this case that, though an

outward force often pushes men on and compels them frequently to advance against their will and to be hurried headlong on, there yet is something in our breast sufficient to struggle against and resist it? And when too this something chooses the store of matter is compelled
5 sometimes to change its course through the limbs and frame, and after it has been forced forward, is reined in and settles back into its place. Wherefore in seeds too you must admit the same, admit that besides blows and weights there is another cause of motions, from which this power of free action has been begotten in us, since we see that nothing
10 can come from nothing. For weight forbids that all things be done by blows through as it were an outward force; but that the mind itself does not feel an internal necessity in all its actions and is not as it were overmastered and compelled to bear and put up with this, is caused by a minute swerving of first beginnings at no fixed part of space and no fixed
15 time.

QUESTIONS TO CONSIDER

- Why does Epicurus insist that we are free, when his philosophy of nature would incline him to determinism, as with his philosophical forebear, Democritus?

- Lucretius applies his doctrine of the swerve to a particular problem: what is the problem, and how does the swerve resolve that problem?

- The first and last sections of this reading contain references to Lucretius' view regarding how we should go about explaining natural events. To which view does Lucretius incline: that we should explain natural occurrences through natural explanations (a view called naturalism), or that we should explain them by references to divine causes (theism)?

ENLIGHTENED MATERIALISM

THOMAS HOBBES—LEVIATHAN

That sense is motion in the organs and interior parts of man's body, caused by the action of the things we see, hear, etc., and that fancy is but the relics of the same motion, remaining after sense, has been already said in the first and second chapters. And because going, speaking, and the
20 like voluntary motions depend always upon a precedent thought of

---

whither, which way, and what, it is evident that the imagination is the first internal beginning of all voluntary motion. And although unstudied men do not conceive any motion at all to be there, where the thing moved is invisible, or the space it is moved in is, for the shortness of it, insensible; yet that does not hinder but that such motions are. For let a space be never so little, that which is moved over a greater space, of which that little one is part, must first be moved over that. These small beginnings of motion within the body of man, before they appear in walking, speaking, striking, and other visible actions, are commonly called endeavor.

"Good, evil, and contemptible are always used with relation to the person that uses them, there being nothing simply and absolutely so."

This endeavor, when it is toward something which causes it, is called appetite, or desire, the latter being the general name, and the other oftentimes restrained to signify the desire of food, namely hunger and thirst. And when the endeavor is from ward something, it is generally called aversion.

That which men desire they are said to love, and to hate those things for which they have aversion. So that desire and love are the same thing; save that by desire, we signify the absence of the object; by love, most commonly the presence of the same. So also by aversion, we signify the absence, and by hate the presence, of the object.

And because the constitution of a man's body is in continual mutation, it is impossible that all the same things should always cause in him the same appetites and aversions: much less can all men consent in the desire of almost any one and the same object.

But whatsoever is the object of any man's appetite or desire, that is it which he for his part calls good; and the object of his hate and aversion, evil; and of his contempt, vile and inconsiderable. For these words of good, evil, and contemptible are always used with relation to the person that uses them: there being nothing simply and absolutely so; nor any common rule of good and evil to be taken from the nature of the objects themselves; but from the person of the man, where there is no Commonwealth; or, in a Commonwealth, from the person that represents it; or from an arbitrator or judge, whom men disagreeing shall by consent set up and make his sentence the rule.

When in the mind of man appetites and aversions, hopes and fears, concerning one and the same thing, arise alternately; and diverse good and evil consequences of the doing or omitting the thing propounded come successively into our thoughts; so that sometimes we have an appetite to it, sometimes an aversion from it; sometimes hope to be able to do it, sometimes despair, or fear to attempt it; the whole sum of desires, aversions, hopes and fears, continued till the thing be either done, or thought impossible, is that we call deliberation.

This alternate succession of appetites, aversions, hopes and fears is no less in other living creatures than in man; and therefore beasts also deliberate.

Every deliberation is then said to end when that about which they deliberate is either done or thought impossible; because till then we retain the liberty of doing, or omitting, according to our appetite, or aversion.

In deliberation, the last appetite, or aversion, immediately adhering to the action, or to its omission, is that we call the will—the act, not the faculty, of willing.

And because in deliberation the appetites and aversions are raised by foresight of the good and evil consequences, and sequels of the action about which we deliberate, the good or evil effect of which depends on the foresight of a long chain of consequences, of which very seldom any man is able to see to the end. But for so far as a man sees, if the good in those consequences be greater than the evil, the whole chain is that which writers call apparent or seeming good. And contrarily, when the evil exceeds the good, the whole is apparent or seeming evil: so that he who has by experience, or reason, the greatest and surest prospect of consequences, deliberates best himself; and is able, when he will, to give the best counsel unto others.

- Life *is* motion, for Hobbes. Following this line of reasoning, what, then, must our choices be? How does Hobbes reduce human choices, then, to literal movements?

- As to desires and aversions, are they objective or subjective, for Hobbes? What, then, of good and evil?

- Are we free, then?

BARON D'HOLBACH—THE SYSTEM OF NATURE

Nature and Her Laws

Man has always deceived himself when he abandoned experience to follow imaginary systems.—He is the work of nature.—He exists in Nature.—He is submitted to the laws of Nature.—He cannot deliver himself from them:—cannot step beyond them even in thought.

5   The universe, that vast assemblage of everything that exists, presents only matter and motion: the whole offers to our contemplation, nothing but an immense, an uninterrupted succession of causes and effects; some of these causes are known to us, because they either strike immediately on our senses, or have been brought under their cognizance, by the
10   examination of long experience; others are unknown to us, because they act upon us by effects, frequently very remote from their primary cause. An immense variety of matter, combined under an infinity of forms, incessantly communicates, unceasingly receives a diversity of impulses. The different qualities of this matter, its innumerable combinations, its
15   various methods of action, which are the necessary consequence of these associations, constitute for man what he calls the essence of beings: it is from these varied essences that spring the orders, the classes, or the systems, which these beings respectively possess, of which the sum total makes up that which is known by the term nature.

Of the System of Man's Free Agency

Those who have pretended that the soul is distinguished from the body, is immaterial, draws its ideas from its own peculiar source, acts by its own energies without the aid of any exterior object; by a consequence of their own system, have enfranchised it from those physical laws, according to which all beings of which we have a knowledge are obliged to act. They have believed that the soul is mistress of its own conduct, is able to regulate its own peculiar operations; has the faculty to determine its will by its own natural energy; in a word, they have pretended man is a free agent.

It has been already sufficiently proved, that the soul is nothing more than the body, considered relatively to some of its functions, more concealed than others: it has been shewn, that this soul, even when it shall be supposed immaterial, is continually modified conjointly with the body; is submitted to all its motion; that without this it would remain inert and dead: that, consequently, it is subjected to the influence of those material, to the operation those physical causes, which give impulse to the body; of which the mode of existence, whether habitual or **"The soul is nothing more than the body."** transitory, depends upon the material elements by which it is surrounded; that form its texture; that constitute its temperament; that enter into it by the means of the aliments; that penetrate it by their subtility; the faculties which are called intellectual, and those qualities which are styled moral, have been explained in a manner purely physical; entirely natural: in the last place, it has been demonstrated, that all the ideas, all the systems, all the affections, all the opinions, whether true or false, which man forms to himself, are to be attributed to his physical powers; are to be ascribed to his material senses. Thus, man is a being purely physical; in whatever manner he is considered, he is connected to universal Nature: submitted to the necessary, to the immutable laws that she imposes on all the beings she contains, according to their peculiar essences; conformable to the respective properties with which, without consulting them, she endows each particular species. Man's life is a line that Nature commands him to describe upon the surface of the earth: without his ever being able to swerve from it even for an instant. He is born without his own consent; his organizations do in no wise depend upon himself; his ideas come to him involuntarily; his habits are in the power of those who cause him to contract them; he is unceasingly modified by causes, whether visible or concealed, over which he has no control; give the hue to his way of thinking and determine his manner of acting. He is good or bad—happy or miserable—wise or foolish—reasonable or irrational, without his will going for anything in these various states. Nevertheless, in despite of the shackles by which he is bound, it is pretended he is a free agent, or that independent of the causes by which he is moved, he determines his own will; regulates his own condition. ...

That which a man is about to do is always a consequence of that which he has been—of that which he is—of that which he has done up to the moment of the action: his total and actual existence, considered under all its possible circumstances, contains the sum of all the motives to the action he is about to commit; this is a principle, the truth of which no thinking, being will be able to refuse accrediting: his life is a series of necessary moments; his conduct, whether good or bad, virtuous or vicious, useful or prejudicial, either to himself or to others, is a concatenation of action, a chain of causes and effects, as necessary as all the moments of his existence. To live is to exist in a necessary mode during the points of its duration, which succeed each other necessarily, to will is to acquiesce or not in remaining such as he is, to be free is to yield to the necessary motives that he carries within himself. ...

The false ideas he has formed to himself upon free-agency, are in general thus founded: there are certain events which he judges necessary; either because he sees they are effects that are constantly, are invariably linked to certain causes, which nothing seems to prevent; or because he believes he has discovered the chain of causes and effects that is put in play to produce those events: whilst he contemplates as contingent, other events, of whose causes he is ignorant; the concatenation of which he does not perceive; with whose mode of acting he is unacquainted: but in Nature, where everything is connected by one common bond, there exists no effect without a cause. In the moral as well as in the physical world, everything that happens is a necessary consequence of causes, either visible or concealed, which are, of necessity, obliged to act after their peculiar essences. In man, free agency is nothing more than necessity contained within himself.

- What is Baron d'Holbach's natural philosophy?
- Does d'Holbach's view regarding our free choices follow his natural philosophy, or has he deviated from that view to carve out a space for human choice?

DUALISM

RENÉ DESCARTES—MEDITATIONS

Meditation IV—Of Truth and Error

8. Whereupon, regarding myself more closely, and considering what my errors are (which alone testify to the existence of imperfection in me), I observe that these depend on the concurrence of two causes, viz, the faculty of cognition, which I possess, and that of election or the power
5 of free choice—in other words, the understanding and the will. For by the understanding alone, I neither affirm nor deny anything but merely apprehend (*percipio*) the ideas regarding which I may form a judgment; nor is any error, properly so called, found in
10 it thus accurately taken. And although

> *"My errors arise from this cause alone, that I do not restrain the will."*

there are perhaps innumerable objects in the world of which I have no idea in my understanding, it cannot, on that account be said that I am deprived of those ideas as of something that is due to my nature, but simply that I do not possess them, because, in truth, there is no ground
15 to prove that Deity ought to have endowed me with a larger faculty of cognition than he has actually bestowed upon me; and however skillful a workman I suppose him to be, I have no reason, on that account, to think that it was obligatory on him to give to each of his works all the perfections he is able to bestow upon some. Nor, moreover, can I
20 complain that God has not given me freedom of choice, or a will sufficiently ample and perfect, since, in truth, I am conscious of will so ample and extended as to be superior to all limits. And what appears to

me here to be highly remarkable is that, of all the other properties I possess, there is none so great and perfect as that I do not clearly discern it could be still greater and more perfect. For, to take an example, if I consider the faculty of understanding which I possess, I find that it is of

5 very small extent, and greatly limited, and at the same time I form the idea of another faculty of the same nature, much more ample and even infinite, and seeing that I can frame the idea of it, I discover, from this circumstance alone, that it pertains to the nature of God. In the same way, if I examine the faculty of memory or imagination, or any other

10 faculty I possess, I find none that is not small and circumscribed, and in God immense and infinite. It is the faculty of will only, or freedom of choice, which I experience to be so great that I am unable to conceive the idea of another that shall be more ample and extended; so that it is chiefly my will which leads me to discern that I bear a certain image and

15 similitude of Deity. For although the faculty of will is incomparably greater in God than in myself, as well in respect of the knowledge and power that are conjoined with it, and that render it stronger and more efficacious, as in respect of the object, since in him it extends to a greater number of things, it does not, nevertheless, appear to me greater,

20 considered in itself formally and precisely: for the power of will consists only in this, that we are able to do or not to do the same thing (that is, to affirm or deny, to pursue or shun it), or rather in this alone, that in affirming or denying, pursuing or shunning, what is proposed to us by the understanding, we so act that we are not conscious of being

25 determined to a particular action by any external force. For, to the possession of freedom, it is not necessary that I be alike indifferent toward each of two contraries; but, on the contrary, the more I am inclined toward the one, whether because I clearly know that in it there is the reason of truth and goodness, or because God thus internally

30 disposes my thought, the more freely do I choose and embrace it; and assuredly divine grace and natural knowledge, very far from diminishing liberty, rather augment and fortify it. But the indifference of which I am conscious when I am not impelled to one side rather than to another for want of a reason, is the lowest grade of liberty, and manifests defect or

35 negation of knowledge rather than perfection of will; for if I always clearly knew what was true and good, I should never have any difficulty in determining what judgment I ought to come to, and what choice I ought to make, and I should thus be entirely free without ever being indifferent.

9. From all this I discover, however, that neither the power of willing, which I have received from God, is of itself the source of my errors, for it is exceedingly ample and perfect in its kind; nor even the power of understanding, for as I conceive no object unless by means of the faculty that God bestowed upon me, all that I conceive is doubtless rightly conceived by me, and it is impossible for me to be deceived in it. Whence, then, spring my errors? They arise from this cause alone, that I do not restrain the will, which is of much wider range than the understanding, within the same limits, but extend it even to things I do not understand, and as the will is of itself indifferent to such, it readily falls into error and sin by choosing the false in room of the true, and evil instead of good.

10. For example, when I lately considered whether aught really existed in the world, and found that because I considered this question, it very manifestly followed that I myself existed, I could not but judge that what I so clearly conceived was true, not that I was forced to this judgment by any external cause, but simply because great clearness of the understanding was succeeded by strong inclination in the will; and I believed this the more freely and spontaneously in proportion as I was less indifferent with respect to it. But now I not only know that I exist, in so far as I am a thinking being, but there is likewise presented to my mind a certain idea of corporeal nature; hence I am in doubt as to whether the thinking nature which is in me, or rather which I myself am, is different from that corporeal nature, or whether both are merely one and the same thing, and I here suppose that I am as yet ignorant of any reason that would determine me to adopt the one belief in preference to the other; whence it happens that it is a matter of perfect indifference to me which of the two suppositions I affirm or deny, or whether I form any judgment at all in the matter.

11. This indifference, moreover, extends not only to things of which the understanding has no knowledge at all, but in general also to all those which it does not discover with perfect clearness at the moment the will is deliberating upon them; for, however probable the conjectures may be that dispose me to form a judgment in a particular matter, the simple knowledge that these are merely conjectures, and not certain and indubitable reasons, is sufficient to lead me to form one that is directly the oppo-site. Of this I lately had abundant experience, when I laid aside as false all that I had before held for true, on the single ground that I could in some degree doubt of it.

12. But if I abstain from judging of a thing when I do not conceive it with sufficient clearness and distinctness, it is plain that I act rightly, and am not deceived; but if I resolve to deny or affirm, I then do not make a right use of my free will; and if I affirm what is false, it is evident that I am deceived; moreover, even although I judge according to truth, I stumble upon it by chance, and do not therefore escape the imputation of a wrong use of my freedom; for it is a dictate of the natural light, that the knowledge of the understanding ought always to precede the determination of the will. And it is this wrong use of the freedom of the will in which is found the privation that constitutes the form of error. Privation, I say, is found in the act, in so far as it proceeds from myself, but it does not exist in the faculty which I received from God, nor even in the act, in so far as it depends on him.

13. For I have assuredly no reason to complain that God has not given me a greater power of intelligence or more perfect natural light than he has actually bestowed, since it is of the nature of a finite understanding not to comprehend many things, and of the nature of a created understanding to be finite; on the contrary, I have every reason to render thanks to God, who owed me nothing, for having given me all the perfections I possess, and I should be far from thinking that he has unjustly deprived me of, or kept back, the other perfections which he has not bestowed upon me.

14. I have no reason, moreover, to complain because he has given me a will more ample than my understanding, since, as the will consists only of a single element, and that indivisible, it would appear that this faculty is of such a nature that nothing could be taken from it without destroying it; and certainly, the more extensive it is, the more cause I have to thank the goodness of him who bestowed it upon me.

15. And, finally, I ought not also to complain that God concurs with me in forming the acts of this will, or the judgments in which I am deceived, because those acts are wholly true and good, in so far as they depend on God; and the ability to form them is a higher degree of perfection in my nature than the want of it would be. With regard to privation, in which alone consists the formal reason of error and sin, this does not require the concurrence of Deity, because it is not a thing or existence, and if it be referred to God as to its cause, it ought not to be called privation, but negation according to the signification of these words in the schools. For

in truth it is no imperfection in Deity that he has accorded to me the power of giving or withholding my assent from certain things of which he has not put a clear and distinct knowledge in my understanding; but it is doubtless an imperfection in me that I do not use my freedom aright, and readily give my judgment on matters which I only obscurely and confusedly conceive. I perceive, nevertheless, that it was easy for Deity so to have constituted me as that I should never be deceived, although I still remained free and possessed of a limited knowledge, viz., by implanting in my understanding a clear and distinct knowledge of all the objects respecting which I should ever have to deliberate; or simply by so deeply engraving on my memory the resolution to judge of nothing without previously possessing a clear and distinct conception of it, that I should never forget it. And I easily understand that, in so far as I consider myself as a single whole, without reference to any other being in the universe, I should have been much more perfect than I now am, had Deity created me superior to error; but I cannot therefore deny that it is not somehow a greater perfection in the universe, that certain of its parts are not exempt from defect, as others are, than if they were all perfectly alike. And I have no right to complain because God, who placed me in the world, was not willing that I should sustain that character which of all others is the chief and most perfect.

16. I have even good reason to remain satisfied on the ground that, if he has not given me the perfection of being superior to error by the first means I have pointed out above, which depends on a clear and evident knowledge of all the matters regarding which I can deliberate, he has at least left in my power the other means, which is, firmly to retain the resolution never to judge where the truth is not clearly known to me: for, although I am conscious of the weakness of not being able to keep my mind continually fixed on the same thought, I can nevertheless, by attentive and oft-repeated meditation, impress it so strongly on my memory that I shall never fail to recollect it as often as I require it, and I can acquire in this way the habitude of not erring.

17. And since it is in being superior to error that the highest and chief perfection of man consists, I deem that I have not gained little by this day's meditation, in having discovered the source of error and falsity. And certainly this can be no other than what I have now explained: for as often as I so restrain my will within the limits of my knowledge, that it forms no judgment except regarding objects which are clearly and

distinctly represented to it by the understanding, I can never be deceived; because every clear and distinct conception is doubtless something, and as such cannot owe its origin to nothing, but must of necessity have God for its author-God, I say, who, as supremely perfect, cannot, without a contradiction, be the cause of any error; and consequently it is necessary to conclude that every such conception or judgment is true. Nor have I merely learned to-day what I must avoid to escape error, but also what I must do to arrive at the knowledge of truth; for I will assuredly reach truth if I only fix my attention sufficiently on all the things I conceive perfectly and separate these from others which I conceive more confusedly and obscurely; to which for the future I shall give diligent heed.

QUESTIONS TO CONSIDER

- Why is error such a problem for Descartes? Is he inclined to say that the mind can simply make mistakes, or is it that we make mistakes only when we think in conjunction with some other power?

- Does it make sense that Descartes would eventually regard the human will as unimpeded by other things—particularly by the body? Could there be any impediment, then, to our freedom of choice?

ARISTOTLE AND THOMAS AQUINAS

ARISTOTLE—METAPHYSICS

IX—2

Since some such originative sources are present in soulless things, and others in things possessed of soul, and in soul, and in the rational part of the soul, clearly some potencies will, be non-rational and some will be non-rational, and some will be accompanied by a rational formula. This is why all arts, i.e., all productive forms of knowledge, are potencies; they are originative sources of change in another thing or in the artist himself considered as other.

And each of those which are accompanied by a rational formula is alike capable of contrary effects, but one non-rational power produces one effect, e.g., the hot is capable only of heating, but the medical art can produce both disease and health. The reason is that science is a rational formula, and the same rational formula explains a thing and its privation, only not in the same way; and in a sense it applies to both, but in a sense it applies rather to the positive fact. Therefore such sciences must deal with contraries, but with one in virtue of their own

> *"There must be, then, something else that decides; I mean by this desire or will."*

nature and with the other not in virtue of their nature; for the rational formula applies to one object in virtue of that object's nature, and to the other, in a sense, accidentally. For it is by denial and removal that it exhibits the contrary; for the contrary is the primary privation, and this is the removal of the positive term. Now since contraries do not occur in the same thing, but science is a potency which depends on the possession of a rational formula, and the soul possesses an originative source of movement; therefore, while the wholesome produces only health and the calorific only heat and the frigorific only cold, the scientific man produces both the contrary effects. For the rational formula is one which applies to both, though not in the same way, and it is in a soul which possesses an originative source of movement; so that the soul will start both processes from the same originative source, having linked them up with the same thing. And so the things whose potency is according to a rational formula act contrariwise to the things whose potency is non-rational; for the products of the former are included under one originative source, the rational formula.

It is obvious also that the potency of merely doing a thing or having it done to one is implied in that of doing it or having it done well, but the latter is not always implied in the former: for he who does a thing well must also do it, but he who does it merely need not also do it well.

IX—5

As all potencies are either innate, like the senses, or come by practice, like the power of playing the flute, or by learning, like artistic power, those which come by practice or by rational formula we must acquire by previous exercise, but this is not necessary with those which are not of this nature and which imply passivity.

Since that which is 'capable' is capable of something and at some time in some way (with all the other qualifications which must be present in the definition), and since some things can produce change according to a rational formula and their potencies involve such a formula, while other things are nonrational and their potencies are non-rational, and the former potencies must be in a living thing, while the latter can be both in the living and in the lifeless; as regards potencies of the latter kind, when the agent and the patient meet in the way appropriate to the potency in question, the one must act and the other be acted on, but with the former kind of potency this is not necessary. For the nonrational potencies are all productive of one effect each, but the rational produce contrary effects, so that if they produced their effects necessarily they would produce contrary effects at the same time; but this is impossible. There must, then, be something else that decides; I mean by this, desire or will. For whichever of two things the animal desires decisively, it will do, when it is present, and meets the passive object, in the way appropriate to the potency in question. Therefore everything which has a rational potency, when it desires that for which it has a potency and in the circumstances in which it has the potency, must do this. And it has the potency in question when the passive object is present and is in a certain state; if not it will not be able to act. (To add the qualification 'if nothing external prevents it' is not further necessary; for it has the potency on the terms on which this is a potency of acting, and it is this not in all circumstances but on certain conditions, among which will be the exclusion of external hindrances; for these are barred by some of the positive qualifications.) And so even if one has a rational wish, or an appetite, to do two things or contrary things at the same time, one will not do them; for it is not on these terms that one has the potency for them, nor is it a potency of doing both at the same time, since one will do the things which it is a potency of doing, on the terms on which one has the potency.

QUESTIONS TO CONSIDER

- What about rational powers distinguishes them from non-rational ones, according to Aristotle? How does this difference address the question of human freedom?

82 1—Does the will desire anything of necessity?

I answer that the word "necessity" is employed in many ways. For that which must be is necessary. Now that a thing must be may belong to it by an intrinsic principle—either material, as when we say that everything composed of contraries is of necessity corruptible—or formal, as when we say that it is necessary for the three angles of a triangle to be equal to two right angles. And this is "natural" and "absolute necessity." In another way, that a thing must be, belongs to it by reason of something extrinsic, which is either the end or the agent. On the part of the end, as when without it the end is not to be attained or so well attained: for instance, food is said to be

"Man has free will, otherwise counsels, commands, prohibitions, rewards, and punishments would be in vain."

necessary for life, and a horse is necessary for a journey. This is called "necessity of end," and sometimes also "utility." On the part of the agent, a thing must be, when someone is forced by some agent, so that he is not able to do the contrary. This is called "necessity of coercion."

Now this necessity of coercion is altogether repugnant to the will. For we call that violent which is against the inclination of a thing. But the very movement of the will is an inclination to something. Therefore, as a thing is called natural because it is according to the inclination of nature, so a thing is called voluntary because it is according to the inclination of the will. Therefore, just as it is impossible for a thing to be at the same time violent and natural, so it is impossible for a thing to be absolutely coerced or violent, and voluntary.

But necessity of end is not repugnant to the will, when the end cannot be attained except in one way: thus from the will to cross the sea, arises in the will the necessity to wish for a ship.

In like manner neither is natural necessity repugnant to the will. Indeed, more than this, for as the intellect of necessity adheres to the first principles, the will must of necessity adhere to the last end, which is happiness: since the end is in practical matters what the principle is in speculative matters. For what befits a thing naturally and immovably must be the root and principle of all else appertaining thereto, since the nature of a thing is the first in everything, and every movement arises from something immovable.

82 2—Does the will desire everything of necessity?

I answer that the will does not desire of necessity whatsoever it desires. In order to make this evident we must observe that as the intellect naturally and of necessity adheres to the first principles, so the will adheres to the last end, as we have said already (1). Now there are some things intelligible which have not a necessary connection with the first principles, such as contingent propositions, the denial of which does not involve a denial of the first principles. And to such the intellect does not assent of necessity. But there are some propositions which have a necessary connection with the first principles: such as demonstrable conclusions, a denial of which involves a denial of the first principles. And to these the intellect assents of necessity, when once it is aware of the necessary connection of these conclusions with the principles; but it does not assent of necessity until through the demonstration it recognizes the necessity of such connection. It is the same with the will. For there are certain individual goods which have not a necessary connection with happiness, because without them a man can be happy: and to such the will does not adhere of necessity. But there are some things which have a necessary connection with happiness, by means of which things man adheres to God, in Whom alone true happiness consists. Nevertheless, until through the certitude of the Divine Vision the necessity of such connection be shown, the will does not adhere to God of necessity, nor to those things which are of God. But the will of the man who sees God in His essence of necessity adheres to God, just as now we desire of necessity to be happy. It is therefore clear that the will does not desire of necessity whatever it desires.

83 1—Does man have free-will?

Objection 1. It would seem that man has not free-will. For whoever has free-will does what he wills. But man does not what he wills; for it is written (Romans 7:19): "For the good which I will I do not, but the evil which I will not, that I do." Therefore man has not free-will.

Objection 2. Further, whoever has free-will has in his power to will or not to will, to do or not to do. But this is not in man's power: for it is written (Romans 9:16): "It is not of him that willeth"—namely, to will—"nor of him that runneth"—namely, to run. Therefore man has not free-will.

Objection 3. Further, what is "free is cause of itself," as the Philosopher says (Metaph. i, 2). Therefore what is moved by another is not free. But God moves the will, for it is written (Proverbs 21:1): "The heart of the king is in the hand of the Lord; whithersoever He will He shall turn it" and (Philippians 2:13): "It is God Who worketh in you both to will and to accomplish." Therefore man has not free-will.

Objection 4. Further, whoever has free-will is master of his own actions. But man is not master of his own actions: for it is written (Jeremiah 10:23): "The way of a man is not his: neither is it in a man to walk." Therefore man has not free-will.

Objection 5. Further, the Philosopher says (Ethic. iii, 5): "According as each one is, such does the end seem to him." But it is not in our power to be of one quality or another; for this comes to us from nature. Therefore it is natural to us to follow some particular end, and therefore we are not free in so doing.

On the contrary, it is written (Sirach 15:14): "God made man from the beginning and left him in the hand of his own counsel"; and the gloss adds: "That is of his free-will."

I answer that man has free-will: otherwise, counsels, exhortations, commands, prohibitions, rewards, and punishments would be in vain. In order to make this evident, we must observe that some things act without judgment; as a stone moves downwards; and in like manner all things which lack knowledge. And some act from judgment, but not a free judgment; as brute animals. For the sheep, seeing the wolf, judges it a thing to be shunned, from a natural and not a free judgment, because it judges, not from reason, but from natural instinct. And the same thing is to be said of any judgment of brute animals. But man acts from judgment, because by his apprehensive power he judges that something should be avoided or sought. But because this judgment, in the case of some particular act, is not from a natural instinct, but from some act of comparison in the reason, therefore he acts from free judgment and retains the power of being inclined to various things. For reason in contingent matters may follow opposite courses, as we see in dialectic syllogisms and rhetorical arguments. Now particular operations are contingent, and therefore in such matters the judgment of reason may follow opposite courses and is not determinate to one. And forasmuch as man is rational is it necessary that man have a free-will.

Reply to Objection 1. As we have said above (81, 3, ad 2), the sensitive appetite, though it obeys the reason, yet in a given case can resist by desiring what the reason forbids. This is therefore the good which man does not when he wishes—namely, "not to desire against reason," as Augustine says.

Reply to Objection 2. Those words of the Apostle are not to be taken as though man does not wish or does not run of his free-will, but because the free-will is not sufficient thereto unless it be moved and helped by God.

Reply to Objection 3. Free-will is the cause of its own movement, because by his free-will man moves himself to act. But it does not of necessity belong to liberty that what is free should be the first cause of itself, as neither for one thing to be cause of another need it be the first cause. God, therefore, is the first cause, Who moves causes both natural and voluntary. And just as by moving natural causes He does not prevent their acts being natural, so by moving voluntary causes He does not deprive their actions of being voluntary: but rather is He the cause of this very thing in them; for He operates in each thing according to its own nature.

Reply to Objection 4. "Man's way" is said "not to be his" in the execution of his choice, wherein he may be impeded, whether he will or not. The choice itself, however, is in us, but presupposes the help of God.

Reply to Objection 5. Quality in man is of two kinds: natural and adventitious. Now the natural quality may be in the intellectual part, or in the body and its powers. From the very fact, therefore, that man is such by virtue of a natural quality which is in the intellectual part, he naturally desires his last end, which is happiness. Which desire, indeed, is a natural desire, and is not subject to free-will, as is clear from what we have said above (82, 1,2). But on the part of the body and its powers man may be such by virtue of a natural quality, inasmuch as he is of such a temperament or disposition due to any impression whatever produced by corporeal causes, which cannot affect the intellectual part, since it is not the act of a corporeal organ. And such as a man is by virtue of a corporeal quality, such also does his end seem to him, because from such a disposition a man is inclined to choose or reject something. But these inclinations are subject to the judgment of reason, which the lower appetite obeys, as we have said (81, 3). Wherefore this is in no way prejudicial to free-will.

The adventitious qualities are habits and passions, by virtue of which a man is inclined to one thing rather than to another. And yet even these inclinations are subject to the judgment of reason. Such qualities, too, are subject to reason, as it is in our power either to acquire them, whether by causing them or disposing ourselves to them, or to reject them. And so there is nothing in this that is repugnant to free-will.

10 2—Is the will moved of necessity by its object?

On the contrary, the rational powers, according to the Philosopher (Metaph. ix, 2) are directed to opposites. But the will is a rational power, since it is in the reason, as stated in De Anima iii, 9. Therefore the will is directed to opposites. Therefore it is not moved, of necessity, to either of the opposites.

I answer that the will is moved in two ways: first, as to the exercise of its act; secondly, as to the specification of its act, derived from the object. As to the first way, no object moves the will necessarily, for no matter what the object be, it is in man's power not to think of it, and consequently not to will it actually. But as to the second manner of motion, the will is moved by one object necessarily, by another not. For in the movement of a power by its object, we must consider under what aspect the object moves the power. For the visible moves the sight, under the aspect of color actually visible. Wherefore if color be offered to the sight, it moves the sight necessarily: unless one turns one's eyes away, which belongs to the exercise of the act. But if the sight were confronted with something not in all respects colored actually, but only so in some respects, and in other respects not, the sight would not of necessity see such an object: for it might look at that part of the object which is not actually colored, and thus it would not see it. Now just as the actually colored is the object of sight, so is good the object of the will. Wherefore if the will be offered an object which is good universally and from every point of view, the will tends to it of necessity, if it wills anything at all, since it cannot will the opposite. If, on the other hand, the will is offered an object that is not good from every point of view, it will not tend to it of necessity. And since lack of any good whatever, is a non-good, consequently, that good alone which is perfect and lacking in nothing, is such a good that the will cannot not-will it: and this is Happiness. Whereas any other particular goods, in so far as they are lacking in some good, can be regarded as non-goods: and from this point of view, they can be set aside or approved by the will, which can tend to one and the same thing from various points of view.

13 6—Does man choose of necessity or freely?

On the contrary, Choice is an act of a rational power, which according to the Philosopher (Metaph. ix, 2) stands in relation to opposites.

I answer that man does not choose of necessity. And this is because that which is possible not to be, is not of necessity. Now the reason why it is possible not to choose, or to choose, may be gathered from a twofold power in man. For man can will and not will, act and not act; again, he can will this or that and do this or that. The reason of this is seated in the very power of the reason. For the will can tend to whatever the reason can apprehend as good. Now the reason can apprehend as good, not only this, viz. "to will" or "to act," but also this, viz. "not to will" or "not to act." Again, in all particular goods, the reason can consider an aspect of some good, and the lack of some good, which has the aspect of evil: and in this respect, it can apprehend any single one of such goods as to be chosen or to be avoided. The perfect good alone, which is Happiness, cannot be apprehended by the reason as an evil, or as lacking in any way. Consequently man wills Happiness of necessity, nor can he will not to be happy, or to be unhappy. Now since choice is not of the end, but of the means, as stated above (Article 3); it is not of the perfect good, which is Happiness, but of other particular goods. Therefore man chooses not of necessity, but freely.

QUESTIONS TO CONSIDER

- Why does Aquinas not answer the question whether we will things of necessity with a simple 'yes' or 'no'? How does this difference bear upon the question of human freedom?

- Finally, what is it about the things we want that makes our choices free in their regard?

6

NATURAL PHILOSOPHY AND THE HUMAN SOUL

Blaise Pascal, the seventeenth-century French philosopher and mathematician, once made the remark that the question of immortality was "our first interest and our first duty". Philosophers from the very earliest times have striven to learn whether any part of us survives bodily death. In this segment, we shall consider the implications the various views regarding nature have for the question of our personal immortality. Does materialism hold out any hope for an afterlife? What does Plato, with his formalist view, think of life after death? What of the hylomorphists, who define human life in terms of body and soul alike?

PASCAL—PENSÉES

---

[194] The immortality of the soul is a matter which is of so great consequence to us, and which touches us so profoundly, that we must have lost all feeling to be indifferent as to knowing what it is. All our actions and thoughts must take such different courses, according as there
5 are or are not eternal joys to hope for, that it is impossible to take one step with sense and judgment, unless we regulate our course by our view of this point which ought to be our ultimate end.

Thus our first interest and our first duty is to enlighten ourselves on this subject, whereon depends all our conduct. Therefore among those who
10 do not believe, I make a vast difference between those who strive with all their power to inform themselves, and those who live without troubling or thinking about it.

I can have only compassion for those who sincerely bewail their doubt, who regard it as the greatest of misfortunes, and who, sparing no effort

---

to escape it, make of this inquiry their principal and most serious occupations.

But as for those who pass their life without thinking of this ultimate end of life, and who, for this sole reason that they do not find within themselves the lights which convince them of it, neglect to seek them elsewhere, and to examine thoroughly whether this opinion is one of those which people receive with credulous simplicity, or one of those which, *"Death, which threatens us every moment, must infallibly place us within a few years under the dreadful necessity of being forever annihilated or unhappy."* although obscure in themselves, have nevertheless a solid and immovable foundation, I look upon them in a manner quite different.

This carelessness in a matter which concerns themselves, their eternity, their all, moves me more to anger than pity; it astonishes and shocks me; it is to me monstrous. I do not say this out of the pious zeal of a spiritual devotion. I expect, on the contrary, that we ought to have this feeling from principles of human interest and self-love; for this we need only see what the least enlightened persons see.

We do not require great education of the mind to understand that here there is no real and lasting satisfaction; that our pleasures are only vanity; that our evils are infinite; and, lastly, that death, which threatens us every moment, must infallibly place us within a few years under the dreadful necessity of being forever either annihilated or unhappy.

There is nothing more real than this, nothing more terrible. Be we as heroic as we like, that is the end which awaits the noblest life in the world. Let us reflect on this, and then say whether it is not beyond doubt that there is no good in this life but in the hope of another; that we are happy only in proportion as we draw near it; and that, as there are no more woes for those who have complete assurance of eternity, so there is no more happiness for those who have no insight into it.

Surely then it is a great evil thus to be in doubt, but it is at least an indispensable duty to seek when we are in such doubt; and thus the doubter who does not seek is altogether completely unhappy and

completely wrong. And if besides this he is easy and content, professes
to be so, and indeed boasts of it; if it is this state itself which is the subject
of his joy and vanity, I have no words to describe so silly a creature.

How can people hold these opinions? What joy can we find in the
expectation of nothing but hopeless misery? What reason for boasting
that we are in impenetrable darkness? And how can it happen that the
following argument occurs to a reasonable man?

"I know not who put me into the world, nor what the world is, nor what
I myself am. I am in terrible ignorance of everything. I know not what
my body is, nor my senses, nor my soul, not even that part of me which
thinks what I say, which reflects on all and on itself, and knows itself no
more than the rest. I see those frightful spaces of the universe which
surround me, and I find myself tied to one corner of this vast expanse,
without knowing why I am put in this place rather than in another, nor
why the short time which is given me to live is assigned to me at this
point rather than at another of the whole eternity which was before me
or which shall come after me. I see nothing but infinites on all sides,
which surround me as an atom, and as a shadow which endures only for
an instant and returns no more. All I know is that I must soon die, but
what I know least is this very death which I cannot escape.

"As I know not whence I come, so I know not whither I go. I know only
that, in leaving this world, I fall for ever either into annihilation or into
the hands of an angry God, without knowing to which of these two states
I shall be forever assigned. Such is my state, full of weakness and
uncertainty. And from all this I conclude that I ought to spend all the
days of my life without caring to inquire into what must happen to me.
Perhaps I might find some solution to my doubts, but I will not take the
trouble, nor take a step to seek it; and after treating with scorn those who
are concerned with this care, I will go without foresight and without fear
to try the great event, and let myself be led carelessly to death, uncertain
of the eternity of my future state."

There are two kinds of people one can call reasonable; those who serve
God with all their heart because they know Him, and those who seek
Him with all their heart because they do not know Him.

But as for those who live without knowing Him and without seeking Him, they judge themselves so little worthy of their own care, that they are not worthy of the care of others; and it needs all the charity of the religion which they despise, not to despise them even to the point of leaving them to their folly. But because this religion obliges us always to regard them, so long as they are in this life, as capable of the grace which can enlighten them, and to believe that they may, in a little time, be more replenished with faith than we are, and that, on the other hand, we may fall into the blindness wherein they are, we must do for them what we would they should do for us if we were in their place, and call upon them to have pity upon themselves, and to take at least some steps in the endeavor to find light. Let them give to reading this some of the hours which they otherwise employ so uselessly; whatever aversion they may bring to the task, they will perhaps gain something, and at least will not lose much. But as for those who bring to the task perfect sincerity and a real desire to meet with truth, those I hope will be satisfied and convinced of the proofs of a religion so divine, which I have here collected, and in which I have followed somewhat after this order.

[195] Before entering into the proofs of the Christian religion, I find it necessary to point out the sinfulness of those men who live in indifference to the search for truth in a matter which is so important to them, and which touches them so nearly.

Of all their errors, this doubtless is the one which most convicts them of foolishness and blindness, and in which it is easiest to confound them by the first glimmerings of common sense, and by natural feelings.

For it is not to be doubted that the duration of this life is but a moment; that the state of death is eternal, whatever may be its nature; and that thus all our actions and thoughts must take such different directions according to the state of that eternity, that it is impossible to take one step with sense and judgment, unless we regulate our course by the truth of that point which ought to be our ultimate end.

There is nothing clearer than this; and thus, according to the principles of reason, the conduct of men is wholly unreasonable, if they do not take another course.

On this point, therefore, we condemn those who live without thought of the ultimate end of life, who let themselves be guided by their own inclinations and their own pleasures without reflection and without concern, and, as if they could annihilate eternity by turning away their thought from it, think only of making themselves happy for the moment.

Yet this eternity exists, and death, which must open into it, and threatens them every hour, must in a little time infallibly put them under the dreadful necessity of being either annihilated or unhappy forever, without knowing which of these eternities is forever prepared for them.

This is a doubt of terrible consequence. They are in peril of eternal woe; and thereupon, as if the matter were not worth the trouble, they neglect to inquire whether this is one of those opinions which people receive with too credulous a facility, or one of those which, obscure in themselves, have a very firm, though hidden, foundation. Thus they know not whether there be truth or falsity in the matter, nor whether there be strength or weakness in the proofs. They have them before their eyes; they refuse to look at them; and in that ignorance they choose all that is necessary to fall into this misfortune if it exists, to await death to make trial of it, yet to be very content in this state, to make profession of it, and indeed to boast of it. Can we think seriously on the importance of this subject without being horrified at conduct so extravagant?

This resting in ignorance is a monstrous thing, and they who pass their life in it must be made to feel its extravagance and stupidity, by having it shown to them, so that they may be confounded by the sight of their folly. For this is how men reason, when they choose to live in such ignorance of what they are, and without seeking enlightenment. "I know not," they say.

QUESTIONS TO CONSIDER

- What does Pascal take to be the most important of all questions? What of those who choose to remain willfully ignorant of the answer?
- Summarize the doubter's argument, as Pascal presents it.
- Who are the two kinds of reasonable people, according to Pascal? Who, then, would the unreasonable person be?

MATERIALISM

LUCRETIUS—ON THE NATURE OF THINGS

First then I say that the mind, which we often call the understanding, in which dwells the directing and governing principle of life, is no less part of the man, than hand and foot and eyes are parts of the whole living creature.

5 Now I assert that the mind and the soul are kept together in close union and make up a single nature, but that the directing principle which we call mind and understanding, is the head so to speak and reigns paramount in the whole body. It has a fixed seat in the middle region of the breast: here throb fear and apprehension, about these spots dwell soothing joys;

10 therefore here is the understanding or mind. All the rest of the soul disseminated through the whole body obeys and moves at the will and inclination of the mind. It by itself alone knows for itself, rejoices for itself, at

15 times when the impression does not move either soul or body together with it. And as when some part of

"For no less long a time will he be no more in being, who beginning with to-day has ended his life, than the man who has died many months and years ago."

us, the head or the eye, suffers from an attack of pain, we do not feel the anguish at the same time over the whole body, thus the mind sometimes

20 suffers pain by itself or is inspirited with joy, when all the rest of the soul throughout the limbs and frame is stirred by no novel sensation. But when the mind is excited by some more vehement apprehension, we see the whole soul feel in unison through all the limbs, sweats and paleness

25 spread over the whole body, the tongue falter, the voice die away, a mist cover the eyes, the ears ring, the limbs sink under one; in short we often see men drop down from terror of mind; so that anybody may easily perceive from this that the soul is closely united with the mind, and, when it has been smitten by the influence of the mind, forthwith pushes and

30 strikes the body.

This same principle teaches that the nature of the mind and soul is bodily; for when it is seen to push the limbs, rouse the body from sleep, and alter

---

the countenance and guide and turn about the whole man, and when we see that none of these effects can take place without touch nor touch without body, must we not admit that the mind and the soul are of a bodily nature? Again you perceive that our mind in our body suffers
5 together with the body and feels in unison with it. When a weapon with a shudder-causing force has been driven in and has laid bare bones and sinews within the body, if it does not take life, yet there ensues a faintness and a lazy sinking to the ground and on the ground the turmoil of mind which arises, and sometimes a kind of undecided inclination to get up.
10 Therefore the nature of the mind must be bodily, since it suffers from bodily weapons and blows.

Now mark me: that you may know that the minds and light souls of living creatures have birth and are mortal, I will go on to set forth verses worthy of your attention, got together by long study and invented with welcome
15 effort. Do you mind to link to one name both of them alike, and when for instance I shall choose to speak of the soul, showing it to be mortal, believe that I speak of the mind as well, inasmuch as both make up one thing and are one united substance.

First of all then since I have shown the soul to be fine and to be formed
20 of minute bodies and made up of much smaller first-beginnings than is the liquid of water or mist or smoke:—for it far surpasses these in nimbleness and is moved when struck by a far more slender cause; inasmuch as it is moved by images of smoke and mist; as when for instance sunk in sleep we see altars steam forth their heat and send up
25 their smoke on high; for beyond a doubt images are begotten for us from these things:—well then, since you see on the vessels being shattered the water flow away on all sides, and since mist and smoke pass away into air, believe that the soul too is shed abroad and perishes much more quickly and dissolves sooner into its first bodies, when once it has been
30 taken out of the limbs of a man and has withdrawn. For, when the body that serves for its vessel cannot hold it, if shattered from any cause and rarefied by the withdrawal of blood from the veins, how can you believe that this soul can be held by any air? How can that air which is rarer than our body hold it in?

35 Again we perceive that the mind is begotten along with the body and grows up together with it and becomes old along with it. For even as children go about with a tottering and weakly body, so slender sagacity

of mind follows along with it; then when their life has reached the maturity of confirmed strength, the judgment too is greater and the power of the mind more developed. Afterwards when the body has been shattered by the mastering might of time and the frame has drooped with its forces dulled, then the intellect halts, the tongue dotes, the mind gives way, all faculties fail and are found wanting at the same time. It naturally follows, then, that the whole nature of the soul is dissolved, like smoke, into the high air; since we see it is begotten along with the body and grows up along with it and, as I have shown, breaks down at the same time worn out with age.

Moreover, we see that even as the body is liable to violent diseases and severe pain, so is the mind to sharp cares and grief and fear; it naturally follows therefore that it is its partner in death as well.

Again in diseases of the body the mind often wanders and goes astray; for it loses its reason and drivels in its speech and often in a profound lethargy is carried into deep and never-ending sleep with drooping eyes and head; out of which it neither bears the voices nor can recognize the faces of those who stand around calling it back to life and bedewing with tears, face and cheeks. Therefore you must admit that the mind too dissolves, since the infection of disease reaches to it; for pain and disease are both forgers of death: a truth we have fully learned ere now by the death of many.

Again, when the pungent strength of wine has entered into a man and its spirit has been infused into and transmitted through his veins, why is it that a heaviness of the limbs follows along with this, his legs are hampered as he reels about, his tongue falters, his mind is besotted, his eyes swim, shouting, hiccupping, wranglings are rife, together with all the other usual concomitants, why is all this, if not because the overpowering violence of the wine disorders the soul within the body? But whenever things can be disordered and hampered, they give token that if a somewhat more potent cause gained an entrance, they would perish and be robbed of all further existence.

Moreover, it often happens that someone constrained by the violence of disease suddenly drops down before our eyes, as by a stroke of lightning, and foams at the mouth, moans and shivers through his frame, loses his reason, stiffens his muscles, is racked, gasps for breath fitfully, and wearies his limbs with tossing. Sure enough, because the violence of the disease spreads itself through his frame and disorders him, he foams as he tries to eject his soul, just as in the salt sea the waters boil with the mastering might of the winds. A moan too is forced out, because the limbs are seized with pain, and mainly because seeds of voice are driven forth and are carried in a close mass out by the mouth, the road which they are accustomed to take and where they have a well-paved way. Loss of reason follows, because the powers of the mind and soul are disordered and, as I have shown, are riven and forced asunder, torn to pieces by the same baneful malady. Then, after the cause of the disease has bent its course back, and the acrid humors of the distempered body return to their biding-places, then he first gets up like one reeling, and by little and little comes back into full possession of his senses and regains his soul. Since therefore even within the body mind and soul are harassed by such violent distempers and so miserably racked by sufferings, why believe that they without the body in the open air can continue existence battling with fierce winds?

And since we perceive that the mind is healed like the sick body, and we see that it can be altered by medicine, this too gives warning that the mind has a mortal existence. For it is natural that whoever attempts to change the mind or seeks to alter any other nature you like, should add new parts or change the arrangement of the present, or withdraw in short some little bit from the sum. But that which is immortal wills not to have its parts transposed nor any addition to be made nor one bit to ebb away; for whenever a thing changes and quits its proper limits, this change is at once the death of that which was before. Therefore the mind, whether it is sick or whether it is altered by medicine, alike, as I have shown, gives forth mortal symptoms. So invariably is truth found to make head against false reason and to cut off all retreat from the assailant and by a two-fold refutation to put falsehood to rout.

Again the quickened powers of body and mind by their joint partnership enjoy health and life; for the nature of the mind cannot by itself alone without the body give forth vital motions nor can the body again bereft of the soul continue to exist and make use of its senses: just, you are to know, as the eye itself torn away from its roots cannot see anything when apart from the whole body, thus the soul and mind cannot it is plain do anything by themselves. Sure enough, because mixed up through veins and flesh, sinews and bones, their first-beginnings are confined by all the body and are not free to bound away leaving great spaces between, therefore thus shut in they make those sense-giving motions which they cannot make after death when forced out of the body into the air by reason that they are not then confined in a like manner; for the air will be a body and a living thing, if the soul shall be able to keep itself together and to enclose in it those motions which it used before to perform in the sinews and within the body.

Moreover even while it yet moves within the confines of life, often the soul shaken from some cause or other is seen to wish to pass out and be loosed from the whole body, the features are seen to droop as at the last hour and all the limbs to sink flaccid over the bloodless trunk: just as happens, when the phrase is used, the mind is in a bad way, or the soul is quite gone; when all is hurry and everyone is anxious to keep from parting the last tie of life; for then the mind and the power of the soul are shaken throughout and both are quite loosened together with the body, so that a cause somewhat more powerful can quite break them up. Why doubt I would ask that the soul when driven forth out of the body, when in the open air, feeble as it is, stripped of its covering, not only cannot continue through eternity, but is unable to hold together the smallest fraction of time? Therefore, again and again I say, when the enveloping body has been all broken up and the vital airs have been forced out, you must admit that the senses of the mind and the soul are dissolved, since the cause of destruction is one and inseparable for both body and soul.

Again a tree cannot exist in the ether, nor clouds in the deep sea nor can fishes live in the fields nor blood exist in woods nor sap in stones. Where each thing can grow and abide is fixed and ordained. Thus the nature of the mind cannot come into being alone without the body nor exist far away from the sinews and blood. But if (for this would be much more likely to happen than that) the force itself of the mind might be in the head or shoulders or heels or might be born in any other part of the body, it would after all be wont to abide in one and the same man or vessel. But since in our body even it is fixed and seen to be ordained where the soul and the mind can severally be and grow, it must still more strenuously be denied that it can abide and be carried out of the body altogether. Therefore when the body has died, we must admit that the soul has perished, wrenched away throughout the body. To link a mortal thing with an everlasting thing and suppose that they can have sense in common and can be reciprocally acted upon, is sheer folly; for what can be conceived more incongruous, more discordant and inconsistent with itself, than a thing which is mortal, linked with an immortal and everlasting thing, trying in such union to weather furious storms? But if perhaps the soul is to be accounted immortal for this reason rather, because it is kept sheltered from death-bringing things, either because things hostile to its existence do not approach at all, or because those which do approach, in some way or other retreat discomfited before we can feel the harm they do, manifest experience proves that this cannot be true. For besides that it sickens in sympathy with the maladies of the body, it is often attacked by that which frets it on the score of the future and keeps it on the rack of suspense and wears it out with cares; and when ill deeds are in the past, remorse for sins yet gnaws: then there is madness peculiar to the mind and forgetfulness of all things; then too it often sinks into the black waters of lethargy.

Death therefore to us is nothing, concerns us not a bit, since the nature of the mind is proved to be mortal; and as in time gone by we felt no distress, when the Poeni from all sides came together to do battle, and all things shaken by war's troublous uproar shuddered and quaked beneath high heaven, and mortal men were in doubt which of the two peoples it should be to whose empire all must fall by sea and land alike, thus when we shall be no more, when there shall have been a separation of body and soul, out of both of which we are each formed into a single being, to us, you may be sure, who then shall be no more, nothing whatever can happen to excite sensation, not if earth shall be mingled with sea and sea with heaven. And even supposing the nature of the mind and power of the soul do feel, after they have been severed from our body, yet that is nothing to us who by the binding tie of marriage between body and soul are formed each into one single being. And if time should gather up our matter after our death and put it once more into the position in which it now is, and the light of life be given to us again, this result even would concern us not at all, when the chain of our self-consciousness has once been snapped asunder. So now we give ourselves no concern about any self which we have been before, nor do we feel any distress on the score of that self. For when you look back on the whole past course of immeasurable time and think how manifold are the shapes which the motions of matter take, you may easily credit this too, that these very same seeds of which we now are formed, have often before been placed in the same order in which they now are; and yet we cannot recover this in memory: a break in our existence has been interposed, and all the motions have wandered to and fro far astray from the sensations they produced. For he whom evil is to befall, must in his own person exist at the very time it comes, if the misery and suffering are even to have any place at all; but since death precludes this, and forbids him to be, upon whom the ills can be brought, you may be sure that we have nothing to fear after death, and that he who exists not, cannot become miserable, and that it matters not a whit whether he has been born into life at any other time, when immortal death has taken away his mortal life.

Therefore when you see a man bemoaning his hard case, that after death he shall either rot with his body laid in the grave or be devoured by flames or the jaws of wild beasts, you may be sure that his ring betrays a flaw and that there lurks in his heart a secret goad, though he himself declare that he does not believe that any sense will remain to him after death. He does not, I think, really grant the conclusion which he professes to grant nor the principle on which he so professes, nor does he take and force himself root and branch out of life, but all unconsciously imagines something of self to survive. For when any one in life suggests to himself that birds and beasts will rend his body after death, he makes moan for himself: he does not separate himself from that self, nor withdraw himself fully from the body so thrown out and fancies himself that other self and stands by and impregnates it with his own sense. Hence he makes much moan that he has been born mortal and sees not that after real death there will be no other self to remain in life and lament to self that his own self has met death, and there to stand and grieve that his own self there lying is mangled or burnt. For if it is an evil after death to be pulled about by the devouring jaws of wild beasts, I cannot see why it should not be a cruel pain to be laid on fires and burn in hot flames, or to be placed in honey and stifled, or to stiffen with cold, stretched on the smooth surface of an icy slab of stone, or to be pressed down and crushed by a load of earth above.

Now no more shall thy house admit thee with glad welcome, nor a most virtuous wife and sweet children run to be the first to snatch kisses and touch thy heart with a silent joy. No more mayst thou be prosperous in thy doings, a safeguard to thine own. One disastrous day has taken from thee luckless man in luckless wise all the many prizes of life.

This do men say, but add not thereto: *and now no longer does any craving for these things beset thee withal.*

For if they could rightly perceive this in thought and follow up the thought in words, they would release themselves from great distress and apprehension of mind.

Thou, even as now thou art, sunk in the sleep of death, shalt continue so to be all time
5 *to come, freed from all distressful pains; but we with a sorrow that would not be sated wept for thee, when close by thou didst turn to an ashen hue on thy appalling funeral pile, and no length of days shall pluck from our hearts our ever-during grief.*

This question therefore should be asked of this speaker, what there is in it so passing bitter, if it come in the end to sleep and rest, that anyone
10 should pine in never-ending sorrow.

This too men often, when they have reclined at table cup in hand and shade their brows with crowns, love to say from the heart, *short is this enjoyment for poor weak men; presently it will have been and never after may it be called back.*

15 As if after their death it is to be one of their principal afflictions that thirst and parching drought is to burn them up hapless wretches, or a craving for anything else is to beset them. What folly! no one feels the want of himself and life at the time when mind and body are together sunk in sleep; for all we care this sleep might be everlasting, no craving whatever
20 for ourselves then moves us. And yet by no means do those first-beginnings throughout our frame wander at that time far away from their sense-producing motions, at the moment when a man starts up from sleep and collects himself. Death therefore must be thought to concern us much less, if less there can be than what we see to be nothing; for a
25 greater dispersion of the mass of matter follows after death, and no one wakes up, upon whom the chill cessation of life has once come.

Once more, what evil lust of life is this which constrains us with such force to be so mightily troubled in doubts and dangers? A sure term of life is fixed for mortals, and death cannot be shunned, but meet it we
30 must. Moreover we are ever engaged, ever involved in the same pursuits, and no new pleasure is struck out by living on; but while what we crave is wanting, it seems to transcend all the rest; then, when it has been gotten, we crave something else, and ever does the same thirst of life possess us, as we gape for it open-mouthed. Quite doubtful it is what
35 fortune the future will carry with it or what chance will bring us or what

end is at hand. Nor by prolonging life do we take one bit from the time past in death nor can we fret anything away, whereby we may haply be a less long time in the condition of the dead. Therefore you may complete as many generations as you please during your life; none the less however will that everlasting death await you; and for no less long a time will he be no more in being, who beginning with to-day has ended his life, than the man who has died many months and years ago.

QUESTIONS TO CONSIDER

- Does Lucretius think of the connection between the human soul (he also calls it the mind or spirit) and the human as being a part / whole relationship, or rather as a spirit inhabiting a body? How does he make his case for that?

- What are some of Lucretius' arguments against the immortality of the human soul?

- What of putting mind and body together again after death (re- animation)? Does Lucretius think it possible? Is it possible?

- What does Lucretius think of the person who complains about the inevitability of death? Would Pascal think Lucretius reasonable, or unreasonable?

- What implication for human action does Lucretius draw from his conclusion about the human soul? (If death is the end of everything, then what should our lives be like, by his account?)

BERTRAND RUSSELL—"WHAT I BELIEVE"

God and immortality, the central dogmas of the Christian religion, find no support in science. It cannot be said that either doctrine is essential to religion, since neither is found in Buddhism. (With regard to immortality, this statement in an unqualified form might be misleading, but it is correct in the last analysis.) But we in the West have come to think of them as the irreducible minimum of theology. No doubt people will continue to entertain these beliefs, because they are pleasant, just as it is pleasant to think ourselves virtuous and our enemies wicked. But for my part I cannot see any ground for either. I do not pretend to be able to prove that there is no God. I equally cannot prove that Satan is a fiction. The Christian God may exist; so may the Gods of Olympus, or of ancient Egypt, or of Babylon. But no one of these hypotheses is more probable than any other: they lie outside the region of even probable knowledge, and therefore there is no reason to consider any of them. I shall not enlarge upon this question, as I have dealt with it elsewhere.

The question of personal immortality stands on a somewhat different footing. Here evidence either way is possible. Persons are part of the everyday world with which science is concerned, and the conditions which determine their existence are discoverable. A drop of water is not immortal; it can be resolved into oxygen and hydrogen. If, therefore, a drop of water were to maintain that it had a quality of "aqueousness" which would survive its dissolution we should be inclined to be skeptical. In like manner we know that the brain is **"I believe that when I die I shall rot."** not immortal, and that the organized energy of a living body becomes, as it were, demobilized at death, and therefore not available for collective action. All the evidence goes to show that what we regard as our mental life is bound up with brain structure and organized bodily energy. Therefore it is rational to suppose that mental life ceases when bodily life ceases. The argument is only one of probability, but it is as strong as those upon which most scientific conclusions are based.

There are various grounds upon which this conclusion might be attacked. Psychical research professes to have actual scientific evidence of survival, and undoubtedly its procedure is, in principle, scientifically correct. Evidence of this sort might be so overwhelming that no one with a scientific temper could reject it. The weight to be attached to the evidence, however, must depend upon the antecedent probability of the hypothesis of survival. There are always different ways of accounting for any set of phenomena and of these we should prefer the one which is antecedently least improbable. Those who already think it likely that we survive death will be ready to view this theory as the best explanation of psychical phenomena. Those who, on other grounds, regard this theory as implausible will seek for other explanations. For my part, I consider the evidence so far adduced by psychical research in favor of survival much weaker than the physiological evidence on the other side. But I fully admit that it might at any moment become stronger, and in that case it would be unscientific to disbelieve in survival.

Survival of bodily death is, however, a different matter from immortality: it may only mean a postponement of psychical death. It is immortality that men desire to believe in. Believers in immortality will object to physiological arguments, such as I have been using, on the ground that soul and body are totally disparate, and that the soul is something quite other than its empirical manifestations through our bodily organs. I believe this to be a metaphysical superstition. Mind and matter alike are for certain purposes convenient terms but are not ultimate realities. Electrons and protons, like the soul, are logical fictions; each is really a history, a series of events, not a single persistent entity. In the case of the soul, this is obvious from the facts of growth. Whoever considers conception, gestation, and infancy cannot seriously believe that the soul is an indivisible something, perfect and complete throughout this process. It is evident that it grows like the body, and that it de- rives both from the spermatozoon and from the ovum, so that it cannot be indivisible. This is not materialism: it is merely the recognition that everything interesting is a matter of organization, not of primal substance.

Metaphysicians have advanced innumerable arguments to prove that the soul must be immortal. There is one simple test by which all these arguments can be demolished. They all prove equally that the soul must pervade all space. But as we are not so anxious to be fat as to live long, none of the meta- physicians in question have ever noticed this application of their reasonings. This is an instance of the amazing power of desire in blinding even very able men to fallacies which would otherwise be obvious at once. If we were not afraid of death, I do not believe that the idea of immortality would ever have arisen.

I believe that when I die I shall rot, and nothing of my ego will survive. I am not young, and I love life. But I should scorn to shiver with terror at the thought of annihilation. Happiness is none the less true happiness because it must come to an end, nor do thought and love lose their value because they are not everlasting. Many a man has borne himself proudly on the scaffold; surely the same pride should teach us to think truly about man's place in the world. Even if the open windows of science at first make us shiver after the cozy indoor warmth of traditional humanizing myths, in the end the fresh air brings vigor, and the great spaces have a splendor of their own.

- How does Russell distinguish between the philosophical questions is there life after death? and does God exist?
- Why, by Russell's account, do people want to believe in immortality?
- What distinction does Russell make between personal immortality and life after death?

PLATONIC FORMALISM

PLATO—THE PHAEDO

LOVERS OF WISDOM

Evenus the poet wanted to know why you, Socrates, who never before wrote a line of poetry, now that you are in prison are turning Aesop's fables into verse, and also composing that hymn in honor of Apollo.

Tell this to Evenus, Cebes, and bid him be of good cheer; say that I would
5   have him come after me if he be a wise man, and not tarry; and that today I am likely to be going, for the Athenians say that I must.

Simmias said: What a message for such a man! having been a frequent companion of his I should say that, as far as I know him, he will never take your advice unless he is obliged.

10   Why, said Socrates—is not Evenus a philosopher?

I think that he is, said Simmias.

Then he, or any man who has the spirit of philosophy, will be willing to die; but he will not take his own life, for that is held to be unlawful.

Here he changed his position and put his legs off the couch on to the
15   ground, and during the rest of the conversation he remained sitting.

And now, my judges, (said Socrates), I desire to prove to you that the real philosopher has reason to be of good cheer when he is about to die, and that after death he may hope to obtain the greatest good in the other world. And how this may be, Simmias and Cebes, I will endeavor to explain. For I deem that the true votary of philosophy is likely to be misunderstood by other men; they do not perceive that he is always pursuing death and dying; and if this be so, and he has had the desire of death all his life long, why when his time comes should he repine at that which he has been always pursuing and desiring?

"The real philosopher has reason to be of good cheer when he is about to die."

Simmias said laughingly: Though not in a laughing humor, you have made me laugh, Socrates; for I cannot help thinking that the many when they hear your words will say how truly you have described philosophers, and our people at home will likewise say that the life which philosophers desire is in reality death, and that they have found them out to be deserving of the death which they desire.

And they are right, Simmias, in thinking so, with the exception of the words they have found them out; for they have not found out either what is the nature of that death which the true philosopher deserves, or how he deserves or desires death. But enough of them:—let us discuss the matter among ourselves. Do we believe that there is such a thing as death?

To be sure, replied Simmias.

Is it not the separation of soul and body? And to be dead is the completion of this; when the soul exists in herself, and is released from the body and the body is released from the soul, what is this but death?

Just so, he replied.

There is another question, which will probably throw light on our present inquiry if you and I can agree about it:—Ought the philosopher to care about the pleasures—if they are to be called pleasures—of eating and drinking?

Certainly not, answered Simmias.

And what about the pleasures of love—should he care for them?

By no means.

And will he think much of the other ways of indulging the body, for example, the acquisition of costly raiment, or sandals, or other adornments of the body? Instead of caring about them, does he not rather despise anything more than nature needs? What do you say?

I should say that the true philosopher would despise them.

Would you not say that he is entirely concerned with the soul and not with the body? He would like, as far as he can, to get away from the body and to turn to the soul.

Quite true.

In matters of this sort philosophers, above all other men, may be observed in every sort of way to dissever the soul from the communion of the body.

Very true.

Whereas Simmias, the rest of the world are of opinion that to him who has no sense of pleasure and no part in bodily pleasure, life is not worth having; and that he who is indifferent about them is as good as dead.

That is also true.

What again shall we say of the actual acquirement of knowledge?—is the body, if invited to share in the inquiry, a hinderer or a helper? I mean to say, have sight and hearing any truth in them? Are they not, as the poets are always telling us, inaccurate witnesses? and yet, if even they are inaccurate and indistinct, what is to be said of the other senses?—for you will allow that they are the best of them?

Certainly, he replied.

Then when does the soul attain truth?—for in attempting to consider anything in company with the body she is obviously deceived.

True.

Then must not true existence be revealed to her in thought, if at all?

Yes.

And thought is best when the mind is gathered into herself and none of
5   these things trouble her—neither sounds nor sights nor pain nor any
pleasure—when she takes leave of the body, and has as little as possible
to do with it, when she has no bodily sense or desire, but is aspiring after
true being?

Certainly.

10   And in this the philosopher dishonors the body; his soul runs away from
his body and desires to be alone and by herself?

That is true.

Well, but there is another thing, Simmias: Is there or is there not an
absolute justice?

15   Assuredly there is.

And an absolute beauty and absolute good?

Of course.

But did you ever behold any of them with your eyes?

Certainly not.

20   Or did you ever reach them with any other bodily sense?—and I speak
not of these alone, but of absolute greatness, and health, and strength,
and of the essence or true nature of everything. Has the reality of them
ever been perceived by you through the bodily organs? or rather, is not
the nearest approach to the knowledge of their several natures made by
25   him who so orders his intellectual vision as to have the most exact
conception of the essence of each thing which he considers?

Certainly.

And he attains to the purest knowledge of them who goes to each with the mind alone, not introducing or intruding in the act of thought sight or any other sense together with reason, but with the very light of the mind in her own clearness searches into the very truth of each; he who has got rid, as far as he can, of eyes and ears and, so to speak, of the whole body, these being in his opinion distracting elements which when they infect the soul hinder her from acquiring truth and knowledge—who, if not he, is likely to attain to the knowledge of true being?

What you say has a wonderful truth in it, Socrates, replied Simmias.

And when real philosophers consider all these things, will they not be led to make a reflection which they will express in words something like the following?

Have we not found, they will say, *a path of thought which seems to bring us and our argument to the conclusion, that while we are in the body, and while the soul is infected with the evils of the body, our desire will not be satisfied? and our desire is of the truth. For the body is a source of endless trouble to us by reason of the mere requirement of food; and is liable also to diseases which overtake and impede us in the search after true being: it fills us full of loves, and lusts, and fears, and fancies of all kinds, and endless foolery, and in fact, as men say, takes away from us the power of thinking at all. Whence come wars, and fighting, and factions? whence but from the body and the lusts of the body? Wars are occasioned by the love of money, and money has to be acquired for the sake and in the service of the body; and by reason of all these impediments we have no time to give to philosophy; and, last and worst of all, even if we are at leisure and betake ourselves to some speculation, the body is always breaking in upon us, causing turmoil and confusion in our enquiries, and so amazing us that we are prevented from seeing the truth. It has been proved to us by experience that if we would have pure knowledge of anything we must be quit of the body—the soul in herself must behold things in themselves: and then we shall attain the wisdom which we desire, and of which we say that we are lovers; not while we live, but after death; for if while in company with the body, the soul cannot have pure knowledge, one of two things follows—either knowledge is not to be attained at all, or, if at all, after death. For then, and not till then, the soul will be parted from the body and exist in herself alone. In this present life, I reckon that we make the nearest approach to knowledge when we have the least possible intercourse or communion with the body, and are not surfeited with the bodily nature, but keep ourselves pure until the hour when God himself is pleased to release us. And thus having got rid of the foolishness of the body we shall be pure and hold converse with the pure, and know of ourselves the clear light everywhere, which is no other than the light of truth. For the impure are not permitted to approach the pure.*

These are the sort of words, Simmias, which the true lovers of knowledge cannot help saying to one another and thinking. You would agree, would you not?

Undoubtedly, Socrates.

But, my friend, if this be true, there is great reason to hope that, going whither I go, when I have come to the end of my journey, I shall attain that which has been the pursuit of my life. And therefore I go on my way rejoicing, and not I only, but every other man who believes that his mind has been made ready and that he is in a manner purified.

Certainly, replied Simmias.

And what is purification but the separation of the soul from the body, as I was saying before; the habit of the soul gathering and collecting herself into herself from all sides out of the body; the dwelling in her own place alone, as in another life, so also in this, as far as she can—the release of the soul from the chains of the body?

Very true, he said.

And this separation and release of the soul from the body is termed death?

To be sure, he said.

And the true philosophers, and they only, are ever seeking to release the soul. Is not the separation and release of the soul from the body their special study?

That is true.

And, as I was saying at first, there would be a ridiculous contradiction in men studying to live as nearly as they can in a state of death, and yet repining when it comes upon them.

Clearly.

And the true philosophers, Simmias, are always occupied in the practice of dying, wherefore also to them least of all men is death terrible. Look at the matter thus—if they have been in every way the enemies of the body, and are wanting to be alone with the soul, when this desire of theirs is granted, how inconsistent would they be if they trembled and repined, instead of rejoicing at their departure to that place where, when they arrive, they hope to gain that which in life they desired—and this was wisdom—and at the same time to be rid of the company of their enemy. Many a man has been willing to go to the world below animated by the hope of seeing there an earthly love, or wife, or son, and conversing with them. And will he who is a true lover of wisdom and is strongly persuaded in like manner that only in the world below he can worthily enjoy her, still repine at death? Will he not depart with joy? Surely he will, my friend, if he be a true philosopher. For he will have a firm conviction that there, and there only, he can find wisdom in her purity. And if this be true, he would be very absurd, as I was saying, if he were afraid of death.

He would indeed, replied Simmias.

And when you see a man who is repining at the approach of death, is not his reluctance a sufficient proof that he is not a lover of wisdom, but a lover of the body, and probably at the same time a lover of either money or power, or both?

Quite so, he replied.

And therefore I maintain that I am right, Simmias and Cebes, in not grieving or repining at parting from you and my masters in this world, for I believe that I shall equally find good masters and friends in another world. But most men do not believe this saying; if then I succeed in convincing you by my defense better than I did the Athenian judges, it will be well.

Cebes answered: I agree, Socrates, in the greater part of what you say. But in what concerns the soul, men are apt to be incredulous; they fear that when she has left the body her place may be nowhere, and that on the very day of death she may perish and come to an end—immediately on her release from the body, issuing forth dispersed like smoke or air and in her flight vanishing away into nothingness. If she could only be collected into herself after she has obtained release from the evils of which you were speaking, there would be good reason to hope, Socrates, that what you say is true. But surely it requires a great deal of argument and many proofs to show that when the man is dead his soul yet exists and has any force or intelligence.

True, Cebes, said Socrates; and shall I suggest that we converse a little of the probabilities of these things?

I am sure, said Cebes, that I should greatly like to know your opinion about them.

I reckon, said Socrates, that no one who heard me now, not even if he were one of my old enemies, the Comic poets, could accuse me of idle talking about matters in which I have no concern—If you please, then, we will proceed with the inquiry.

BEYOND QUESTION

Tell me, then, what is that of which the inherence will render the body alive?

The soul, he replied.

And is this always the case?

Yes, he said, of course.

Then whatever the soul possesses, to that she comes bearing life?

Yes, certainly.

And is there any opposite to life?

There is, he said.

And what is that?

Death.

Then the soul, as has been acknowledged, will never receive the opposite of what she brings.

Impossible, replied Cebes.

And now, he said, what did we just now call that principle which repels the even?

The odd.

And that principle which repels the musical or the just?

The unmusical, he said, and the unjust.

And what do we call that principle which does not admit of death?

The immortal, he said.

And does the soul admit of death?

No.

Then the soul is immortal?

Yes, he said.

And may we say that this has been proven?

Yes abundantly proven, Socrates, he replied.

Supposing that the odd were imperishable, must not three be imperishable?

Of course.

And if that which is cold were imperishable, when the warm principle came attacking the snow, must not the snow have retired whole and unmelted—for it could never have perished, nor could it have remained and admitted the heat?

True, he said.

166

Again, if the uncooling or warm principle were imperishable, then fire when assailed by cold would not have perished or have been extinguished, but would have gone away unaffected?

Certainly, he said.

And the same may be said of the immortal: if the immortal is also imperishable, the soul when attacked by death cannot perish; for the preceding argument shows that the soul will not admit of death, or ever be dead, any more than three or the odd number will admit of the even, or fire, or the heat in the fire, of the cold. Yet a person may say: 'But although the odd will not become even at the approach of the even, why may not the odd perish /and the even take the place of the odd?' Now to him who makes this objection, we cannot answer that the odd principle is imperishable; for this has not been acknowledged, but if this had been acknowledged, there would have been no difficulty in contending that at the approach of the even the odd principle and the number three took their departure; and the same argument would have held good of fire and heat and any other thing.

Very true.

And the same may be said of the immortal: if the immortal is also imperishable, then the soul will be imperishable as well as immortal; but if not, some other proof of her imperishableness will have to be given.

No other proof is needed, he said; for if the immortal, being eternal, is liable to perish, then nothing is imperishable.

Yes, replied Socrates, and yet all men will agree that God, and the essential form of life, and the immortal in general, will never perish.

Yes, all men, he said—that is true; and what is more, gods, if I am not mistaken, as well as men.

Seeing then that the immortal is indestructible, must not the soul, if she is immortal, be also imperishable?

Most certainly.

Then when death attacks a man, the mortal portion of him may be supposed to die, but the immortal retires at the approach of death and is preserved safe and sound?

True.

5 Then, Cebes, beyond question, the soul is immortal and imperishable, and our souls will truly exist in another world!

I am convinced, Socrates, said Cebes, and have nothing more to object.

THE NEXT LIFE

But then, my friends, he said, if the soul is really immortal, what care should be taken of her, not only in respect of the portion of time which 10 is called life, but of eternity! And the danger of neglecting her from this point of view does indeed appear to be awful. If death had only been the end of all, the wicked would have had a good bargain in dying, for they would have been happily quit not only of their body, but of their own evil together with their souls. But now, inasmuch as the soul is manifestly 15 immortal, there is no release or salvation from evil except the attainment of the highest virtue and wisdom. For the soul when on her progress to the world below takes nothing with her but nurture and education; and these are said greatly to benefit or greatly to injure the departed, at the very beginning of his journey there.

20 For after death, as they say, the genius of each individual, to whom he belonged in life, leads him to a certain place in which the dead are gathered together, whence after judgment has been given they pass into the world below, following the guide, who is appointed to conduct them from this world to the other: and when they have there received their due 25 and remained their time, another guide brings them back again after many revolutions of ages. Now this way to the other world is not, as Aeschylus says in the Telephus, a single and straight path—if that were so no guide would be needed, for no one could miss it; but there are many partings of the road, and windings, as I infer from the rites and 30 sacrifices which are offered to the gods below in places where three ways meet on earth. The wise and orderly soul follows in the straight path and is conscious of her surroundings; but the soul which de- sires the body,

and which, as I was relating before, has long been fluttering about the lifeless frame and the world of sight, is after many struggles and many sufferings hardly and with violence carried away by her attendant genius; and when she arrives at the place where the other souls are gathered, if she be impure and have done impure deeds, whether foul murders or other crimes which are the brothers of these, and the works of brothers in crime—from that soul every one flees and turns away; no one will be her companion, no one her guide, but alone she wanders in extremity of evil until certain times are fulfilled, and when they are fulfilled, she is borne irresistibly to her own fitting habitation; as every pure and just soul which has passed through life in the company and under the guidance of the gods has also her own proper home.

THE DEATH OF SOCRATES

You, Simmias and Cebes, and all other men, will depart at some time or other. Me already, as a tragic poet would say, the voice of fate calls. Soon I must drink the poison; and I think that I had better repair to the bath first, in order that the women may not have the trouble of washing my body after I am dead.

When he had done speaking, Crito said: And have you any commands for us, Socrates—anything to say about your children, or any other matter in which we can serve you?

Nothing particular, Crito, he replied: only, as I have always told you, take care of yourselves; that is a service which you may be ever rendering to me and mine and to all of us, whether you promise to do so or not. But if you have no thought for yourselves, and care not to walk according to the rule which I have prescribed for you, not now for the first time, however much you may profess or promise at the moment, it will be of no avail.

We will do our best, said Crito: And in what way shall we bury you?

In any way that you like; but you must get hold of me and take care that I do not run away from you. Then he turned to us, and added with a smile:—I cannot make Crito believe that I am the same Socrates who have been talking and conducting the argument; he fancies that I am the other Socrates whom he will soon see, a dead body—and he asks, how shall he bury me? And though I have spoken many words, in the endeavor to show that when I have drunk the poison I shall leave you and go to the joys of the blessed,—these words of mine, with which I was comforting you and myself, have had, as I perceive, no effect upon Crito. And therefore I want you to be surety for me to him now, as at the trial he was surety to the judges for me: but let the promise be of another sort; for he was surety for me to the judges that I would remain, and you must be my surety to him that I shall not remain but go away and depart; and then he will suffer less at my death, and not be grieved when he sees my body being burned or buried. I would not have him sorrow at my hard lot, or say at the burial, thus we lay out Socrates, or thus we follow him to the grave or bury him; for false words are not only evil in themselves, but they infect the soul with evil. Be of good cheer then, my dear Crito, and say that you are burying my body only, and do with that whatever is usual, and what you think best.

When he had spoken these words, he arose and went into a chamber to bathe; Crito followed him and told us to wait. So we remained behind, talking and thinking of the subject of discourse, and also of the greatness of our sorrow; he was like a father of whom we were being bereaved, and we were about to pass the rest of our lives as orphans. When he had taken the bath his children were brought to him—(he had two young sons and an elder one); and the women of his family also came, and he talked to them and gave them a few directions in the presence of Crito; then he dismissed them and returned to us.

Now the hour of sunset was near, for a good deal of time had passed while he was within. When he came out, he sat down with us again after his bath, but not much was said. Soon the jailer, who was the servant of the Eleven, entered and stood by him, saying:—To you, Socrates, whom I know to be the noblest and gentlest and best of all who ever came to this place, I will not impute the angry feelings of other men, who rage and swear at me, when, in obedience to the authorities, I bid them drink the poison—indeed, I am sure that you will not be angry with me; for others, as you are aware, and not I, are to blame. And so fare you well and try to bear lightly what must needs be—you know my errand. Then bursting into tears he turned away and went out.

Socrates looked at him and said: I return your good wishes and will do as you bid. Then turning to us, he said, how charming the man is: since I have been in prison he has always been coming to see me, and at times he would talk to me, and was as good to me as could be, and now see how generously he sorrows on my account. We must do as he says, Crito; and therefore let the cup be brought, if the poison is prepared: if not, let the attendant prepare some.

Yet, said Crito, the sun is still upon the hill-tops, and I know that many a one has taken the draught late, and after the announcement has been made to him, he has eaten and drunk, and enjoyed the society of his beloved; do not hurry—there is time enough.

Socrates said: Yes, Crito, and they of whom you speak are right in so acting, for they think that they will be gainers by the delay; but I am right in not following their example, for I do not think that I should gain anything by drinking the poison a little later; I should only be ridiculous in my own eyes for sparing and saving a life which is already forfeit. Please then to do as I say, and not to refuse me.

Crito made a sign to the servant, who was standing by; and he went out, and having been absent for some time, returned with the jailer carrying the cup of poison. Socrates said: You, my good friend, who are experienced in these matters, shall give me directions how I am to proceed. The man answered: You have only to walk about until your legs are heavy, and then to lie down, and the poison will act. At the same time, he handed the cup to Socrates, who in the easiest and gentlest manner, without the least fear or change of color or feature, looking at the man with all his eyes, Echecrates, as his manner was, took the cup and said: What do you say about making a libation out of this cup to any god? May I, or not? The man answered: We only prepare, Socrates, just so much as we deem enough. I understand, he said: but I may and must ask the gods to prosper my journey from this to the other world—even so—and so be it according to my prayer. Then raising the cup to his lips, quite readily and cheerfully he drank off the poison. And hitherto most of us had been able to control our sorrow; but now when we saw him drinking, and saw too that he had finished the drought, we could no longer forbear, and in spite of myself my own tears were flowing fast; so that I covered my face and wept, not for him, but at the thought of my own calamity in having to part from such a friend. Nor was I the first; for Crito, when he found himself unable to restrain his tears, had got up, and I followed; and at that moment, Apollodorus, who had been weeping all the time, broke out in a loud and passionate cry which made cowards of us all. Socrates alone retained his calmness: What is this strange outcry? he said. I sent away the women mainly in order that they might not misbehave in this way, for I have been told that a man should die in peace. Be quiet then and have patience. When we heard his words we were ashamed, and refrained our tears; and he walked about until, as he said, his legs began to fail, and then he lay on his back, according to the directions, and the man who gave him the poison now and then looked at his feet and legs; and after a while he pressed his foot hard, and asked him if he could feel; and he said, No; and then his leg, and so upwards and upwards, and showed us that he was cold and stiff. And he felt them himself, and said: When the poison reaches the heart, that will be the end. He was beginning to grow cold about the groin, when he uncovered his face, for he had covered himself up, and said—they were his last words—he said: Crito, I owe a cock to Asclepius; will you remember to pay the debt? The debt shall be paid, said Crito; is there anything else? There was no answer to this question; but in a minute or two a movement was heard, and the attendants uncovered him; his eyes were set, and Crito closed his eyes and mouth.

Such was the end, Echecrates, of our friend; concerning whom I may truly say, that of all the men of his time whom I have known, he was the wisest and most just and best.

QUESTIONS TO CONSIDER

- Why does Socrates insist that philosophers (literally, "lovers of wisdom") are not concerned with the body? What has this to do with the allegory of the cave?
- In a long, italicized speech, Socrates presents his audience with a dilemma concern the philosopher's acquisition of knowledge. What is the dilemma, and what has it to do with life after death?
- Socrates' argument for the immortality of the soul centers upon a characteristic of opposites (hot vs. cold, even vs. odd, life vs. death). What does Socrates observe about such pairs?
- Assuming the common definition of soul, the principle of life, what would seem to follow, given the above observation concerning opposites?

- Like Lucretius, Socrates also draws ethical implications from his conclusion that the soul is immortal. What are those conclusions, that is, if Socrates is right about life after death, how ought we to live this life?

- Socrates' friend, Crito, asks Socrates "how shall we bury you?" Socrates makes a joke in reply. What's the joke?

- What are Socrates' last words, and why are they significant? (Who was Asclepius, and why would Socrates owe him something now, at the very end of his life?)

DUALISM

RENÉ DESCARTES—MEDITATIONS

Synopsis of the Second Meditation

In the Second [Meditation], the mind which, in the exercise of the freedom peculiar to itself, supposes that no object is, of the existence of which it has even the slightest doubt, finds that, meanwhile, it must itself exist. And this point is likewise of the highest moment, for the mind is
5   thus enabled easily to distinguish what pertains to itself, that is, to the intellectual nature, from what is to be referred to the body. But since some, perhaps, will expect, at *"The body may perish without* this stage of our progress, a *difficulty, but the mind is in* statement of the reasons which *its own nature immortal."*
10   establish the doctrine of the immortality of the soul, I think it proper here to make such aware, that it was my aim to write nothing of which I could not give exact demonstration, and that I therefore felt myself obliged to adopt an order similar to that in use among the geometers, viz., to premise all upon
15   which the proposition in question depends, before coming to any conclusion respecting it. Now, the first and chief prerequisite for the knowledge of the immortality of the soul is our being able to form the clearest possible conception (conceptus, concept) of the soul itself, and such as shall be absolutely distinct from all our notions of body; and how
20   this is to be accomplished is there shown. There is required, besides this, the assurance that all objects which we clearly and distinctly think are true (really exist) in that very mode in which we think them; and this could not be established previously to the Fourth Meditation. Farther, it is necessary, for the same purpose, that we possess a distinct conception of

corporeal nature, which is given partly in the Second and partly in the Fifth and Sixth Meditations. And, finally, on these grounds, we are necessitated to conclude, that all those objects which are clearly and distinctly conceived to be diverse substances, as mind and body, are substances really reciprocally distinct; and this inference is made in the Sixth Meditation. The absolute distinction of mind and body is, besides, confirmed in this Second Meditation, by showing that we cannot conceive body unless as divisible; while, on the other hand, mind cannot be conceived unless as indivisible. For we are not able to conceive the half of a mind, as we can of any body, however small, so that the natures of these two substances are to be held, not only as diverse, but even in some measure as contraries. I have not, however, pursued this discussion further in the present treatise, as well for the reason that these considerations are sufficient to show that the destruction of the mind does not follow from the corruption of the body, and thus to afford to men the hope of a future life, as also because the premises from which it is competent for us to infer the immortality of the soul, involve an explication of the whole principles of Physics: in order to establish, in the first place, that generally all substances, that is, all things which can exist only in consequence of having been created by God, are in their own nature incorruptible, and can never cease to be, unless God himself, by refusing his concurrence to them, reduce them to nothing; and, in the second place, that body, taken generally, is a substance, and therefore can never perish, but that the human body, in as far as it differs from other bodies, is constituted only by a certain configuration of members, and by other accidents of this sort, while the human mind is not made up of accidents, but is a pure substance. For although all the accidents of the mind be changed—although, for example, it think certain things, will others, and perceive others, the mind itself does not vary with these changes; while, on the contrary, the human body is no longer the same if a change take place in the form of any of its parts: from which it follows that the body may, indeed, without difficulty perish, but that the mind is in its own nature immortal.

A QUESTION TO CONSIDER

- In this section Descartes notes that, unlike the body, we cannot think of the mind as being divided. What relevant conclusion does he take as following from this observation?

ARISTOTLE AND THOMAS AQUINAS

ARISTOTLE—ON THE SOUL

III—4

Turning now to the part of the soul with which the soul knows and thinks (whether this is separable from the others in definition only, or spatially as well) we have to inquire (1) what differentiates this part, and (2) how thinking can take place.

If thinking is like perceiving, it must be either a process in which the soul is acted upon by what is capable of being thought, or a process different from but analogous to that. The thinking part of the soul must therefore be, while impassible, *"This alone is immortal and eternal."* capable of receiving the form of an object; that is, must be potentially identical in character with its object without being the object. Mind must be related to what is thinkable, as sense is to what is sensible.

Therefore, since everything is a possible object of thought, mind in order, as Anaxagoras says, to dominate, that is, to know, must be pure from all admixture; for the co-presence of what is alien to its nature is a hindrance and a block: it follows that it too, like the sensitive part, can have no nature of its own, other than that of having a certain capacity. Thus that in the soul which is called mind (by mind I mean that whereby the soul thinks and judges) is, before it thinks, not actually any real thing. For this reason it cannot reasonably be regarded as blended with the body: if so, it would acquire some quality, e.g., warmth or cold, or even have an organ like the sensitive faculty: as it is, it has none. It was a good idea to call the soul 'the place of forms', though (1) this description holds only of the intellective soul, and (2) even this is the forms only potentially, not actually.

Observation of the sense-organs and their employment reveals a distinction between the impassibility of the sensitive and that of the intellective faculty. After strong stimulation of a sense we are less able to exercise it than before, as e.g. in the case of a loud sound we cannot hear

175

easily immediately after, or in the case of a bright color or a powerful odor we cannot see or smell, but in the case of mind thought about an object that is highly intelligible renders it more and not less able afterwards to think objects that are less intelligible: the reason is that while the faculty of sensation is dependent upon the body, mind is separable from it.

Once the mind has become each set of its possible objects, as a man of science has, when this phrase is used of one who is actually a man of science (this happens when he is now able to exercise the power on his own initiative), its condition is still one of potentiality, but in a different sense from the potentiality which preceded the acquisition of knowledge by learning or discovery: the mind too is then able to think itself.

Since we can distinguish between a spatial magnitude and what it is to be such, and between water and what it is to be water, and so in many other cases (though not in all; for in certain cases the thing and its form are identical), flesh and what it is to be flesh are discriminated either by different faculties, or by the same faculty in two different states: for flesh necessarily involves matter and is like what is snub-nosed, a this in a this. Now it is by means of the sensitive faculty that we discriminate the hot and the cold, i.e., the factors which combined in a certain ratio constitute flesh: the essential character of flesh is apprehended by something different either wholly separate from the sensitive faculty or related to it as a bent line to the same line when it has been straightened out.

Again in the case of abstract objects what is straight is analogous to what is snub-nosed; for it necessarily implies a continuum as its matter: its constitutive essence is different, if we may distinguish between straightness and what is straight: let us take it to be two-ness. It must be apprehended, therefore, by a different power or by the same power in a different state. To sum up, in so far as the realities it knows are capable of being separated from their matter, so it is also with the powers of mind.

The problem might be suggested: if thinking is a passive affection, then if mind is simple and impassible and has nothing in common with anything else, as Anaxagoras says, how can it come to think at all? For interaction between two factors is held to require a precedent community of nature between the factors. Again it might be asked, is mind a possible object of thought to itself? For if mind is thinkable per se and what is thinkable is in kind one and the same, then either (a) mind will belong to everything, or (b) mind will contain some element common to it with all other realities which makes them all thinkable.

(1) Have not we already disposed of the difficulty about interaction involving a common element, when we said that mind is in a sense potentially whatever is thinkable, though actually it is nothing until it has thought? What it thinks must be in it just as characters may be said to be on a writing tablet on which as yet nothing actually stands written: this is exactly what happens with mind.

(Mind is itself thinkable in exactly the same way as its objects are. For (a) in the case of objects which involve no matter, what thinks and what is thought are identical; for speculative knowledge and its object are identical. (Why mind is not always thinking we must consider later., b) In the case of those which contain matter each of the objects of thought is only potentially present. It follows that while they will not have mind in them (for mind is a potentiality of them only in so far as they are capable of being disengaged from matter) mind may yet be thinkable.

III 5

Since in every class of things, as in nature as a whole, we find two factors involved, (1) a matter which is potentially all the particulars included in the class, (2) a cause which is productive in the sense that it makes them all (the latter standing to the former, as e.g., an art to its material), these distinct elements must likewise be found within the soul.

And in fact mind as we have described it is what it is what it is by virtue of becoming all things, while there is another which is what it is by virtue of making all things: this is a sort of positive state like light; for in a sense light makes potential colors into actual colors.

Mind in this sense of it is separable, impassible, unmixed, since it is in its essential nature activity (for always the active is superior to the passive factor, the originating force to the matter which it forms).

Actual knowledge is identical with its object: in the individual, potential knowledge is in time prior to actual knowledge, but in the universe as a whole it is not prior even in time. Mind is not at one time knowing and at another not. When mind is set free from its present conditions it appears as just what it is and nothing more: this alone is immortal and eternal (we do not, however, remember its former activity because, while mind in this sense is impassible, mind as passive is destructible), and without it nothing thinks.

5

QUESTIONS TO CONSIDER

- How is mind unlike the senses—indeed, any of the body's powers—as regards their capacity to be affected? What has this to do with immortality?
- What has the distinction between the active mind and the passive mind to do with Aristotle's argument for immortality?

AQUINAS—SUMMA THEOLOGIAE

---

75 1—Is the soul a body?

Objection 1. It would seem that the soul is a body. For the soul is the moving principle of the body. Nor does it move unless moved. First, because seemingly nothing can move unless it is itself moved, since nothing gives what it has not; for instance, what is not hot does not give heat. Secondly, because if there be anything that moves and is not moved, it must be the cause of eternal, unchanging movement, as we find proved Phys. viii, 6; and this does not appear to be the case in the movement of an animal, which is caused by the soul. Therefore the soul is a mover moved. But every mover moved is a body. Therefore the soul is a body.

10

"The intellectual principle, which we call the human soul, is incorruptible."

15

Objection 2. Further, all knowledge is caused by means of a likeness. But there can be no likeness of a body to an incorporeal thing. If, therefore, the soul were not a body, it could not have knowledge of corporeal things.

20

Objection 3. Further, between the mover and the moved there must be contact. But contact is only between bodies. Since, therefore, the soul moves the body, it seems that the soul must be a body.

25

On the contrary, Augustine says (De Trin. vi, 6) that the soul "is simple in comparison with the body, inasmuch as it does not occupy space by its bulk."

I answer that, to seek the nature of the soul, we must premise that the soul is defined as the first principle of life of those things which live: for we call living things "animate," [i.e., having a soul], and those things which have no life, "inanimate." Now life is shown principally by two actions, knowledge and movement. The philosophers of old, not being able to rise above their imagination, supposed that the principle of these actions was something corporeal: for they asserted that only bodies were real things; and that what is not corporeal is nothing: hence they maintained that the soul is something corporeal. This opinion can be proved to be false in many ways; but we shall make use of only one proof, based on universal and certain principles, which shows clearly that the soul is not a body.

It is manifest that not every principle of vital action is a soul, for then the eye would be a soul, as it is a principle of vision; and the same might be applied to the other instruments of the soul: but it is the "first" principle of life, which we call the soul. Now, though a body may be a principle of life, or to be a living thing, as the heart is a principle of life in an animal, yet nothing corporeal can be the first principle of life. For it is clear that to be a principle of life, or to be a living thing, does not belong to a body as such; since, if that were the case, every body would be a living thing, or a principle of life. Therefore a body is competent to be a living thing or even a principle of life, as "such" a body. Now that it is actually such a body, it owes to some principle which is called its act. Therefore the soul, which is the first principle of life, is not a body, but the act of a body; thus heat, which is the principle of calefaction, is not a body, but an act of a body.

Reply to Objection 1. As everything which is in motion must be moved by something else, a process which cannot be prolonged indefinitely, we must allow that not every mover is moved. For, since to be moved is to pass from potentiality to actuality, the mover gives what it has to the thing moved, inasmuch as it causes it to be in act. But, as is shown in Phys. viii, 6, there is a mover which is altogether immovable, and not moved either essentially, or accidentally; and such a mover can cause an invariable movement. There is, however, another kind of mover, which, though not moved essentially, is moved accidentally; and for this reason it does not cause an invariable movement; such a mover, is the soul. There is, again, another mover, which is moved essentially—namely, the body. And because the philosophers of old believed that nothing existed but bodies, they maintained that every mover is moved; and that the soul is moved directly and is a body.

Reply to Objection 2. The likeness of a thing known is not of necessity actually in the nature of the knower; but given a thing which knows potentially, and afterwards knows actually, the likeness of the thing known must be in the nature of the knower, not actually, but only potentially; thus color is not actually in the pupil of the eye, but only potentially. Hence it is necessary, not that the likeness of corporeal things should be actually in the nature of the soul, but that there be a potentiality in the soul for such a likeness. But the ancient philosophers omitted to distinguish between actuality and potentiality; and so they held that the soul must be a body in order to have knowledge of a body; and that it must be composed of the principles of which all bodies are formed in order to know all bodies.

Reply to Objection 3. There are two kinds of contact; of "quantity," and of "power." By the former a body can be touched only by a body; by the latter a body can be touched by an incorporeal thing, which moves that body.

75 2—Is the human soul something subsistent?

Objection 1. It would seem that the human soul is not something subsistent. For that which subsists is said to be "this particular thing." Now "this particular thing" is said not of the soul, but of that which is composed of soul and body. Therefore the soul is not something subsistent.

Objection 2. Further, everything subsistent operates. But the soul does not operate; for, as the Philosopher says (De Anima i, 4), "to say that the soul feels or understands is like saying that the soul weaves or builds." Therefore the soul is not subsistent.

Objection 3. Further, if the soul were subsistent, it would have some operation apart from the body. But it has no operation apart from the body, not even that of understanding: for the act of understanding does not take place without a phantasm, which cannot exist apart from the body. Therefore the human soul is not something subsistent.

On the contrary, Augustine says (De Trin. x, 7): "Who understands that the nature of the soul is that of a substance and not that of a body, will see that those who maintain the corporeal nature of the soul, are led astray through associating with the soul those things without which they are unable to think of any nature—i.e., imaginary pictures of corporeal things." Therefore the nature of the human intellect is not only incorporeal, but it is also a substance, that is, something subsistent.

I answer that, it must necessarily be allowed that the principle of intellectual operation which we call the soul, is a principle both incorporeal and subsistent. For it is clear that by means of the intellect man can have knowledge of all corporeal things. Now whatever knows certain things cannot have any of them in its own nature; because that which is in it naturally would impede the knowledge of anything else. Thus we observe that a sick man's tongue being vitiated by a feverish and bitter humor, is insensible to anything sweet, and everything seems bitter to it. Therefore, if the intellectual principle contained the nature of a body it would be unable to know all bodies. Now every body has its own determinate nature. Therefore it is impossible for the intellectual principle to be a body. It is likewise impossible for it to understand by means of a bodily organ; since the determinate nature of that organ would impede knowledge of all bodies; as when a certain determinate color is not only in the pupil of the eye, but also in a glass vase, the liquid in the vase seems to be of that same color.

Therefore the intellectual principle which we call the mind or the intellect has an operation "per se" apart from the body. Now only that which subsists can have an operation "per se." For nothing can operate but what is actual: for which reason we do not say that heat imparts heat, but that what is hot gives heat. We must conclude, therefore, that the human soul, which is called the intellect or the mind, is something incorporeal and subsistent.

Reply to Objection 1. "This particular thing" can be taken in two senses.

Firstly, for anything subsistent, secondly, for that which subsists, and is complete in a specific nature. The former sense excludes the inherence of an accident or of a material form; the latter excludes also the imperfection of the part, so that a hand can be called "this particular thing" in the first sense, but not in the second. Therefore, as the human soul is a part of human nature, it can indeed be called "this particular thing," in the first sense, as being something subsistent; but not in the second, for in this sense, what is composed of body and soul is said to be "this particular thing."

Reply to Objection 2. Aristotle wrote those words as expressing not his own opinion, but the opinion of those who said that to understand is to be moved, as is clear from the context. Or we may reply that to operate "per se" belongs to what exists "per se." But for a thing to exist "per se," it suffices sometimes that it be not inherent, as an accident or a material form; even though it be part of something. Nevertheless, that is rightly said to subsist "per se," which is neither inherent in the above sense, nor part of anything else. In this sense, the eye or the hand cannot be said to subsist "per se"; nor can it for that reason be said to operate "per se." Hence the operation of the parts is through each part attributed to the whole. For we say that man sees with the eye, and feels with the hand, and not in the same sense as when we say that what is hot gives heat by its heat; for heat, strictly speaking, does not give heat. We may therefore say that the soul understands, as the eye sees; but it is more correct to say that man understands through the soul.

Reply to Objection 3. The body is necessary for the action of the intellect, not as its origin of action, but on the part of the object; for the phantasm is to the intellect what color is to the sight. Neither does such a dependence on the body prove the intellect to be non-subsistent; otherwise it would follow that an animal is non-subsistent, since it requires external objects of the senses in order to perform its act of perception.

75 3—Are the souls of brute animals subsistent?

Objection 1. It would seem that the souls of brute animals are subsistent. For man is of the same 'genus' as other animals; and, as we have just shown (2), the soul of man is subsistent. Therefore the souls of other animals are subsistent.

Objection 2. Further, the relation of the sensitive faculty to sensible objects is like the relation of the intellectual faculty to intelligible objects. But the intellect, apart from the body, apprehends intelligible objects. Therefore the sensitive faculty, apart from the body, perceives sensible objects. Therefore, since the souls of brute animals are sensitive, it follows that they are subsistent; just as the human intellectual soul is subsistent.

Objection 3. Further, the soul of brute animals moves the body. But the body is not a mover but is moved. Therefore the soul of brute animals has an operation apart from the body.

On the contrary, is what is written in the book De Eccl. Dogm. xvi, xvii: "Man alone we believe to have a subsistent soul: whereas the souls of animals are not subsistent."

I answer that, the ancient philosophers made no distinction between sense and intellect, and referred both a corporeal principle, as has been said (1). Plato, however, drew a distinction between intellect and sense; yet he referred both to an incorporeal principle, maintaining that sensing, just as understanding, belongs to the soul as such. From this it follows that even the souls of brute animals are subsistent. But Aristotle held that of the operations of the soul, understanding alone is performed without a corporeal organ. On the other hand, sensation and the consequent operations of the sensitive soul are evidently accompanied with change in the body; thus in the act of vision, the pupil of the eye is affected by a reflection of color: and so with the other senses. Hence it is clear that the sensitive soul has no *per se* operation of its own, and that every operation of the sensitive soul belongs to the composite. Wherefore we conclude that as the souls of brute animals have no *per se* operations they are not subsistent. For the operation of anything follows the mode of its being.

Reply to Objection 1. Although man is of the same "genus" as other animals, he is of a different "species." Specific difference is derived from the difference of form; nor does every difference of form necessarily imply a diversity of "genus."

Reply to Objection 2. The relation of the sensitive faculty to the sensible object is in one way the same as that of the intellectual faculty to the intelligible object, in so far as each is in potentiality to its object. But in another way their relations differ, inasmuch as the impression of the object on the sense is accompanied with change in the body; so that excessive strength of the sensible corrupts sense; a thing that never occurs in the case of the intellect. For an intellect that understands the highest of intelligible objects is more able afterwards to understand those that are lower. If, however, in the process of intellectual operation the body is weary, this result is accidental, inasmuch as the intellect requires the operation of the sensitive powers in the production of the phantasms.

Reply to Objection 3. Motive power is of two kinds. One, the appetitive power, commands motion. The operation of this power in the sensitive soul is not apart from the body; for anger, joy, and passions of a like nature are accompanied by a change in the body. The other motive power is that which executes motion in adapting the members for obeying the appetite; and the act of this power does not consist in moving, but in being moved. Whence it is clear that to move is not an act of the sensitive soul without the body.

75 6—Is the human soul incorruptible?

Objection 1. It would seem that the human soul is corruptible. For those things that have a like beginning and process seemingly have a like end. But the beginning, by generation, of men is like that of animals, for they are made from the earth. And the process of life is alike in both; because "all things breathe alike, and man hath nothing more than the beast," as it is written (Ecclesiastes 3:19). Therefore, as the same text concludes, "the death of man and beast is one, and the condition of both is equal." But the souls of brute animals are corruptible. Therefore, also, the human soul is corruptible.

Objection 2. Further, whatever is out of nothing can return to nothingness, because the end should correspond to the beginning. But as it is written (Wisdom 2:2), "We are born of nothing"; which is true, not only of the body, but also of the soul. Therefore, as is concluded in the same passage, "After this we shall be as if we had not been," even as to our soul.

Objection 3. Further, nothing is without its own proper operation. But the operation proper to the soul, which is to understand through a phantasm, cannot be without the body. For the soul understands nothing without a phantasm; and there is no phantasm without the body as the Philosopher says (De Anima i, 1). Therefore the soul cannot survive the dissolution of the body.

On the contrary, Dionysius says (Div. Nom. iv) that human souls owe to Divine goodness that they are "intellectual," and that they have "an incorruptible substantial life."

I answer that, we must assert that the intellectual principle which we call the human soul is incorruptible. For a thing may be corrupted in two ways—"per se," and accidentally. Now it is impossible for any substance to be generated or corrupted accidentally, that is, by the generation or corruption of something else. For generation and corruption belong to a thing, just as existence belongs to it, which is acquired by generation and lost by corruption. Therefore, whatever has existence "per se" cannot be generated or corrupted except 'per se'; while things which do not subsist, such as accidents and material forms, acquire existence or lost it through the generation or corruption of composite things. Now it was shown above (2,3) that the souls of brutes are not self-subsistent, whereas the human soul is; so that the souls of brutes are corrupted, when their bodies are corrupted; while the human soul could not be corrupted unless it were corrupted "per se." This, indeed, is impossible, not only as regards the human soul, but also as regards anything subsistent that is a form alone. For it is clear that what belongs to a thing by virtue of itself is inseparable from it; but existence belongs to a form, which is an act, by virtue of itself. Wherefore matter acquires actual existence as it acquires the form; while it is corrupted so far as the form is separated from it. But it is impossible for a form to be separated from itself; and therefore it is impossible for a subsistent form to cease to exist.

Granted even that the soul is composed of matter and form, as some pretend, we should nevertheless have to maintain that it is incorruptible. For corruption is found only where there is contrariety, since generation and corruption are from contraries and into contraries. Wherefore the heavenly bodies, since they have no matter subject to contrariety, are incorruptible. Now there can be no contrariety in the intellectual soul; for it receives according to the manner of its existence, and those things which it receives are without contrariety; for the notions even of contraries are not themselves contrary, since contraries belong to the same knowledge. Therefore it is impossible for the intellectual soul to be corruptible. Moreover we may take a sign of this from the fact that everything naturally aspires to existence after its own manner. Now, in things that have knowledge, desire ensues upon knowledge. The senses indeed do not know existence, except under the conditions of "here" and "now," whereas the intellect apprehends existence absolutely, and for all time; so that everything that has an intellect naturally desires always to exist. But a natural desire cannot be in vain. Therefore every intellectual substance is incorruptible.

Reply to Objection 1. Solomon reasons thus in the person of the foolish, as expressed in the words of Wisdom 2. Therefore the saying that man and animals have a like beginning in generation is true of the body; for all animals alike are made of earth. But it is not true of the soul. For the souls of brutes are produced by some power of the body, whereas the human soul is produced by God. To signify this it is written as to other animals: "Let the earth bring forth the living soul" (Genesis 1:24): while of man it is written (Genesis 2:7) that "He breathed into his face the breath of life." And so in Ecclesiastes 12:7 it is concluded: "(Before) the dust return into its earth from whence it was; and the spirit return to God Who gave it." Again the process of life is alike as to the body, concerning which it is written (Ecclesiastes 3:19): "All things breathe alike," and (Wisdom 2:2), "The breath in our nostrils is smoke." But the process is not alike of the soul; for man is intelligent, whereas animals are not. Hence it is false to say: "Man has nothing more than beasts." Thus death comes to both alike as to the body, by not as to the soul.

Reply to Objection 2. As a thing can be created by reason, not of a passive potentiality, but only of the active potentiality of the Creator, Who can produce something out of nothing, so when we say that a thing can be reduced to nothing, we do not imply in the creature a potentiality to non-existence, but in the Creator the power of ceasing to sustain existence. But a thing is said to be corruptible because there is in it a potentiality to non-existence.

Reply to Objection 3. To understand through a phantasm is the proper operation of the soul by virtue of its union with the body. After separation from the body it will have another mode of understanding, similar to other substances separated from bodies, as will appear later on.

- In the first article, is Aquinas speaking of the human soul or of all souls? Does it make sense for Aquinas to say the soul is a form? If so, with which principle would we associate the body?

- Is Aquinas speaking of the human soul exclusively in article two? What does it mean, then, to say that the human soul is subsistent, that is, it can exist independently? Independently of what? So why are the souls of the other animals not subsistent, then?

- Why is article six needed? Has Aquinas not already proved that the human soul can exist independently?

7

NATURAL PHILOSOPHY AND THE EXISTENCE OF GOD

Finally, we turn to matters which go beyond the natural order of things. We have chosen God, and in particular the existence of God, as a matter which finds itself near the absolute limit of philosophical thought. What would a materialist have to tell us about whether God exists, or not? Would Plato agree with them? The Cartesian dualist? And what would Aristotle and Aquinas have to say?—from a philosophical perspective, that is, from the perspective of reason alone, and not from the privileged viewpoint of faith. It may well be that one's notion of what nature is necessarily leads to a corresponding notion of the supernatural.

MATERIALISTIC ATHEISM AND AGNOSTICISM

EPICURUS

Is God willing to prevent evil, but not able? Then he is not omnipotent. Is he able, but not willing? Then he is malevolent. Is he both able and willing? Then whence cometh evil? Is he neither able nor willing? Then why call him God?

LUCRETIUS—ON THE NATURE OF THINGS

5 This too you cannot possibly believe, that the holy seats of the gods exist in any parts of the world: the fine nature of the gods far withdrawn from our senses is hardly seen by the thought of the mind; and since it has ever eluded the touch and stroke of the hands, it must touch nothing which is tangible for us; for that cannot touch which does not admit of being
10 touched in turn. And therefore their seats as well must be unlike our seats, fine, even as their bodies are fine. All which I will prove to you later in

copious argument. To say again that for the sake of men they have willed
to set in order the glorious nature of the world and therefore it is right to
praise the work of the gods,
calling as it does for all praise, *"The nature of things has not*
and to believe that it will be *been made for us by divine*
eternal and immortal, and that it *power, so great are the defects*
is an unholy thing ever to shake *with which it is encumbered."*
by any force from its fixed seats
that which by the forethought of the gods in ancient days has been
established on everlasting foundations for mankind, or to assail it by
speech and utterly overturn it from top to bottom; and to invent and add
other figments of the kind, Memmius, is all sheer folly. For what
advantage can our gratitude bestow on immortal and blessed beings, that
for our sakes they should take in hand to administer anything? And what
novel incident should have induced them at rest so long up to now to
desire to change their former life? For it seems natural he should rejoice
in a new state of things, whom old things annoy; but for him whom no
ill has befallen in times gone by, when he passed a pleasant existence,
what could have kindled in such a one a love of change? Did life lie
groveling in darkness and sorrow, until the first dawn of the birth of
things? Or what evil had it been for us never to have been born?
Whoever has been born must want to continue in life, so long as fond
pleasure shall keep him; but for him who has never tasted the love, never
been on the lists, of life, what harm not to have been born? Whence again
was first implanted in the gods a pattern for begetting things in general
as well as the preconception of what men are, so that they knew and saw
in mind what they wanted to make? And in what way was the power of
first beginnings ever ascertained, and what they could effect by a change
in their mutual arrangements, unless nature herself gave the model for
making things? For in this way the first beginnings of things many in
number in many ways impelled by blows for infinite ages back and kept
in motion by their own weights have been carried along and to unite in
all manner of ways and thoroughly test every kind of production possible
by their mutual combinations; that it is not strange if they have also fallen
into arrangements and have come into patterns like to those out of which
this sum of things is now carried on by constant renewing.

But if I did not know what the first beginnings of things are, yet this
judging by the very arrangements of heaven I would venture to affirm,

and led by many other facts to maintain, that the nature of things has by no means been made for us by divine power: so great are the defects with which it is encumbered. In the first place of all the space which the vast reach of heaven covers, a portion greedy mountains and forests of wild beasts have occupied, rocks and wasteful pools take up and the sea which holds wide apart the coasts of different lands. Next of nearly two thirds burning heat and the constant fall of frost rob mortals. What is left for tillage, even that nature by its power would overrun with thorns, unless the force of man-made head against it, accustomed for the sake of a livelihood to groan beneath the strong hoe and to cut through the earth by pressing down the plough. Unless by turning up the fruitful clods with the share and laboring the soil of the earth we stimulate things to rise, they could not spontaneously come up into the clear air; and even then sometimes when things earned with great toil now put forth their leaves over the lands and are all in blossom, either the ethereal sun burns them up with excessive heats or sudden rains and cold frosts cut them off, and the blasts of the winds waste them by a furious hurricane. Again why does nature give food and increase to the frightful race of wild beasts dangerous to mankind both by sea and land? Why do the seasons of the year bring diseases in their train? Why stalks abroad untimely death? Then too the baby, like to a sailor cast away by the cruel waves, lies naked on the ground, speechless, wanting every furtherance of life, soon as nature by the throes of birth has shed him forth from his mother's womb into the borders of light: he fills the room with a rueful wailing, as well he may whose destiny it is to go through in life so many ills. But the different flocks, herds, and wild beasts grow up; they want no rattles; to none of them need be addressed the fond broken accents of the fostering nurse; they ask not different dresses according to the season; no, nor do they want arms or lofty walls whereby to protect their own, the earth itself and nature manifold in her works producing in plenty all things for all.

But in what ways the concourse of matter founded earth and heaven and the deeps of the sea, the courses of the sun and moon, I will next in order describe. For verily not by design did the first-beginnings of things station themselves each in its right place by keen intelligence, nor did they bargain to say what motions each should assume, but because the first-beginnings of things many in number in many ways impelled by blows for infinite ages back and kept in motion by their own weights have been carried along and to unite in all manner of ways and thoroughly to test every kind of production possible by their mutual combinations, therefore it is that spread abroad through great time after trying unions and motions of every kind they at length meet together in those masses which suddenly brought together become often the rudiments of great things, of earth, sea, and heaven and the race of living things.

QUESTIONS TO CONSIDER

- To what conclusion does the argument ascribed to Epicurus lead? If we take his words at face value, is Lucretius an atheist? If not, what is his objection to the gods?

- What arguments does Lucretius supply toward his claim that the gods did not make the world, nor can they destroy it?

- Should Lucretius even be able to speak of the defects in the world?

- The last paragraph of this reading references Lucretius proposed explanation for the universe. What does he offer in place of God (or gods) who created the universe in accordance with some plan? (You may want to review his natural philosophy before addressing this question.)

DAVID HUME—DIALOGUES CONCERNING NATURAL RELIGION

Part II

Not to lose any time in circumlocutions, said Cleanthes, addressing himself to Demea, much less in replying to the pious declamations of Philo; I shall briefly explain how I conceive this matter. Look round the world: contemplate the whole and every part of it: you will find it to be nothing but one great machine, subdivided into an infinite number of lesser machines, which again admit of subdivisions to a degree beyond what human senses and faculties can trace and explain. All these various machines, and even their *"What if I should revive the old epicurean hypothesis?"* most minute parts, are adjusted to each other with an accuracy which ravishes into admiration all men who have ever contemplated them. The curious adapting of means to ends, throughout all nature, resembles exactly, though it much exceeds, the productions of human contrivance;

of human designs, thought, wisdom, and intelligence. Since, therefore, the effects resemble each other, we are led to infer, by all the rules of analogy, that the causes also resemble; and that the Author of Nature is somewhat similar to the mind of man, though possessed of much larger faculties, proportioned to the grandeur of the work which he has executed. By this argument *a posteriori*, and by this argument alone, do we prove at once the existence of a Deity, and his similarity to human mind and intelligence.

VIII

What you ascribe to the fertility of my invention, replied Philo, is entirely owing to the nature of the subject. In subjects adapted to the narrow compass of human reason, there is commonly but one determination, which carries probability or conviction with it; and to a man of sound judgment, all other suppositions, but that one, appear entirely absurd and chimerical. But in such questions as the present, a hundred contradictory views may preserve a kind of imperfect analogy; and invention has here full scope to exert itself. Without any great effort of thought, I believe that I could, in an instant, propose other systems of cosmogony, which would have some faint appearance of truth, though it is a thousand, a million to one, if either yours or any one of mine be the true system.

For instance, what if I should revive the old epicurean hypothesis? This is commonly, and I believe justly, esteemed the most absurd system that has yet been proposed; yet I know not whether, with a few alterations, it might not be brought to bear a faint appearance of probability. Instead of supposing matter infinite, as Epicurus did, let us suppose it finite. A finite number of particles is only susceptible of finite transpositions: and it must happen, in an eternal duration, that every possible order or position must be tried an infinite number of times. This world, therefore, with all its events, even the most minute, has before been produced and destroyed, and will again be produced and destroyed, without any bounds and limitations. No one, who has a conception of the powers of infinite, in comparison of finite, will ever scruple this determination.

But this supposes, said Demea, that matter can acquire motion, without any voluntary agent or first mover.

And where is the difficulty, replied Philo, of that supposition? Every event, before experience, is equally difficult and incomprehensible; and every event, after experience, is equally easy and intelligible. Motion, in many instances, from gravity, from elasticity, from electricity, begins in matter, without any known voluntary agent: and to suppose always, in these cases, an unknown voluntary agent, is mere hypothesis; and hypothesis attended with no advantages. The beginning of motion in matter itself is as conceivable a priori as its communication from mind and intelligence.

Besides, why may not motion have been propagated by impulse through all eternity, and the same stock of it, or nearly the same, be still upheld in the universe? As much is lost by the composition of motion, as much is gained by its resolution. And whatever the causes are, the fact is certain, that matter is, and always has been, in continual agitation, as far as human experience or tradition reaches. There is not probably, at present, in the whole universe, one particle of matter at absolute rest.

And this very consideration too, continued Philo, which we have stumbled on in the course of the argument, suggests a new hypothesis of cosmogony, that is not absolutely absurd and improbable. Is there a system, an order, an economy of things, by which matter can preserve that perpetual agitation which seems essential to it, and yet maintain a constancy in the forms which it produces? There certainly is such an economy; for this is actually the case with the present world. The continual motion of matter, therefore, in less than infinite transpositions, must produce this economy or order; and by its very nature, that order, when once established, supports itself, for many ages, if not to eternity. But wherever matter is so poised, arranged, and adjusted, as to continue in perpetual motion, and yet preserve a constancy in the forms, its situation must, of necessity, have all the same appearance of art and contrivance which we observe at present. All the parts of each form must have a relation to each other, and to the whole; and the whole itself must have a relation to the other parts of the universe; to the element in which the form subsists; to the materials with which it repairs its waste and decay; and to every other form which is hostile or friendly. A defect in any of these particulars destroys the form; and the matter of which it is composed is again set loose, and is thrown into irregular motions and fermentations, till it unite itself to some other regular form. If no such form be prepared to receive it, and if there be a great quantity of this corrupted matter in the universe, the universe itself is entirely disordered; whether it be the feeble embryo of a world in its first beginnings that is thus destroyed, or the rotten carcass of one languishing in old age and infirmity. In either case, a chaos ensues; till finite, though innumerable revolutions produce at last some forms, whose parts and organs are so adjusted as to support the forms amidst a continued succession of matter.

Suppose (for we shall endeavor to vary the expression), that matter were thrown into any position, by a blind, unguided force; it is evident that this first position must, in all probability, be the most confused and most disorderly imaginable, without any resemblance to those works of human contrivance, which, along with a symmetry of parts, discover an adjustment of means to ends, and a tendency to self-preservation. If the actuating force cease after this operation, matter must remain forever in disorder, and continue an immense chaos, without any proportion or activity. But suppose that the actuating force, whatever it be, still continues in matter, this first position will immediately give place to a second, which will likewise in all probability be as disorderly as the first, and so on through many successions of changes and revolutions. No particular order or position ever continues a moment unaltered. The original force, still remaining in activity, gives a perpetual restlessness to matter. Every possible situation is produced, and instantly destroyed. If a glimpse or dawn of order appears for a moment, it is instantly hurried away, and confounded, by that never-ceasing force which actuates every part of matter.

Thus the universe goes on for many ages in a continued succession of chaos and disorder. But is it not possible that it may settle at last, so as not to lose its motion and active force (for that we have supposed inherent in it), yet so as to preserve a uniformity of appearance, amidst the continual motion and fluctuation of its parts? This we find to be the case with the universe at present. Every individual is perpetually changing, and every part of every individual; and yet the whole remains, in appearance, the same. May we not hope for such a position, or rather be assured of it, from the eternal revolutions of unguided matter; and may not this account for all the appearing wisdom and contrivance which is in the universe? Let us contemplate the subject a little, and we shall find, that this adjustment, if attained by matter of a seeming stability in

194

the forms, with a real and perpetual revolution or motion of parts, affords a plausible, if not a true solution of the difficulty.

It is in vain, therefore, to insist upon the uses of the parts in animals or vegetables, and their curious adjustment to each other. I would fain know, how an animal could subsist, unless its parts were so adjusted? Do we not find that it immediately perishes whenever this adjustment ceases, and that its matter corrupting tries some new form? It happens indeed, that the parts of the world are so well adjusted, that some regular form immediately lays claim to this corrupted matter: and if it were not so, could the world subsist? Must it not dissolve as well as the animal, and pass through new positions and situations, till in great, but finite succession, it falls at last into the present or some such order?

It is well, replied Cleanthes, you told us, that this hypothesis was suggested on a sudden, in the course of the argument. Had you had leisure to examine it, you would soon have perceived the insuperable objections to which it is exposed. No form, you say, can subsist, unless it possess those powers and organs requisite for its subsistence: some new order or economy must be tried, and so on, without intermission; till at last some order, which can support and maintain itself, is fallen upon. But according to this hypothesis, whence arise the many conveniences and advantages which men and all animals possess? Two eyes, two ears, are not absolutely necessary for the subsistence of the species. Human race might have been propagated and preserved, without horses, dogs, cows, sheep, and those innumerable fruits and products which serve to our satisfaction and enjoyment. If no camels had been created for the use of man in the sandy deserts of Africa and Arabia, would the world have been dissolved? If no lodestone had been framed to give that wonderful and useful direction to the needle, would human society and the human kind have been immediately extinguished? Though the maxims of Nature be in general very frugal, yet instances of this kind are far from being rare; and any one of them is a sufficient proof of design, and of a benevolent design, which gave rise to the order and arrangement of the universe.

At least, you may safely infer, said Philo, that the foregoing hypothesis is so far incomplete and imperfect, which I shall not scruple to allow. But can we ever reasonably expect greater success in any attempts of this nature? Or can we ever hope to erect a system of cosmogony, that will be liable to no exceptions, and will contain no circumstance repugnant to our limited and imperfect experience of the analogy of Nature? Your theory itself cannot surely pretend to any such advantage, even though you have run into Anthropomorphism, the better to preserve a conformity to common experience. Let us once more put it to trial. In all instances which we have ever seen, ideas are copied from real objects, and are ectypal, not archetypal, to express myself in learned terms: You reverse this order and give thought the precedence. In all instances which we have ever seen, thought has no influence upon matter, except where that matter is so conjoined with it as to have an equal reciprocal influence upon it. No animal can move immediately anything but the members of its own body; and indeed, the equality of action and reaction seems to be a universal law of nature: But your theory implies a contradiction to this experience. These instances, with many more, which it were easy to collect, (particularly the supposition of a mind or system of thought that is eternal, or, in other words, an animal ingenerable and immortal); these instances, I say, may teach all of us sobriety in condemning each other, and let us see, that as no system of this kind ought ever to be received from a slight analogy, so neither ought any to be rejected on account of a small incongruity. For that is an inconvenience from which we can justly pronounce no one to be exempted.

All religious systems, it is confessed, are subject to great and insuperable difficulties. Each disputant triumphs in his turn; while he carries on an offensive war, and exposes the absurdities, barbarities, and pernicious tenets of his antagonist. But all of them, on the whole, prepare a complete triumph for the Skeptic, who tells them, that no system ought ever to be embraced with regard to such subjects: For this plain reason, that no absurdity ought ever to be assented to with regard to any subject. A total suspense of judgment is here our only reasonable resource. And if every attack, as is commonly observed, and no defense, among Theologians, is successful; how complete must be his victory, who remains always, with all mankind, on the offensive, and has himself no fixed station or abiding city, which he is ever, on any occasion, obliged to defend?

QUESTIONS TO CONSIDER

- In the selection from Part II, Cleanthes presents what is commonly called a "design" argument. How does the argument proceed? To what sort of God does the argument conclude?

- In Part VIII, Demea offers an objection to Philo: how can matter ever acquire motion without a first mover? Does Epicurus himself address this objection? Does Lucretius?

- In the remaining selections, Philo (likely Hume himself) offers an explanation for an ordered universe arising from disorder, apart from any first mover (God). How like contemporary explanations is this?

- What is Philo's ultimate philosophical position on the question of the origins of the universe, then? Is he an atheist? An agnostic?

BERTRAND RUSSELL—WHAT I BELIEVE

Fear is the basis of religious dogma, as of so much else in human life. Fear of human beings, individually or collectively, dominates much of our social life, but it is fear of nature that gives rise to religion. The antithesis of mind and matter is, as we have seen, more or less illusory; but there is another antithesis which is more important—that, namely, between things that can be affected by our desires and things that cannot be so affected. The line between the two is neither sharp nor immutable—as science advances, more and more things are brought under human control. Nevertheless there remain things definitely on the other side. Among these are all the large facts of our world, the sort of facts that are dealt with by astronomy. It is only facts on or near the surface of the earth that we can, to some extent, mold to suit our desires. And even on the surface of the earth our powers are very limited. Above all, we cannot prevent death, although we can often delay it.

Religion is an attempt to overcome this antithesis. If the world is controlled by God, and God can be moved by prayer, we acquired a share in omnipotence. In former days, miracles happened in answer to prayer; they still do in the Catholic Church, but Protestants have lost this power. However, it is possible to dispense with miracles, since Providence has de- creed that the operation of natural laws shall produce the best possible results. Thus belief in God still serves to humanize the world of nature and to make men feel that physical forces are really their allies. In like manner immortality removes the terror from death. People who believe that when they die they will inherit eternal bliss may be expected to view death without horror, though, fortunately for medical men, this does not invariably happen. It does, however, soothe men's fears somewhat even when it cannot allay them wholly.

Religion, since it has its source in terror, has dignified certain kinds of fear, and made people think them not disgraceful. In this it has done mankind a great disservice: all fear is bad.

QUESTIONS TO CONSIDER

- Is Russell decidedly a theist? An atheist? Neither?
- Apart from the question of God, what is Russell's view of religion?

PLATONIC FORMALISM

PLATO—THE LAWS

Athenian—And now having spoken of assaults, let us sum up all acts of violence under a single law, which shall be as follows:—No one shall take or carry away any of his neighbor's goods, neither shall he use anything which is his neighbor's without the consent of the owner; for these are the offenses which are and have been, and will ever be, the source of all the aforesaid evils. The greatest of them are excesses and insolences of

"Nearly all of themseem to be ignorant of the nature and power of the soul, especially in what relates to her origin."

youth, and are offenses against the greatest when they are done against religion; and especially great when in violation of public and holy rites, or of the partly-common rites in which tribes and phratries share; and in the second degree great when they are committed against private rites and sepulchers, and in the third degree (not to repeat the acts formerly mentioned), when insults are offered to parents; the fourth kind of violence is when any one, regardless of the authority of the rulers, takes or carries away or makes use of anything which belongs to them, not having their consent; and the fifth kind is when the violation of the civil rights of an individual demands reparation. There should be a common law embracing all these cases. For we have already said in general terms what shall be the punishment of the sacrilege, whether fraudulent or violent, and now we have to determine what is to be the punishment of those who speak or act insolently toward the Gods. But first we must give them an admonition which may be in the following terms:—No one who in obedience to the laws believed that there were Gods, ever intentionally do any unholy act, or uttered any unlawful word; but he who did must have supposed one of three things,—either that they did not exist,—which is the first possibility, or secondly, that, if they did, they took no care of man, or thirdly, that they were easily appeased and turned aside from their purpose by sacrifices and prayers.

Cleinias—What shall we say or do to these persons?

Athenian—My good friend, let us first hear the jests which I suspect that they in their superiority will utter against us.

Cleinias—What jests?

Athenian—They will make some irreverent speech of this sort—*O inhabitants of Athens, and Sparta, and Cnosus, they will reply, in that you speak truly; for some of us deny the very existence of the Gods, while others, as you say, are of opinion that they do not care about us; and others that they are turned from their course by gifts. Now we have a right to claim, as you yourself allowed, in the matter of laws, that before you are hard upon us and threaten us, you should argue with us and convince us—you should first attempt to teach and persuade us that there are Gods by reasonable evidences, and also that they are too good to be unrighteous, or to be propitiated, or turned from their course by gifts. For when we hear such things said of them by those who are esteemed to be the best of poets, and orators, and prophets, and priests, and by innumerable others, the thoughts of most of us are not set upon abstaining from unrighteous acts, but upon doing them and atoning for them. When lawgivers profess that they are gentle and not stern, we think that they should first of all use persuasion to us, and show us the existence of Gods, if not in a better manner than other men, at any rate in a truer; and who knows but that we shall hearken to you? If then our request is a fair one, please to accept our challenge.*

Cleinias—But is there any difficulty in proving the existence of the Gods?

Athenian—How would you prove it?

Cleinias—How? In the first place, the earth and the sun, and the stars and the universe, and the fair order of the seasons, and the division of them into years and months, furnish proofs of their existence; and also there is the fact that all Hellenes and barbarians believe in them.

Athenian—I fear, my sweet friend, though I will not say that I much regard, the contempt with which the profane will be likely to assail us. For you do not understand the nature of their complaint, and you fancy that they rush into impiety only from a love of sensual pleasure.

Cleinias—Why, Stranger, what other reason is there?

Athenian—One which you who live in a different atmosphere would never guess.

Cleinias—What is it?

Athenian—A very grievous sort of ignorance which is imagined to be the greatest wisdom.

Cleinias—What do you mean?

Athenian—At Athens there are tales preserved in writing which the virtue of your state, as I am informed, refuses to admit. They speak of the Gods in prose as well as verse, and the oldest of them tell of the origins of the heavens and of the world, and not far from the beginning of their story they proceed to narrate the birth of the Gods, and how after they were born they behaved to one another. Whether these stories have in other ways a good or a bad influence, I should not like to be severe upon them, because they are ancient; but, looking at them with reference to the duties of children to their parents, I cannot praise them, or think that they are useful, or at all true. Of the words of the ancients I have nothing more to say; and I should wish to say of them only what is pleasing to the Gods. But as to our younger generation and their wisdom, I cannot let them off when they do mischief. For do but mark the effect of their words: when you and I argue for the existence of the Gods, and produce the sun, moon, stars, and earth, claiming for them a divine being, if we would listen to the aforesaid philosophers we should say that they are earth and stones only, which can have no care at all of human affairs, and that all religion is a cooking up of words and a make-believe. ...

Cleinias—What a dreadful picture, Stranger, have you given, and how great is the injury which is thus inflicted on young men to the ruin both of states and families!

Athenian—True, Cleinias; but then what should the lawgiver do when this evil is of long standing? should he only rise up in the state and threaten all mankind, proclaiming that if they will not say and think that the Gods are such as the law ordains (and this may be extended generally to the honorable, the just, and to all the highest things, and to all that relates to virtue and vice), and if they will not make their actions conform to the copy which the law gives them, then he who refuses to obey the law shall die, or suffer stripes and bonds, or privation of citizenship, or in some cases be punished by loss of property and exile? Should he not rather, when he is making laws for men, at the same time infuse the spirit of persuasion into his words, and mitigate the severity of them as far as he can?

Cleinias—Why, Stranger, if such persuasion be at all possible, then a legislator who has anything in him ought never to weary of persuading men; he ought to leave nothing unsaid in support of the ancient opinion that there are Gods, and of all those other truths which you were just now mentioning; he ought to support the law and also art, and acknowledge that both alike exist by nature, and no less than nature, if they are the creations of mind in accordance with right reason, as you appear to me to maintain, and I am disposed to agree with you in thinking.

Athenian—Yes, my enthusiastic Cleinias; but are not these things when spoken to a multitude hard to be understood, not to mention that they take up a dismal length of time?

Cleinias—Why, Stranger, shall we, whose patience failed not when drinking or music were the themes of discourse, weary now of discoursing about the Gods, and about Divine things? And the greatest help to rational legislation is that the laws when once written down are always at rest; they can be put to the test at any future time, and therefore, if on first hearing they seem difficult, there is no reason for apprehension about them, because any man however dull can go over them and consider them again and again; nor if they are tedious but useful, is there any reason or religion, as it seems to me, in any man refusing to maintain the principles of them to the utmost of his power.

Megillus—Stranger, I like what Cleinias is saying.

Athenian—Yes, Megillus, and we should do as he proposes; for if impious discourses were not scattered, as I may say, throughout the world, there would have been no need for any vindication of the existence of the Gods—but seeing that they are spread far and wide, such arguments are needed; and who should come to the rescue of the greatest laws, when they are being undermined by bad men, but the legislator himself?

Megillus—There is no more proper champion of them.

Athenian—Well, then, tell me, Cleinias,—for I must ask you to be my partner,—does not he who talks in this way conceive fire and water and earth and air to be the first elements of all things? these he calls nature, and out of these he supposes the soul to be formed afterwards; and this is not a mere conjecture of ours about his meaning, but is what he really means.

Cleinias—Very true.

Athenian—Then, by Heaven, we have discovered the source of this vain opinion of all those physical investigators; and I would have you examine their arguments with the utmost care, for their impiety is a very serious matter; they not only make a bad and mistaken use of argument, but they lead away the minds of others: that is my opinion of them.

Cleinias—You are right, but I should like to know how this happens.

Athenian—I fear that the argument may seem singular.

Cleinias—Do not hesitate, Stranger; I see that you are afraid of such a discussion carrying you beyond the limits of legislation. But if there be no other way of showing our agreement in the belief that there are Gods, of whom the law is said now to approve, let us take this way, my good sir.

Athenian—Then I suppose that I must repeat the singular argument of those who manufacture the soul according to their own impious notions; they affirm that which is the first cause of the generation and destruction of all things, to be not first, but last, and that which is last to be first, and hence they have fallen into error about the true nature of the Gods.

Cleinias—Still I do not understand you.

Athenian—Nearly all of them, my friends, seem to be ignorant of the nature and power of the soul, especially in what relates to her origin: they do not know that she is among the first of things, and before all bodies, and is the chief author of their changes and transpositions. And if this is true, and if the soul is older than the body, must not the things which are of the soul's kindred be of necessity prior to those which appertain to the body?

Cleinias—Certainly.

Athenian—Then thought and attention and mind and art and law will be prior to that which is hard and soft and heavy and light; and the great and primitive works and actions will be works of art; they will be the first, and after them will come nature and works of nature, which however is a wrong term for men to apply to them; these will followand will be under the government of art and mind.

Cleinias—But why is the word 'nature' wrong?

Athenian—Because those who use the term mean to say that nature is the first creative power; but if the soul turned out to be the first primeval element, and not fire or air, then in the truest sense and beyond other things the soul may be said to exist by nature; and this would be true if you proved that the soul is older than the body, but not otherwise.

Cleinias—You are quite right.

Athenian—Shall we, then, take this as the next point to which our attention should be directed?

Cleinias—By all means.

Athenian—Come, then, and if ever we are to call upon the Gods, let us call upon them now in all seriousness to come to the demonstration of their own existence. And so holding fast to the rope we will venture upon the depths of the argument. When questions of this sort are asked of me, my safest answer would appear to be as follows:—Someone says to me, 'O Stranger, are all things at rest and nothing in motion, or is the exact opposite of this true, or are some things in motion and others at rest?'— To this I shall reply that some things are in motion and others at rest....

Athenian—Everything which is thus changing and moving is in process of generation; only when at rest has it real existence, but when passing into another state it is destroyed utterly. Have we not mentioned all motions that there are, and comprehended them under their kinds and numbered them with the exception, my friends, of two?

Cleinias—Which are they?

Athenian—Just the two, with which our present inquiry is concerned.

Cleinias—Speak plainer.

Athenian—I suppose that our inquiry has reference to the soul?

Cleinias—Very true.

Athenian—Let us assume that there is a motion able to move other things, but not to move itself;—that is one kind; and there is another kind which can move itself as well as other things, working in composition and decomposition, by increase and diminution and generation and destruction,—that is also one of the many kinds of motion.

Cleinias—Granted.

Athenian—And we will assume that which is moved by other, and is changed by other, to be the ninth, and that which changes itself and others, and is coincident with every action and every passion, and is the true principle of change and motion in all that is,—that we shall be inclined to call the tenth.

Cleinias—Certainly.

Athenian—And which of these ten motions ought we to prefer as being the mightiest and most efficient?

Cleinias—I must say that the motion which is able to move itself is ten thousand times superior to all the others.

Athenian—Very good; but may I make one or two corrections in what I have been saying?

Cleinias—What are they?

Athenian—When I spoke of the tenth sort of motion, that was not quite correct.

Cleinias—What was the error?

Athenian—According to the true order, the tenth was really the first in generation and power; then follows the second, which was strangely enough termed the ninth by us.

Cleinias—What do you mean?

Athenian—I mean this: when one thing changes another, and that another, of such will there be any primary changing element? How can a thing which is moved by another ever be the beginning of change? Impossible. But when the self-moved changes another, and that again another, and thus thousands upon tens of thousands of bodies are set in motion, must not the principle of all this motion be the change of the self-moving principle?

Cleinias—Very true, and I quite agree.

Athenian—Or, to put the question in another way, making answer to ourselves:—If, as most of these philosophers have the audacity to affirm, all things were at rest in one mass, which of the above-mentioned principles of motion would first spring up among them?

5   Cleinias—Clearly, the self-moving; for there could be no change in them arising out of any external cause; the change must first take place in themselves.

Athenian—Then we must say that self-motion being the origin of all motions, and the first which arises among things at rest as well as among
10   things in motion, is the eldest and mightiest principle of change, and that which is changed by another and yet moves another is second.

QUESTIONS TO CONSIDER

- Cleinias supplies two arguments for the existence of the gods at the outset of this reading. Summarize the two. What do you think: are these good arguments?

- According to the Athenian, what is the source of the materialists' error regarding matter and the gods?

- Between the two main types of motion, one able to move other things but not itself and one able to also move itself, which would the Athenian take as being prior? What sort of mover presents itself as a better explanation of the origins of the universe: a self-mover, or something which must be moved by something else?

- What is the obvious answer to the question: "if all things were at rest in one mass, which of these principles would first spring up among them"?

DUALISM

RENÉ DESCARTES—MEDITATIONS

V Of the Essence of Material Things; and Again of God: That He Exists

1. Several other questions remain for consideration respecting the attributes of God and my own nature or mind. I will, however, on some

other occasion perhaps resume the investigation of these. Meanwhile, as I have discovered what must be done and what avoided to arrive at the knowledge of truth, what I have chiefly to do is to essay to emerge from the state of doubt in which I have for some time been, and to discover whether anything can be known with certainty regarding material objects.

2. But before considering whether such objects as I conceive exist without me, I must examine their ideas in so far as these are to be found in my consciousness and discover which of them are distinct and which confused.

3. In the first place, I distinctly imagine that quantity which the philosophers commonly call continuous, or the extension in length, breadth, and depth that is in this quantity, or rather in the object to which it is attributed. Further, I can enumerate in it many diverse parts, and attribute to each of these all sorts of sizes, figures, situations, and local motions; and, in fine, I can assign to each of these motions all degrees of duration.

4. And I not only distinctly know these things when I thus consider them in general; but besides, by a little attention, I discover innumerable particulars respecting figures, numbers, motion, and the like, which are so evidently true, and so accordant with my nature, that when I now discover them I do not so much appear to learn anything new, as to call to remembrance what I before knew, or for the first time to remark what was before in my mind, but to which I had not hitherto directed my attention.

5. And what I here find of most importance is, that I discover in my mind innumerable ideas of certain objects, which cannot be esteemed pure negations, although perhaps they possess no reality beyond my thought, and which are not framed by me though it may be in my power to think, or not to think them, but possess true

"I no less find the idea of a God in my consciousness than that of any figure or number whatever."

and immutable natures of their own. As, for example, when I imagine a triangle, although there is not perhaps and never was in any place in the universe apart from my thought one such figure, it remains true nevertheless that this figure possesses a certain determinate nature, form, or essence, which is immutable and eternal, and not framed by me, nor in any degree dependent on my thought; as appears from the circumstance, that diverse properties of the triangle may be demonstrated, viz, that its three angles are equal to two right, that its greatest side is subtended by its greatest angle, and the like, which, whether I will or not, I now clearly discern to belong to it, although before I did not at all think of them, when, for the first time, I imagined a triangle, and which accordingly cannot be said to have been invented by me.

6. Nor is it a valid objection to allege, that perhaps this idea of a triangle came into my mind by the medium of the senses, through my having. seen bodies of a triangular figure; for I am able to form in thought an innumerable variety of figures with regard to which it cannot be supposed that they were ever objects of sense, and I can nevertheless demonstrate diverse properties of their nature no less than of the triangle, all of which are assuredly true since I clearly conceive them: and they are therefore something, and not mere negations; for it is highly evident that all that is true is something, truth being identical with existence]; and I have already fully shown the truth of the principle, that whatever is clearly and distinctly known is true. And although this had not been demonstrated, yet the nature of my mind is such as to compel me to assert to what I clearly conceive while I so conceive it; and I recollect that even when I still strongly adhered to the objects of sense, I reckoned among the number of the most certain truths those I clearly conceived relating to figures, numbers, and other matters that pertain to arithmetic and geometry, and in general to the pure mathematics.

7. But now if because I can draw from my thought the idea of an object, it follows that all I clearly and distinctly apprehend to pertain to this object, does in truth belong to it, may I not from this derive an argument for the existence of God? It is certain that I no less find the idea of a God in my consciousness, that is the idea of a being supremely perfect, than that of any figure or number whatever: and I know with not less clearness and distinctness that an actual and] eternal existence pertains to his nature than that all which is demonstrable of any figure or number really belongs to the nature of that figure or number; and, therefore, although all the conclusions of the preceding Meditations were false, the existence of

God would pass with me for a truth at least as certain as I ever judged any truth of mathematics to be.

8. Indeed such a doctrine may at first sight appear to contain more sophistry than truth. For, as I have been accustomed in every other matter to distinguish between existence and essence, I easily believe that the existence can be separated from the essence of God, and that thus God may be conceived as not actually existing. But, nevertheless, when I think of it more attentively, it appears that the existence can no more be separated from the essence of God, than the idea of a mountain from that of a valley, or the equality of its three angles to two right angles, from the essence of a rectilinear] triangle; so that it is not less impossible to conceive a God, that is, a being supremely perfect, to whom existence is wanting, or who is devoid of a certain perfection, than to conceive a mountain without a valley.

9. But though, in truth, I cannot conceive a God unless as existing, any more than I can a mountain without a valley, yet, just as it does not follow that there is any mountain in the world merely because I conceive a mountain with a valley, so likewise, though I conceive God as existing, it does not seem to follow on that account that God exists; for my thought imposes no necessity on things; and as I may imagine a winged horse, though there be none such, so I could perhaps attribute existence to God, though no God existed.

10. But the cases are not analogous, and a fallacy lurks under the semblance of this objection: for because I cannot conceive a mountain without a valley, it does not follow that there is any mountain or valley in existence, but simply that the mountain or valley, whether they do or do not exist, are inseparable from each other; whereas, on the other hand, because I cannot conceive God unless as existing, it follows that existence is inseparable from him, and therefore that he really exists: not that this is brought about by my thought, or that it imposes any necessity on things, but, on the contrary, the necessity which lies in the thing itself, that is, the necessity of the existence of God, determines me to think in this way: for it is not in my power to conceive a God without existence, that is, a being supremely perfect, and yet devoid of an absolute perfection, as I am free to imagine a horse with or without wings.

11. Nor must it be alleged here as an objection, that it is in truth necessary to admit that God exists, after having supposed him to possess all perfections, since existence is one of them, but that my original supposition was not necessary; just as it is not necessary to think that all quadrilateral figures can be inscribed in the circle, since, if I supposed this, I should be constrained to admit that the rhombus, being a figure of four sides, can be therein inscribed, which, however, is manifestly false. This objection is, I say, incompetent; for although it may not be necessary that I shall at any time entertain the notion of Deity, yet each time I happen to think of a first and sovereign being, and to draw, so to speak, the idea of him from the storehouse of the mind, I am necessitated to attribute to him all kinds of perfections, though I may not then enumerate them all, nor think of each of them in particular. And this necessity is sufficient, as soon as I discover that existence is a perfection, to cause me to infer the existence of this first and sovereign being; just as it is not necessary that I should ever imagine any triangle, but whenever I am desirous of considering a rectilinear figure composed of only three angles, it is absolutely necessary to attribute those properties to it from which it is correctly inferred that its three angles are not greater than two right angles, although perhaps I may not then advert to this relation in particular. But when I consider what figures are capable of being inscribed in the circle, it is by no means necessary to hold that all quadrilateral figures are of this number; on the contrary, I cannot even imagine such to be the case, so long as I shall be unwilling to accept in thought aught that I do not clearly and distinctly conceive; and consequently there is a vast difference between false suppositions, as is the one in question, and the true ideas that were born with me, the first and chief of which is the idea of God. For indeed I discern on many grounds that this idea is not factitious depending simply on my thought, but that it is the representation of a true and immutable nature: in the first place because I can conceive no other being, except God, to whose essence existence necessarily] pertains; in the second, because it is impossible to conceive two or more gods of this kind; and it being supposed that one such God exists, I clearly see that he must have existed from all eternity, and will exist to all eternity; and finally, because I apprehend many other properties in God, none of which I can either diminish or change.

QUESTIONS TO CONSIDER

- What is the gist of the argument Descartes presents here, beginning roughly with section seven? With what, exactly, does the argument begin? How does it conclude? To what does it conclude, by Descartes' account?

- Descartes himself raises an objection to his own argument. What is the objection, and how does he respond to it?

ARISTOTLE AND THOMAS AQUINAS

ARISTOTLE—PHYSICS

2—3

Having defined these things, let us consider the causes: both what they are and how many: for since this inquiry is for the sake of knowledge, and we do not think that we know anything until we understand 'why' it is so (and this is to have a grasp of its first cause,) we must do the same as regards generation and corruption and every sort of physical change, so that, knowing their principles, we may try to refer each of those things that we seek to them.

> *"We do not think that we know anything until we understand why it is so."*

In one way, then, a cause is said to be that from which something comes into being, and which remains, for example, bronze is the cause of the statue, silver of the bowl, as well as the genera of these.

In another way, cause is the form or the paradigm, that is, the definition of the essence [of a thing] and its genus (for example, the form of the octave is two to one, and in general, number), as well as the parts which are contained in the definition.

Further, cause is said to be the first principle of change or of coming to rest, for example, an advisor is [such] a cause, a father is a cause of his child, and, in general, the maker is the cause of that which is made and that which brings about a change is the cause of that which is changed.

Again, cause is the end, that is, that for the sake of which, for example, health is a cause of walking: for why does he walk? We answer, 'in order to be healthy', and having said this, we think that we have given the cause. So it is among such things as are for the sake of the end but are intermediate, for example, losing weight, or purging, or medicines, or instruments, are for the sake of health: for all these are for the sake of the end, yet they differ from each other insofar as some of them are activities, while others are instruments. 'Cause', then, has about this many meanings.

Yet, since 'cause' has many meanings, it happens that there may be several non-accidental causes of the same thing, for example, the art of the sculptor and bronze are both causes of the statue as a statue (and not as something else) but not in the same way: one is a cause as matter, while the other as that from which the change began.

And some things are causes of each other, for example, work is the cause of good bodily condition, and good bodily condition is a cause of work, yet not in the same way: one is the end, while the other is the principle of motion.

Again, the same thing can be the cause of contraries: for that which when present is the cause of some effect is sometimes said by us to be the cause of a contrary effect when it is absent, for example, we say that the cause of the shipwreck is the absence of the pilot, whose presence is the cause of its safety.

And all the causes just mentioned fall into four clear groups. For letters are the causes of syllables, the material of artificial things, fire and such things of bodies, parts of the whole, and premises of the conclusion as that from which something comes. And of these, some are causes as subjects, for example, parts, while others are causes as essences: the whole, and composition, and form. But seed, a physician, an advisor, and in general the maker, are all causes as a principle of change, or of coming to rest, or of motion. Still others are causes as the end, or what is good for other things: for that for the sake of which is what is best, and the end of the other things; and it makes no difference here whether we say the end is the good itself or the apparent good. Such, then, and so many are the types of cause.

The modes of the causes, however, are many, though they are fewer when summarized. For 'cause' is said in many ways, and one of those which are of a similar type may be prior or posterior to another, for example, the physician and the artist are causes of health, the double and number are causes of the octave, and whatever contains is related to the particulars in this way. Causes, as well as their genera, are also said accidentally, for example, in one way Polyclitus is the cause of the statue and in another way the sculptor is the cause, since the sculptor happens to be Polyclitus. Similarly, those things which contain what is accidental are said to be causes [in this way], as if man, or, in general, animal, were the cause of the statue. And some of these accidents are more or less remote than others, as if the white or the musician were said to be the cause of the statue.

But all the causes, both proper and accidental, are also said to be either potential or actual, for example, the builder who is about to build a house, or the builder who is building one now.

The like may also be said about the effects brought about by these causes, for example, about this particular statue, or about a statue, or, in general, about an image, or about this brass, or about brass, or, in general, about matter; and this holds for accidents also. And all these may be said in combination, for example, not Polyclitus, nor a sculptor, but Polyclitus the sculptor.

All these [modes], however, are six in number, and each is said in two ways: for [they are said] either as a particular or as a genus, as accidental or as the genus of an accident, or in combination or singly—and all these either as actual or as potential. And the difference is this: that causes which are actual and particular exist or do not exist at the same time as their effects, for example, this man who heals exists at the same time as the one who is being healed, and this builder exists at the same time as the building which is being built. But this is not always so for potential causes: for the house and the builder do not cease to exist at the same time.

Now one ought always to consider the highest cause here, as with other things, (for example, a man builds because he is a builder, but he is a builder according to the art of building: this, then, is the prior cause; and so it is with every other thing.)

Further, one ought to consider general [causes] of general [effects], and particular [causes] of particular [effects], for example, a sculptor is the cause of a statue, and this sculptor is the cause of this statue. And one ought also to consider potential [causes] of potential [effects], and actual [causes] of actual [effects].

Let this be a sufficient description, then, of how many causes there are and in what ways they are causes.

QUESTIONS TO CONSIDER

- Why does Aristotle take up causes next? What is the relation between the question why is it so? and a cause?

- List and describe the four causes. Give examples of each. Which of the four causes are also principles of nature? Which cause is matter? Which might be called an agent (acting) cause? What do we call that which brings about an end?

- Can a single effect have more than one cause? If so, give an example. If not, why not? Can causes cause each other? Can the same thing be a cause of contrary effects?

II—8

First, then, we must say why nature is one of the causes which [act] for the sake of something, then how necessity is found in physical things: for all come back to this cause, saying that since what is hot is naturally a thing of this kind, as is what is cold, and so on, certain things necessarily are and will necessarily come about: for even though they refer to another cause (one [speaking of] friendship and strife, another, mind), yet they merely mention it, and then dismiss it.

There is a doubt: what prevents nature from operating, not for the sake of something and because it is better to do so, but just as it rains, not that corn may grow, but of necessity (for what is drawn up must be cooled; and what has been cooled, upon becoming water, must fall, and it

---

214

happens that the corn grows as a consequence of this), and similarly, if the corn on the ground were spoiled, it does not rain in order that it might be spoiled, but this is accidental—so that what prevents the parts in nature also coming about in this way, for example, that our teeth should come up of necessity, the front ones sharp and able to tear, and the back teeth broad and able to grind the food—since they did not come about for the sake of this, but it merely happened? And similarly for the other parts of the body which seem to be for the sake of something. And whenever all such things came about as if for the sake of something, they survived, being suitably put together by chance, whereas the things which were not put together in this way died off, and continue to die off, as Empedocles says of the 'man-faced offspring of oxen'.

"That nature is a cause, then, and that it acts for the sake of something, is clear."

This, then, (and any other such), is the argument which might cause someone difficulties.

Yet it is impossible that things should be in this way. For these things, and everything which is produced by nature, come about either always or usually in the same way, whereas this is not so with anything coming about by luck or chance. For it does not seem to be due to luck or coincidence that it frequently rains in the winter, but in the summer, nor heat in the summer, but in the winter. Now if these things seem either due to chance or for the sake of something, but they are not due to chance or coincidence, they must be for the sake of something. But all such things exist by nature, as is acknowledged by those who say these things. Therefore, there is 'that for the sake of which' among things which come about and exist by nature.

Further, among things in which there is some end, what is prior and what follows that are for the sake of that end. As it happens, so it is naturally [designed to occur], and as it is naturally [designed to occur], so it happens, if nothing prevents it. But it happens for the sake of something, and therefore it is naturally [designed to be] for the sake of this. For example, if a house were among the things which come about by nature, it would come about by nature in the same way as it now comes about by art: and if things which come about by nature not only came about by nature but also by art, they would come about in the same way as they come about by nature. The one, then, is for the sake of the other. And, in general, art partly completes what nature cannot complete, and partly imitates nature. If, then, artificial things are for the sake of something, so also are natural things. For the latter [stages] are related to the former in the same way in both natural and artificial things.

This is even more clear in the other animals, which make things neither by art nor by inquiry or deliberation. And so some wonder whether spiders, and ants, and animals of this sort, work by intellect or by something else. But to the one who proceeds gradually in this way it is apparent that even in plants certain things come about for the sake of the end, for example, leaves are for the sake of protecting the fruit. And so, if the swallow makes her nest, and the spider her web, both by nature and for the sake of something, and if plants make leaves for the sake of the fruit, and if roots grow, not up, but down, for the sake of nourishment, it is clear that there is a cause of this sort among things which come about and exist by nature. And since nature is twofold, matter and form, and [form] is the end, and the others are for the sake of the end, this [the form] will be the cause, and 'that for the sake of which'.

Now mistakes occur even among artificial things (for a grammarian has not written correctly and a doctor has not administered the medicine correctly), so that this may clearly also happen among natural things. If, then, there are some artificial things which, rightly made, are for the sake of something, but which, mistakenly made, were produced for the sake of something, which was not attained, the same will also occur among natural things, and monstrosities would be mistakes with respect to that for the sake of which [it was done]. In the original combinations of things, then, the 'offspring of oxen', if they were unable to attain a certain limit, or end, must have come about from the corruption of some principle, as [such] things now come about from the corruption of seed.

Further, the seed must have come about first, and not the animals all at once: and the expression "first the whole-natured" referred to the seed.

Again, we also find 'that for the sake of which' among plants, though it is less distinct. Would there have come about in plants, then, 'olive-headed offspring of vines', much as the 'man-faced offspring of oxen'?

But this is ridiculous, yet it must have, since it also occurred among the animals.

Again, things must have come about by chance among the seeds of things. But he who asserts this completely destroys both natural things and nature itself: for those things are natural which are continuously moved by reason of a certain principle within themselves, and so arrive at a specific end. Yet the same thing does not come about by reason of each principle, nor does any chance thing, but the same [principle] always arrives at the same end, unless it is impeded.

But 'that for the sake of which' [the end], and what is for the sake of this [the means], may also come about by chance, for example, we say that a stranger came by chance, paid the ransom, and left, when he did so as if he came for the sake of this, yet did not actually come for this reason. And this is accidental (for chance is found among accidental causes, as we said earlier), but when this comes about either always or usually in this way, then it is neither accidental, nor by chance: and among natural things it always comes about in this way, unless something prevents it.

It is also absurd to think that things do not come about for the sake of something unless the agent is seen to deliberate. For neither does art deliberate: and if the ship-building art were in the wood, it would make [the same thing] by nature. So that if there is 'that for the sake of which' in art, this will also be found in nature. And this is especially clear when someone heals himself: for nature is like this.

That nature is a cause, then, and that it acts for the sake of something, is clear.

QUESTIONS TO CONSIDER

- As to whether the universe has a point or not, which of these alternatives did the philosophers prior to Aristotle tend to choose?
- How might one explain the relation between rain falling and wheat growing, or the structure of our teeth, in terms of necessity? How might the same be explained in terms of purpose?

- Aristotle next describes a position which has gained popular support in our time. What is the modern counterpart of the position he summarizes here?

- One reason why someone might think that natural occurrences come about by chance is that certain things happen outside the normal course of things (such as birth defects, for example.) How does Aristotle use this very fact to prove that, given these errors in nature, nature must act for the sake of an end?

THOMAS AQUINAS—THE PRINCIPLES OF NATURE

3—What are the four types of cause?

From what has been said it is clear that there are three principles of nature: namely, matter, form, and privation. But these [principles] are not sufficient for generation. For whatever is in potency cannot reduce itself to act: for example, that bronze which is in potency to a statue does not
5 make itself into a statue, but requires some worker, so that the form of the statue might be brought forth from potency into act. Nor is the form able to bring itself forth from potency into act (and I speak of the form of what is generated, which *"The end is the cause of causes."* we say is the term of
10 generation); for the form only exists in the thing made: but what acts is in coming to be while the thing comes about. Therefore it is necessary that there be some principle, in addition to matter and form, which acts, and this is called the efficient cause, or the mover, or the agent, or that from which there is a beginning of motion.

15 And since, as Aristotle says in the second book of the Metaphysics, everything which acts only acts by intending something, it is necessary that there be a fourth [principle], namely, that which is intended by what acts: and this is called the end. It must also be noted that, although every agent, both natural and voluntary, intends an end, nevertheless it does
20 not follow that every agent knows the end, or deliberates about the end. Knowing the end is necessary among those [agents] whose actions are not determinate, but are related to opposite things, as with voluntary agents; and thus it is necessary that these [agents] know the end through which they might determine their actions. But with natural agents the

actions are determinate: whence it is not necessary [that they] choose the means to the end. And Avicenna gives an example about the lute-player: it is not necessary that he deliberate about each and every striking of chords, since those strikings are determined with him; otherwise there
5   would be a delay in the strikings, which would be dissonant. But it seems [to pertain] more to the voluntary agent, that he deliberate, than to the natural agent. And so it is clear, by [an argument] *a maiori*, that if a voluntary agent, to which it seems [to pertain] more [to deliberate] does not deliberate sometimes, therefore neither does a natural agent.
10   Therefore it is possible for a natural agent to intend an end without deliberation: and this 'intention' is nothing other than to have a natural inclination to that [end]. From what has been said, it is clear that there are four causes: namely, the material cause, the efficient [or agent] cause, the formal cause, and the final cause.

15   Now, although principle and cause are [sometimes] interchangeable, as is said in the fourth book of the Metaphysics, nevertheless, Aristotle gives four causes and three principles in the Physics. For he takes causes both for extrinsic and intrinsic principles. But matter and form are said to be intrinsic to a thing, because they are parts which make something up;
20   while the efficient and final causes are said to be extrinsic, since they are outside the thing. But he takes principles only for intrinsic causes. (Privation is not named among the causes, since it is an accidental principle, as was said. And when we say there are four causes, we understand this to be about those which are *per se* causes, to which all *per*
25   *accidens* causes, however, are reduced, since everything which is *per accidens* is reduced to that which is *per se*.)

QUESTIONS TO CONSIDER

- Can change be explained in terms of the three principles alone? What cause is needed beyond the material, formal, and agent?

- Some agents do not deliberate about the purpose of their actions. Does it follow that they do not intend those purposes?

- What do matter and form have in common as causes? What do the agent and the end have in common as causes? What sort of cause are elements?

4—On the coincidence and priority of the causes.

Having seen that there are four kinds of cause, we must also know that it is not impossible for the same thing to have many causes: for example, a statue, the cause of which is bronze and an artist: the artist as the efficient cause and bronze as the matter. Nor is it impossible for the same thing to be a cause of contrary things: for example, the pilot is the cause of the safety of the ship as well as of its sinking: of its sinking through his absence and of its safety through his presence, as the Philosopher [Aristotle] says in the second book of the Physics.

It must also be noted that it is not impossible for the same thing to be both the cause and what is caused [the effect] with respect to the same thing: but in different ways: just as walking is sometimes the cause of health as an efficient cause, but health is a cause of walking as a final cause: for walking is sometimes the [agent] cause of health, as well as for the sake of health. Also, the body is the matter of the soul, and the soul is the form of the body.

Now the efficient cause is called a cause with respect to the end [final cause], since the end is actual only through the activity of the agent: but the end [final cause] is called the cause of the efficient cause, since the efficient cause only acts through intending the end. Whence the efficient cause is the cause of that which is the end: for example, walking, that there may be health; nevertheless, it does not make the end to be an end, and therefore it is not a cause of the causality of the end, that is, it does not make the end a final cause: for example, the doctor causes health to be in act, but he does not make health an end.

And the end is not a cause of that which is the efficient cause but makes that which is the efficient cause to be an efficient cause: for health does not make a doctor a doctor (and I speak of the health which comes about by the activity of the doctor,) but makes the doctor an efficient cause. Whence the end [final cause] is a cause of the causality of the efficient cause, since it makes the efficient cause an efficient cause: and in the same way, it makes the matter, matter and the form, form, since matter only receives a form for the sake of some end, and form perfects matter only through an end. Hence it is said that the end is the cause of causes, since it is the cause of the causality in all the causes. Matter is also said to be a cause of form, insofar as form can only exist in matter; and similarly form is a cause of matter, insofar as matter only has being in act through form. For matter and form are said relatively to each other, as is said in the second book of the *Physics*.

QUESTIONS TO CONSIDER

- How can the same thing have more than one cause? How can the same thing be both cause and effect?
- Which of the causes is the cause of all the others?

ARISTOTLE—ON THE SOUL

2—4

It follows that first of all we must treat of nutrition and reproduction, for the nutritive soul is found along with all the others and is the most primitive and widely distributed power of soul, being indeed that one in virtue of which all are said to have life. The acts in which it manifests itself are reproduction and the use of food—reproduction, I say, because for any living thing that has reached its normal development and which is unmutilated, and whose mode of generation is not spontaneous, the most natural act is the production of another like itself, an animal producing an animal, a plant a plant, in order that, as far as its nature allows, it may partake in the eternal and divine. That is the goal towards which all things strive, that for the sake of which they do whatsoever their nature renders possible. The phrase 'for the sake of which' is ambiguous; it may mean either (a) the end to achieve which, or (b) the being in whose interest, the act is done. Since then no living thing is able to partake in what is eternal and divine by uninterrupted continuance (for nothing perishable can forever remain one and the same), it tries to achieve that end in the only way possible to it, and success is possible in varying degrees; so it remains not indeed as the self-same individual but continues its existence in something like itself—not numerically but specifically one.

ARISTOTLE—POLITICS

1—8

In like manner we may infer that, after the birth of animals, plants exist for their sake, and that the other animals exist for the sake of man, the tame for use and food, the wild, if not all at least the greater part of them, for food, and for the provision of clothing and various instruments. Now
5   if nature makes nothing incomplete, and nothing in vain, the inference must be that she has made all animals for the sake of man.

What claim does Aristotle make regarding the end (that for the sake of which) for which all living things strive? Would Aristotle be thereby required to claim that all living things are intelligent?

10   Is the end of plants something belonging to the plants, by Aristotle's account? What of the end of animals? What does this suggest about Aristotle's conception of the universe as a whole?

QUESTIONS TO CONSIDER

- In these two selections, Aristotle is making a case that the final cause— purpose—extends beyond the good of the individual. This is called 'extrinsic finality'. What case does he make that natural things act for an end which is greater than themselves?

ARISTOTLE—METAPHYSICS

XII—7

On such a principle, then, depend the heavens and the world of nature. And it is a life such as the best which we enjoy and enjoy for but a
15   short time (for it is ever in this state, which we cannot be), since its actuality is also pleasure. (And for this reason are waking, perception, and thinking most pleasant, and hopes and memories are so on account of these.) And thinking in itself deals with that which is best in itself, and that which is thinking in the fullest sense with that which is best in the

fullest sense. And thought thinks on itself because it shares the nature of the object of thought; for it becomes an object of thought in coming into contact with and thinking its objects, so that thought and the object of thought are the same. For that which is capable of receiving the object of thought, i.e., the essence, is thought. But it is active when it possesses this object. Therefore the possession rather than the receptivity is the divine element which thought seems to contain, and the act of contemplation is what is most pleasant and best. If, then, God is always in that good state in which we sometimes are, this compels our wonder; and if in a better this compels it yet more. And God is in a better state. And life also belongs to God; for the actuality of thought is life, and God is that actuality; and God's self-dependent actuality is life most good and eternal. We say therefore that God is a living being, eternal, most good, so that life and duration continuous and eternal belong to God; for this is God.

"God is a living being, eternal and most good, so that life and duration continuous and eternal belong to God—for this is God."

Those who suppose, as the Pythagoreans and Speusippus do, that supreme beauty and goodness are not present in the beginning, because the beginnings both of plants and of animals are causes, but beauty and completeness are in the effects of these, are wrong in their opinion. For the seed comes from other individuals which are prior and complete, and the first thing is not seed but the complete being, e.g., we must say that before the seed there is a man,-not the man produced from the seed, but another from whom the seed comes.

It is clear then from what has been said that there is a substance which is eternal and unmovable and separate from sensible things. It has been shown also that this substance cannot have any magnitude but is without parts and indivisible (for it produces movement through infinite time, but nothing finite has infinite power; and, while every magnitude is either infinite or finite, it cannot, for the above reason, have finite magnitude, and it cannot have infinite magnitude because there is no infinite magnitude at all). But it has also been shown that it is impassive and unalterable; for all the other changes are posterior to change of place.

- Is God beautiful? Is God good? Is God alive? Is God intelligent? Does God have a body? Does God ever change? What sort of arguments does Aristotle supply for his conclusions here?

THOMAS AQUINAS—SUMMA THEOLOGIAE

---

2 3—Does God exist?

OBJ 1: It seems that God does not exist; because if one of two contraries be infinite, the other would be altogether destroyed. But the word God means that He is infinite goodness. If, therefore, God existed, there would be no evil discoverable; but there is evil in the world. Therefore God does not exist.

OBJ 2: Further, it is superfluous to suppose that what can be accounted for by a few principles has been produced by many. But it seems that everything we see in the world can be accounted for by other principles, supposing God did not exist. For all natural things can be reduced to one principle which is nature; and all voluntary things can be reduced to one principle which is human reason, or will. Therefore there is no need to suppose God's existence.

On the contrary, it is said in the person of God: "I am Who am." (Exodus 3:14)

I answer that the existence of God can be proved in five ways.

The first and more manifest way is the argument from motion. It is certain, and evident to our senses, that in the world somethings are in motion. Now whatever is in motion is put in motion by another, for nothing can be in motion except it is in potentiality to that towards which it is in motion; whereas a thing moves inasmuch as it is in act. For motion is nothing else than the reduction of something from potentiality to actuality. But nothing can be reduced from potentiality to actuality,

---

except by something in a state of actuality. Thus that which is actually hot, as fire, makes wood, which is potentially hot, tobe actually hot, and thereby moves and changes it. Now it is not possible that the same thing should be at once in actuality

> *"The existence of God can be proved in five ways."*

and potentiality in the same respect, but only in different respects. For what is actually hot cannot simultaneously be potentially hot; but it is simultaneously potentially cold. It is therefore impossible that in the same respect and in the same way a thing should be both mover and moved, i.e., that it should move itself. Therefore, whatever is in motion must be put in motion by another. If that by which it is put in motion be itself put in motion, then this also must needs be put in motion by another, and that by another again. But this cannot goon to infinity, because then there would be no first mover, and, consequently, no other mover; seeing that subsequent movers move only inasmuch as they are put in motion by the first mover, as the staff moves only because it is put in motion by the hand. Therefore it is necessary to arrive at a first mover, put in motion by no other; and this everyone understands to be God.

The second way is from the nature of the efficient cause. In the world of sense we find there is an order of efficient causes. There is no case known (neither is it, indeed, possible) in which a thing is found to be the efficient cause of itself; for so it would be prior to itself, which is impossible. Now in efficient causes it is not possible to go on to infinity, because in all efficient causes following in order, the first is the cause of the intermediate cause, and the intermediate is the cause of the ultimate cause, whether the intermediate cause be several, or only one. Now to take away the cause is to take away the effect. Therefore, if there be no first cause among efficient causes, there will be no ultimate, nor any intermediate cause. But if in efficient causes it is possible to go on to infinity, there will be no first efficient cause, neither will there be an ultimate effect, nor any intermediate efficient causes; all of which is plainly false. Therefore it is necessary to admit a first efficient cause, to which everyone gives the name of God.

The third way is taken from possibility and necessity and runs thus. We find in nature things that are possible to be and not to be, since they are found to be generated, and to corrupt, and consequently, they are possible to be and not to be. But it is impossible for these always to exist, for that which is possible not to be at some time is not. Therefore, if everything is possible not to be, then at one time there could have been nothing in existence. Now if this were true, even now there would be nothing in existence, because that which does not exist only begins to exist by something already existing. Therefore, if at one time nothing was in existence, it would have been impossible for anything to have begun to exist; and thus even now nothing would be in existence—which is absurd. Therefore, not all beings are merely possible, but there must exist something the existence of which is necessary. But every necessary thing either has its necessity caused by another, or not. Now it is impossible to go on to infinity in necessary things which have their necessity caused by another, as has been already proved in regard to efficient causes. Therefore we cannot but postulate the existence of some being having of itself its own necessity, and not receiving it from another, but rather causing in others their necessity. This all men speak of as God.

The fourth way is taken from the gradation to be found in things. Among beings there are some more and some less good, true, noble and the like. But "more" and "less" are predicated of different things, according as they resemble in their different ways something which is the maximum, as a thing is said to be hotter according as it more nearly resembles that which is hottest; so that there is something which is truest, something best, something noblest and, consequently, something which is uttermost being, for those things that are greatest in truth are greatest in being, as it is written in De Metaphysica ii. Now the maximum in any genus is the cause of all in that genus; as fire, which is the maximum heat, is the cause of all hot things. Therefore there must also be something which is to all beings the cause of their being, goodness, and every other perfection; and this we call God.

The fifth way is taken from the governance of the world. We see that things which lack intelligence, such as natural bodies, act for an end, and this is evident from their acting always, or nearly always, in the same way, so as to obtain the best result. Hence it is plain that not fortuitously, but designedly, do they achieve their end. Now whatever lacks intelligence cannot move towards an end, unless it be directed by some being endowed with knowledge and intelligence, as the arrow is shot to its mark by the archer. Therefore some intelligent being exists by whom all natural things are directed to their end; and this being we call God.

Reply OBJ 1: As Augustine says (Enchiridion 11): "Since God is the highest good, He would not allow any evil to exist in His works, unless His omnipotence and goodness were such as to bring good even out of evil." This is part of the infinite goodness of God, that He should allow evil to exist, and out of it produce good.

Reply OBJ 2: Since nature works for a determinate end under the direction of a higher agent, whatever is done by nature must needs be traced back to God, as to its first cause. So also whatever is done voluntarily must also be traced back to some higher cause other than human reason or will, since these can change or fail; for all things that are changeable and capable of defect must be traced back to an immovable and self-necessary first principle, as was shown in the body of the Article.

QUESTIONS TO CONSIDER

- What two objections does Aquinas raise to the objection of God? Have we seen objections like these before?
- What is the starting point of each of the five ways? To what sort of God does each conclude?
- How does Aquinas respond to the two objections he initially raised?

8

ELEMENTS OF LOGIC

Logic is how philosophers go about their business. In the course of carefully reading and analyzing the arguments contained in this book, you will inevitably need to ask yourself about logic: what distinctions philosophers make, what distinguishes a good argument from a bad one, and so on. Some of those sorts of distinction are contained in the pages which follow.

UNIVOCAL | EQUIVOCAL | ANALOGOUS

Most commonly, when we use a single word to signify two concepts, or two things, we use the word in a univocal way (from the Latin, *univoce*, with a single voice). For example, when we use the word bear to describe both a polar bear and a grizzly, we use the word univocally. Both are
5 bears, and the word bear has the same meaning (the single voice of the Latin word univocal) in each case. This is not to say that a polar bear and a grizzly bear are the same—only that they are both bears. Examples could be multiplied: isosceles triangle and equilateral triangle are equally triangles, oak and aspen are both trees, salesman and accountant are both
10 occupations, and so on. This is the most common way in which we use words.

We use words in an equivocal way (from the Latin, *equivoce*, with an equal voice) when the same word is used to signify two entirely different concepts. This is quite possible. Since we give words their meanings (which is to say, we use vocal or written signs to bring to mind whatever
15 concepts we choose, as a group, to bring out,) it can very well happen(and it does) that the same sign is used to bring to mind very different concepts.

When we used the word bear above in a univocal way, we used it to
20 describe two different species of animal. The word bear, in that context,

228

had the same meaning, or signification. We can use the word bear, however, to signify things in an equivocal way as well—different context, different manner of signifying. For example, bear as describing an animal and bear as describing the act of carrying a load do not mean the same thing. Same word, differently used.

We cannot overemphasize the importance of seeing these distinctions as distinctions in the way we use words. There is no such thing as a univocal word, as such. A word may be used univocally; but it may then be used equivocally, or analogously. The simple fact is that words do have many different meaning and coming to realize this is one of the most important beginnings one can make in philosophy.

One might think at this point that the distinctions in the way in which we use words have been made. Either we use words with the same meaning, or not. If they have the same meaning, we use them univocally, otherwise they are being used equivocally. But there is still another distinction to be made. For we can see, in our usage of words, that we sometimes use words with different meanings, but consciously maintain some connection between one of the two meanings and another. Thus, when using the same word with different meanings, we can recognize that the meanings can be entirely different, or they can be related.

Words that are used analogously have meanings which differ, to be sure, but which retain a reasonable connection to one another none the less. In fact, usually there is a first meaning, to which an extended meaning is then related. The first meaning is called the prime analogate.

For example, one might use the word tree to describe, in a univocal manner, any number of species of certain types of plant. Oak, aspen, maple, birch, yew—all are trees. One might also use the word tree to describe an action taken by a hound dog when chasing a possum or other prey. Here, tree is a verb. The two meanings differ: a plant is not an action; yet the meanings are consciously related to one another. However much the action of treeing a possum has to do with cornering it, one crucial aspect of treeing is where it occurs: in a tree. The word tree, used to describe both the plant and the action, then, is being used in an analogous manner.

ESSENTIAL AND NON-ESSENTIAL

There are only a few ways in which a predicate (some descriptive term) can truly describe a subject. These ways of describing or ways of predicating (technically called predicables) fall out into two groups. Some are essential, others are non-essential.

5　Alpacas are mammals is an example of essential predication. What this simply means is that we are referring to some part of the essence of the thing. Essential predicates provide a direct answer to the question what is it. What is an alpaca? An alpaca is a mammal. The response supplies at least part of the answer to one of the most basic questions we ask: what
10　is that thing? In sum, then, essential predicates give a direct (though perhaps not complete) answer to the question what is it.

We know that Pomeranians and Great Danes are types of dog, but are they essentially the same animal? Pomeranians and Great Danes do differ greatly from one another, so much so that one might think they are
15　essentially different things. But even great and significant differences between things do not make them essentially different. Not all differences are essential: that is, not all differences serve to tell us what something is. The simple fact that Pomeranians are small dogs and Great Danes are large dogs is not enough to distinguish them from one another
20　in an essential way. We would say, rather, that such differences in size are accidental, not essential. In sum, then, non-essential predicates, however true, do not give a direct answer to the question what is it.

THE CATEGORIES

Speaking universally, the things we predicate (the things we use to describe other things, whether essentially or accidentally) fall out into ten
25　classes, or groups, which are called the predicaments or categories. The first and most fundamental distinction among the categories is rooted in the way they exist.

First, to exist in a subject means to be incapable of existing apart from that subject. For example, the quality of a thing which we call red is
30　incapable of existence apart from some subject. Red does not have

existence in its own right. It must exist in something in order to exist at all. Such things are called accidents.

At first glance, it might seem that everything exists in other things; but, upon reflection, we see that this could not possibly be so—for if there were no subjects for things to exist in, nothing would exist! Things which exist in their own right in this way, which do not rely upon another thing in which to exist, are called substances. Of course, substances do depend upon other things for their existence in certain ways. How could living things survive without other substances to eat, for instance? The point we wish to make, however, is that some things exist in others, they depend upon them, not for survival, but for being there in the first place.

The first of the categories, then, is substance. As we just noted, substances do not exist in other things, but they are themselves the basis for the existence of all else. Remember also that we are speaking here of substance as a category, as something which can be predicated, and hence of substance as a universal. Examples of substances abound, since all living and natural things are substances.

The second category is quantity. Within this category are contained such things as we normally associate with quantity, such as numbers and measures. But quantity is of two different sorts, corresponding to two different questions we ask concerning the quantity of a thing: for we ask both how much and how many. And just as it would be incorrect to ask concerning the number of people in a room how much are in the room?, so it would be incorrect to ask concerning a continuous quantity, such as a length, how many is it? The distinction between the questions is an indication of an underlying difference in the types of quantity: there are discrete quantities and continuous quantities. Discrete quantities are the how many of parts which are actually distinct from one another, while continuous quantities are the basis for the how much question we ask of parts which are not actually distinct.

The third category is quality. Less well-defined than the previous two categories, a direct translation of the Greek word Aristotle uses to name it, *to poion*, might be of what sort. What quality signifies is best seen in the four types into which it is immediately divided.

Some qualities are habits, or dispositions, such as the quality of being a smoker or an artist, others are abilities, or inabilities, such as sighted or blind, still others are sense qualities, such as sweet or white, and, finally, others are the shapes of substances, such as triangular or spherical.

5   Next is the category of relation, or reference to another. Relations occur only between two things. Examples are greater and smaller, parent and child, identical and similar. In each case, note that the relation entails a connection between one thing and another.

The fifth category is action, the doing of something to another. So, we
10   are not speaking of all actions, but only of transitive actions (you will find the grammatical distinction between transitive and intransitive verbs of use here). Further, since this sort of action is the doing of something to another, the category of action is associated with the category of relation (as well as with the category of being passive, which we take up now.)

15   The sixth category, being passive, necessarily implies that there is something which is acting, which is doing something. So, we have action, the doing of something to another, being passive, receiving the action done, and the relation established between the two. (Keep in mind that not all relations depend upon the categories of action and being passive;
20   some depend upon quantity, such as greater and taller.) An example of things which are connected as action, being passive, and relation is: cutting, the action, being cut, the being passive, and cutter, the relation between them.

Next come the two categories of when and where. Things are contained
25   in these groupings which answer the questions where is it and when is it. Do not confuse when and where with the quantities of place and time. A minute is a quantity: it tells us how much with respect to duration. In a minute tells us when something will occur. Similarly, an acre is a quantity: it tells us how much with respect to size. On that acre, on the other hand,
30   tells us where something is, and so it would be contained in the category of where.

The ninth category is position, that is, the order that the parts of a thing have. This is not position in the sense of location (for example, we might say someone's position is twenty miles west of town,) since that reduces to the category of where, but in the sense of the arrangement of bodily parts. Examples of positions are kneeling, laying down, upside-down, and so on. Note also that, in this context, verb-forms can express position and not action. To kneel upon is an action (to be knelt upon would be the being passive,) while the verb form derived from it describes the posture, or position, of kneeling.

Last among the categories is habit. (Note that we listed habit among the types of quality above. Here, we use the word in a different sense.) Though English usage frowns upon it, habit here means something like the having of something. This type of accident is peculiar to humans, insofar as only we can have things through acquisition.

In some sense, animals do have things: birds have feathers and mammals have fur, but these things are parts of their substances. Only humans have possessions which they acquire through reason and art. Thus, corresponding to the protection afforded a bird by feathers and a mammal by fur is clothing, which humans acquire through the arts of weaving and sewing. What animals have by nature humans possess by means of a special category, which is called habit. Examples of habits, then, are being clothed, armed (having weapons), wearing glasses, and so on.

SIMPLE OPPOSITION

At the very heart of human knowledge is our basic ability to see that this is not that—to distinguish one thing from another.

This recognition (that one thing is not another) is seen more clearly when we consider simple opposition. For when we try to understand the world around us, we often discover an opposition between the thing in question and other things. (This is not to say that all things are opposed to one another—some things are merely other.) There are a number of different ways in which one simple expression (we are not speaking of statements here) can be opposed to another. We will address three of them.

First, two simple expressions can be opposed by way of contradictory opposition. When such expressions contradict one another, one of them simply and entirely takes away what the other says. Contradictory opposition is based upon the absolute opposition between being and non-being. The contradictory opposite of alpaca would be that which says everything which alpaca does not say—the absolute opposite. In this case that would be non-alpaca, everything which is not an alpaca. This is the clearest and most complete type of opposition. Here there is no middle ground, as is sometimes found with other types of opposition. Every conceivable thing is either an alpaca or a non-alpaca. This, then, is characteristic of contradictory opposition: it divides all things into two in this absolute way. Such a division is sometimes called a dichotomy, from the Greek, meaning cut in two.

The next type of opposition is not as absolute. It is called privative opposition. While contradictory opposition is absolute, the opposition of being and non-being, this type of opposition is qualified: it is the opposition between being and nonbeing in a certain thing. While it seems obvious that there are beings which belong only to certain types of subjects (for example, only mammals have mammary glands,) what does it mean to speak of a non-being as restricted to a certain type of subject?

Actually, there are countless examples of such things, though we tend not to bring them to mind as examples of non-being.

Take, for instance, the sense of sight. Not all things are sighted, and it is obvious that sight can only exist in something which has eyes. So much, then, for a being which exists in some determinate subject. What is the opposite of sighted? Well, we should ask, what type of opposite are we interested in? Its contradictory would be non-sighted. Is there anything which represents the non-being of sight in things which have sight? Such a question at first sounds contradictory, but there is such a thing.

Let us consider a human being and a stone. A stone has no sight. Yet we do not, on that account, say that it is blind. Blindness cannot apply to a stone. Why is this? Because blindness is conceived as the lack of sight in a thing which has the natural ability to see. Blindness is conceptually different from not seeing. A stone does not see. Neither does a person who is blind. Yet we do not say of both that they are blind. Blindness is that peculiar type of non-being which we call a privation. It is the non-being of a thing in a determinate subject. Blindness is the non-being of sight, not absolutely (that is simply non-sighted,) but in a thing which naturally has the ability to see. Illiteracy is the non-being of the ability to read, not in just anything (we would not call a tree illiterate, even though it cannot read,) but in something which has the natural ability to read. And so privative opposition, though like contradictory opposition insofar as we speak of being and non-being, is still a limited type of opposition. Its limitation is exactly where it can be found. Blindness and sight are not found everywhere, while non-sighted and sighted together encompass all possible things. There can be nothing which is neither sighted nor non-seeing; many things, however, are neither sighted nor blind.

The third sort of opposition is even more limited than the previous two. Both contradictory and privative opposition entail being versus non-being. The third type, contrary opposition, is an opposition between one being and another being. Contraries are conceptually inseparable. For example, hot is conceptually inseparable from cold. As extremes with respect to temperature, each is necessary for the understanding of the other. One cannot conceive of hot, as such, without also conceiving of cold, as such.

It might seem, at this point, that these things are not opposites at all—in fact, they seem to rely upon one another. But their opposition is not in whether one can be understood without the other (for, as we just said, they cannot,) but in whether one can exist along with the other, at the same time, and in the same place. And here we see the distinct type of opposition which contrary opposition expresses: it is an opposition between one being and another in the same thing, but not at the same time.

The same thing cannot be both hot and cold simultaneously. (This is not to say that different parts cannot be hot and cold at the same time, but that the same part cannot.) Note that hot and cold are at the extremes within a class, that is, that hot and cold have something in common: they belong to the same genus, namely, temperature. This is another characteristic of contraries. One could say that contraries are extremes within a genus, were it not for the existence of contraries which are not extremes. Certainly, many of the familiar types of contrary opposition are extremes within a common genus: hot and cold, black and white, sweet and sour, rough and smooth. Even and odd are also contraries, however, yet they cannot be called extremes, since there is no intermediate state between them. In many cases, then, but not in all, contraries are extremes within a genus, such that there are intermediate states between them.

5   The very possibility of intermediate states distinguishes contrary opposition from the previous two types also. For, in contradictory opposition, something either is an alpaca or it is not, and, given that we are speaking of things which have the natural ability to see, something is either sighted or blind. Yet this is not so with all contraries. Given that
10   we are speaking of temperature, it is not the case that something is either hot or cold, for there is an infinite number of temperatures between these extremes. The only characteristic of opposition which remains for contraries is that the same thing cannot be both of them at the same time—it is possible that it is neither.

CONTRARIES VS. CONTRADICTORIES

Propositional Quality

15   The most fundamental way in which statements can differ has to do with what is called their quality. A statement (or proposition) claims either that some predicate belongs to some subject, or that it does not. Propositions of the first sort are said to be affirmative, while propositions of the second sort are negative.

20   In the abstract, taking s as any subject whatsoever and p as any predicate, the form of an affirmative proposition is

s is p

while the form of a negative proposition is

s is not p.

25   Bear in mind that the quality of a proposition depends upon whether one is joining or separating the predicate and subject. Is the statement no maple is an oak tree affirmative, then, or negative? We need simply ask whether the predicate

236

of the proposition given, oak tree, is being associated with, or distinguished from, the subject, maple. Clearly, a separation between the two is being expression. Therefore, this proposition is negative.

Propositional Quantity

The second characteristic of a proposition is its quantity. The quantity of a proposition as a whole is based upon the quantity of its subject. Though there are four types of quantity a subject can have, we are directly concerned only with two: universal and particular.

The proposition

> every dog is a four-legged animal

is a universal proposition (or a proposition with universal quantity.) This not only means that it is referring to more than a single individual, but also that it is referring to each and every individual signified by the word dog. In this case, the quantifier every is what signifies the proposition's universal quantity.

Now consider the proposition

> no dog is a cat.

This is also a universal proposition. Why? Because the quantity of a proposition is based solely upon the quantity of a subject. If we are referring to each and every dog in the proposition, then it must have universal quantity. In this case, the quantifier no indicates universality. Now, the word no, we just saw, is also a sign that this proposition has negative quality: in this case, this word serves two functions, indicating both its quality and the quantity of the proposition as a whole.

Particular quantity is usually indicated by the quantifier some, whether we are speaking affirmatively or negatively. For example

> some dogs have fleas

is a common affirmative form, while

---

some dogs do not have fleas

is a common form of the particular negative proposition.

Propositional Type

The type of a proposition comes down to a combination of its quantity and its quality. Given our summary of quality and quantity above, then, four sorts of propositional type are possible. This can be easily seen by making reference to the following grid

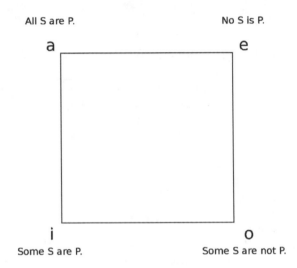

(The letters A, E, I, and O come from the two first vowels of each of the Latin words *affirmo*, I affirm, and *nego*, I deny.)

Opposition

Let us now use these distinctions to speak of two of the ways in which propositions can be opposed to one another. For purposes of clarification, we can represent these four propositions on a square, with the universals at the top and the affirmatives at the left. This device is called the square of opposition.

First, assume that the four propositions represented on the square have the same subject and predicate; thus, they are all talking about the same thing. To find opposed propositions, then, we need only look for pairs of affirmative and negative propositions.

The first such pair we will discuss is A and E. Putting these in terms of a common subject and predicate, we would be considering the relation
5 between all s is p and no s is p, where s and p can refer to anything whatsoever, as long as it is the same thing in the case of each proposition.

All s is p and no s is p, then, are opposites. This is more than to say that they are saying different things, although they certainly are. It is to say that a person claiming that all s is p and a person claiming that no s is p
10 are disagreeing with one another, in the strict sense of the word.

This sort of disagreement, or opposition, is called contrary opposition, and the propositions all s is p and no s is p are called contraries. It is the opposition between universal propositions, one affirmative, the other negative.

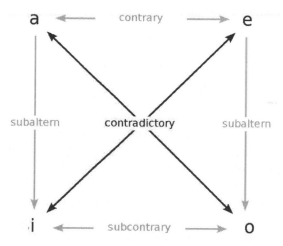

15 We have seen contrary opposition before, not as an opposition between propositions, but as an opposition between simple expressions. Earlier, we spoke of hot and cold as being opposed in this way, as contraries. At that point, we defined such opposition as being between extremes within the same group, or class. Thus, hot and cold are contraries because they
20 are at extremes within the class of temperatures. We also pointed out that, though it is not necessary that things have one or the other of these

contraries at any given time, nevertheless, it is impossible for both to be present simultaneously. With contraries, as opposed to contradictories, it is possible to have neither one, but impossible to have both at the same time. (The exact same thing cannot be both hot and cold simultaneously, but it can be neither one.)

There is a good reason why we call the opposition between type A and type E contrary opposition also. Type A and type E can be seen as extremes with respect to those propositions which make claims about the same subject and predicate. Let us take a concrete example.

With respect to the color of swans, one person might make the claim that every swan is white. This is a logically extreme claim. (Note that a logically extreme claim need not be false; it is extreme not in the common sense where we use it to mean unreasonable, but only in a logical sense.) Type A is extreme here because it is the most one can say affirmatively of swans and whiteness. One can say no more, in an affirmative way, about swans being white; and it makes no sense to say more than every swan is white.

With respect to denying whiteness of swans, the most one can say is no swans are white. Again, it makes no sense to say even fewer than none of the swans are white.

It makes sense, then, to speak of the opposition between type A and type E as contrary opposition, since it is very much like the opposition between simple expressions of which we have already spoken.

The next type of opposition which concerns us is that between a universal and a particular proposition, one of which is affirmative, the other negative. There are two instances of this opposition represented on the square, namely, the opposition between type A and type O, and the opposition between type E and type I. This type is called contradictory opposition, and it is the greatest opposition two propositions can have to one another. In other words, two people cannot disagree more than when they contradict one another.

We also saw this type of opposition earlier. There also it was taken as the strictest type of opposition which can occur—in that case, it was between two simple expressions. Here, it is between two propositions.

When we considered contradictory opposition earlier, we saw that everything must be either one of the opposites, or the other. For example, everything must be either hot or non-hot. This either-or characteristic also applies to contradictory propositions, as we will shortly see.

Rules for Truth and Falsity

What remains is to look at the rules for the truth and falsity of contraries and contradictories.

The rule for contradictories is immediately seen and simple: in fact, this rule is one of the basic truths upon which all human thought is based.. Simply put, one of two contradictory propositions must be true, the other false; they cannot both be true, and they cannot both be false. Here we can see the reason why this opposition is called contradictory, since it is very much like contradictory opposition among simple expressions. Among simple expressions, as we saw, something must be either one of two contradictories or the other—there is no third alternative, and it cannot be both. (For instance, something must be either hot or non-hot. It cannot be both at the same time, nor can it be neither one nor the other, since, between them, they encompass all things.)

Though we depend upon the truth of this rule for all our reasoning, it can be made manifest through examples. Suppose it were false that all swans were white. What, at the very least, must be true? That no swans are white? No, what we can be certain is true is that some swans are not white. It does not follow from saying it is false that all swans are white that no swans are white is true. All that necessarily follows is that some are not white. Now suppose that every swan was in fact white. The proposition some swans are not white would necessarily be false. (How could any swan not be white if it were true that all swans are white?) The same can be easily seen using examples of the opposition between types E and I.

What does this rule imply? Consider the situation where persons are disagreeing in this way: they are contradicting one another. Apart from the truth of the matter, we do know one thing: one of them must be right and the other wrong. Contradictories cannot both be true, nor can they both be false. Of course, this logical truth does not settle the important matter of who is right and who is wrong. Nevertheless, we do know so much about the situation.

The rule for the truth and falsity of contraries is what one would expect, given what we have said of contrary terms already. Though both propositions cannot be true, they can both be false; and there are intermediates between these contraries (namely, the particular affirmative and the particular negative proposition).

Though it is not possible that every swan is white and that no swan is white, it is possible that both are false, in which casethe intermediates some swan is white and some swan is not white would be true.

While one can tell from a true or a false proposition whether its contradictory is true or false, that is not the case with contraries. If the first of two contraries is true, then the other is false; but if the first is false, the other could be true, but it could also be false. Logically, we say that the other contrary is undecided (or unknown), which is merely to say that we do not know whether it is true or false. (Obviously, it must be one or the other, but we cannot tell which using logic alone.) Contraries cannot both be true, though they can both be false.

NECESSITY AND CONTINGENCY

One thing which some descriptive terms (or predicates) have in common is that each is necessary to the subject of which it is predicated, which is to say that it must belong to that thing. For example, humans are animals, triangles are three-sided, and potentiality is needed for change are all necessary propositions.

Other predicates, however, are not related to the subject in this way; in fact, some things are decidedly unnecessary to the subjects to which they belong. For example, it is not necessary that humans are tall, or that triangles are blue or that things change slowly. This second sort of proposition is called contingent, contingent being the opposite of necessary. While necessary things must belong to their subjects, contingent things may or may not belong. Every true proposition, then, is possible on account of either a necessary or a contingent connection between the subject and the predicate.

INFERENCE SIGNS, VALIDITY, AND SOUNDNESS

In every argument, one is going from one thing to another. This process of going from one to another is what distinguishes argumentation (formulating arguments) from mere predication (making propositions.) The part of an argument one is going from is generally called a premise (arguments will generally have two premises). The part of an argument one is going to is called the conclusion.

Suppose, for example, we were given the following argument

> *Could these be common porpoises? Stanton asked. They sure had the look of the breed. But since common porpoises are found exclusively in the southern latitudes and these animals had been with him for many miles as he journeyed south across the equator, they could not be common porpoises. They must be a similar species.*

An argument is being made here; a simple argument, but an argument none the less. Can we identify which parts are the premises and which is the conclusion? The keys to doing this are what are called inference signs. Inference signs are certain words we use to indicate to our listeners or readers how propositions in our arguments are to be taken. The use of such signs arose from the necessity of distinguishing the different parts of arguments in order that they be understood. Consider these three propositions

> human is mortal
> animal is mortal
> human is animal.

Without inference signs, it is impossible to decide whether this person is trying to conclude that humans are animals or that animals are mortal or that humans are mortal—in fact, there is no indication here of whether an argument is even being made. These could be three simple statements which the speaker intends to be taken separately. But consider this way of expressing the same three statements

> since every human is an animal,
> every human is mortal,
> for every animal is mortal.

Several things become clear upon reflection, the first of which is that this speaker is definitely making an argument. The use of the words since and for makes this clear. That is because since and for can be used as inference signs. Here, they are meant to point out that the propositions every human is an animal and every animal is mortal are to be taken as the premises of the argument. The proposition every human is mortal is seen to be the conclusion by process of elimination.

Returning to the example we gave above

> *Could these be common porpoises? Stanton asked. They sure had the look of the breed. But since common porpoises are found exclusively in the southern latitudes and these animals had been with him for many miles as he journeyed south across the equator, they could not be common porpoises. They must be a similar species.*

We can now see that the proposition

> common porpoises are found exclusively in the southern latitudes

is being taken as a premise of the argument. The same is true for the proposition which follows it

> these animals had been with him for many miles as he journeyed south across the equator

since it is preceded by the conjunction and (as if one were to say since this is so and [since] that is so...). The conclusion is

> they [the animals he is looking at] could not be common porpoises.

5   Inference signs are crucial for the study of philosophy, since philosophers present arguments for what they hold. Words like 'since' and 'therefore' enable us to distinguish between the point the author is trying to make (his conclusion) and the reasons (premises) he uses to justify his view.

When its process of reasoning is good (logical, reasonable,) then an
10 argument is said to be valid. When propositions correspond to the way things are, then those propositions are said to be true. Though there is something distinctly right about both truth and validity, they are also different from one another. In fact, an argument can be valid even though the propositions it contains are false, and invalid even though the
15 propositions it contains are true. Consider this example

> every fish is a mammal
> every whale is a fish
> ∴ every whale is a mammal

Notice that the first two propositions (which are where the argument is
20 going from, the part of an argument we call the premises) are false while the third proposition (which is where the argument is going to, the part of an argument we call the conclusion) is true. One might think that false propositions could not lead us to a true conclusion; nevertheless, this argument is valid, as can be shown using a diagram.

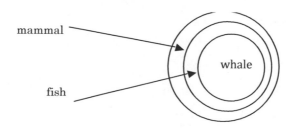

Clearly, then, the validity (logical correctness) of the process of reasoning contained in an argument is independent of the truth of the propositions it contains; in other words, how it goes (that is, well or poorly) from the premises to the conclusion has nothing to do with whether the premises and conclusion are true.

Here is an invalid argument containing true propositions:

> every car is a vehicle
> every station wagon is a vehicle
> ∴ every station wagon is a car.

In this case, the problem is not what is being claimed (for, in fact, all these statements are true,) but in the way the argument tries to go from one part to another. Again, diagrams make it clear that one cannot get from the first two statements to the third in a logical manner.

We could diagram every car is a vehicle in this way

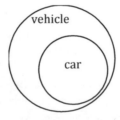

Yet, when we come to diagram every station wagon is a vehicle, we realize that we cannot be certain of the position of the one term, station wagon in relation to the other, car. The only requirement is that we place station wagon wholly within vehicle. Since there are three possible (and logically incompatible) ways to do this, it does not necessarily follow that every station wagon is a car.

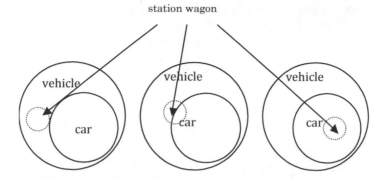

This should suffice to show that the truth or falsity of propositions is something very different from the validity or invalidity of arguments.

Soundness is the goal of argumentation. One might ask what do we expect from our arguments, truth, or validity? The answer, of course, is both. Valid arguments, though correct in one respect, are of little value if one is proceeding from a false antecedent. Similarly, true propositions lead nowhere if one's reasoning is not correct. We want to reason 1) in a correct way 2) about true things. This is to say that we want our arguments to be sound. An argument is unsound, then, if it is invalid, or if it has a false premise, or both.

ENTHYMEMES

An enthymeme is an argument with a missing (or unstated) premise. It is not, strictly speaking, a different form of reasoning at all, but a different way in which to present an argument.

There are several reasons why someone may choose to leave a premise unstated. Perhaps it is obvious, as in the example: all kangaroos are marsupials because they carry their young in a pouch. The missing premise is that all animals which carry their young in a pouch are marsupials—an obvious enough fact, and so one which does not need to be explicitly stated. The motivation for leaving a premise unstated in this case is efficiency and brevity—it is much more wordy to bring out explicitly what is obvious to everyone anyway, and which (incidentally) everyone automatically supplies in their own mind when they see that the argument is valid.

There are other, less praiseworthy, reasons for leaving a premise unstated. One might leave it out because it is either false or highly questionable. For example, one might say

> Obviously the current administration is dishonest: they're politicians, aren't they?

Of course, the unstated claim is that all politicians are dishonest, which is either false or highly questionable.

Regardless of the reason for leaving a premise unstated, however, no argument can conclude validly without it; in fact, enthymemes are conclusive only to the extent that the person who hears them can supply mentally the premise which is left unstated. In any other case, someone may be persuaded by an enthymeme to accept the conclusion (as in the example just given,) but they have not accepted it because they have seen it proved. Such a use (or, better, misuse) of enthymemes for rhetorical purposes is quite common, especially in the political, social, and ethical realms, where persuasion oftentimes leads directly to action, with relatively little time allowed for one to reflect upon the soundness of arguments presented. An enthymeme in, say, mathematics, on the other hand, will soon be discovered, since there is ample time to reflect upon whether thearguments provided are or are not sound. Since an argument cannot reach a valid conclusion without its premises, it is the function of logic to supply what is missing in enthymemes.

CONDITIONAL ARGUMENTS

The main premise in a conditional argument (technically called a conditional syllogism) is a conditional (if... then) proposition. Conditional propositions have two main parts: the portion following the if, which is called the antecedent, and the portion following the then (or the other portion if the then is omitted), which is called the consequent. This distinction ought to borne in mind, both for understanding what a conditional syllogism is and for deciding whether it is or is not valid.

The other premise in a conditional syllogism is a statement with one of four possible functions: it can either affirm or deny the antecedent of the main premise, or it can affirm or deny the consequent of the main premise. It is very important to realize that to affirm here does not mean to make an affirmative proposition, nor does to deny mean to make a negative statement. This is best seen in an example

> if it is raining then something is getting wet
> it is raining.

In this case, the minor premise affirms the antecedent contained in the major premise. This is not to say that it affirms the antecedent because it is an affirmative proposition, (which it happens to be), but because it re-states what the antecedent is claiming. The following is also an example of a minor premise affirming the antecedent of the major premise

> if it is not raining then nothing is getting wet
> it is not raining.

Even though the minor premise has negative quality, it still affirms the antecedent because the antecedent is also negative—one re-states a negative only in a negative. Here is an instance in which the minor premise denies the antecedent

> if it is raining then something is getting wet
> it is not raining.

Here are examples in which the consequent is affirmed and denied, respectively

> if it is raining then something is getting wet
> something is getting wet

> if it is raining then something is getting wet
> nothing is getting wet.

These, then, are the four possible forms of the conditional syllogism. It is one of the simpler forms of argumentation. The rules for the validity of conditional syllogisms are also quite simple, and we will derive them here. Let us take the first form, in which the minor premise affirms the antecedent contained in the major premise.

> if it is raining then something is getting wet
> it is raining.

In this instance, one can intuitively see that a valid conclusion can be drawn from these premises. One might ask: does anything necessarily follow from the premises given? Clearly:

> if it is raining then something is getting wet;
> it is raining;
> ∴ something is getting wet.

This valid form of reasoning, in which the minor premise affirms the antecedent and the conclusion affirms the consequent, simply makes explicit the already-existing connection between antecedent and consequent in the major premise.

This valid argument form is called *modus ponens* (*modus ponens* is Latin for 'the way of setting something down as so'.) We can explicitly give the conditions for *modus ponens* as follows

> when one affirms the antecedent of a conditional proposition as a premise, one can validly affirm the consequent as a conclusion.

Let us turn to the second possible conditional form of argument, in which the minor premise denies the antecedent

> if it is raining then something is getting wet
> it is not raining.

In this instance, one might be led to conclude that nothing is getting wet—it certainly sounds like that ought to be the conclusion. Yet this conclusion does not follow, as can be easily seen by asking whether something might not be getting wet on account of something other than the rain—sprinklers, for example. It simply does not follow that nothing is getting wet from the simple fact that it is not raining. This very common logical mistake is called the fallacy of denying the antecedent (for obvious reasons). The truth is that this second form of conditional reasoning has no valid conclusion.

The third form we mentioned was an argument in which the minor premise affirms the consequent contained in the major premise.

> if it is raining then something is getting wet
> something is getting wet.

As in the last case, it is fairly easy to see that nothing follows from this combination of premises. The fact that something happens to be getting wet is no proof that it must be raining: it could arise from an altogether different source. This logical mistake, which is also very common, is called the fallacy of affirming the consequent, again, for obvious reasons.

The last form of conditional argument had the minor premise denying the consequent contained in the major premise.

> if it is raining then something is getting wet
> nothing is getting wet.

In this instance, it is not as clear whether something follows of necessity, or not. One might think it possible to conclude that it is not raining—and this does follow, in fact.

> if it is raining then something is getting wet
> nothing is getting wet
> ∴ it is not raining.

Nevertheless, it is not as clear as in the case of *modus ponens* exactly why it follows. There is a way to prove that this argument form, which is called *modus tollens* (*modus tollens* is Latin for 'the way of taking something away',) is in fact valid—and the argument uses *modus ponens* to do so.

Let us suppose that the conclusion does not follow: it would then be possible for the premises to be true and the conclusion false. So, if it is raining then something is getting wet and nothing is getting wet, is it possible that it is raining? No—because if it were raining, then something would be getting wet. We know this already, through the argument called *modus ponens*. In this indirect way, then, we can prove that *modus tollens* is also a valid form of conditional reasoning. We can explicitly give the conditions for modus tollens as follows

5   when one denies the consequent of a conditional proposition as a premise, one can validly deny the antecedent as a conclusion.

Of the four possible forms, then, two are valid and two are invalid. It is important to distinguish among them, both because the fallacies are 10 common and because conditional arguments in general are used often in our everyday speaking and writing.

Bibliography

Anaximenes, Anaximander, Parmenides, Melissus, Zeno, Empedocles, Anaxagoras, and Heraclitus. *Early Greek Philosophy*. Translated by John Burnet. London and Edinburgh: A. and C. Black, 1892.

Aristotle. *Metaphysics, De Anima*. Translated by W. D. Ross. Oxford: Clarendon, 1928.

———. *On the Soul*. Translated by J. A. Smith. Oxford: Clarendon, 1928.

———. *Politics*. translated by Benjamin Jowett. Oxford: Clarendon, 1928.

Descartes, René. *The Method, Meditations and Philosophy of Descartes*. Translated by John Veitch. Washington DC; London: M. W. Dunne, 1901.

d'Holbach, Baron. *The System of Nature*. Translated by Samuel Wilkinson. London: Thomas Davison, 1820.

Epicurus. *The Extant Remains, Letter to Menoeceus*. Translated by C. Bailey. Oxford: Clarendon, 1926.

Hobbes, Thomas. *Leviathan*. London: William Wilson for Andrew Crooke, at the Green Dragon in St. Paul's Churchyard, 1651.

Hume, David. *Dialogues Concerning Natural Religion*. 1779.

———. *An Enquiry Concerning Human Understanding*. 1748.

Lucretius. *On the Nature of Things*. Translated by H. A. J. Munro London: Routledge, 1886.

Pascal, Blaise. *Pensées*. Translated by W. F. Trotter. New York: P. F. Collier & Son, 1910.

Pinker, Stephen, and Richard Dawkins. "Is Science Killing the Soul?" Guardian-Dillons Debate, February 10, 1999, Westminster Central Hall, London.

Plato. *The Cratylus, the Timaeus, the Republic, the Laws, the Phaedo*, in *The Dialogues of Plato*. Translated by Benjamin Jowett. Oxford: Oxford University Press, 1892.

Russell, Bertrand. *What I Believe*. London: Routledge, 1925.

Sextus Empiricus. *Outlines of Pyrrhonism*, Book 1. Translated by Rev. R. G. Bury. Cambridge, MA: Harvard University Press, 1933.

Thomas Aquinas. *Summa Theologiae*. Translated by Fathers of the English Dominican Province. New York: Benziger, Brothers 1911.